Click Start

Computer Science for Schools

2nd Edition

Anjna Virmani   Shalini Harisukh

CAMBRIDGE
UNIVERSITY PRESS

CAMBRIDGE
UNIVERSITY PRESS

4381/4 Ansari Road, Daryaganj, Delhi 110002, India

Cambridge University Press is part of the University of Cambridge.

It furthers the University's mission by disseminating knowledge in the pursuit of education, learning and research at the highest international levels of excellence.

www.cambridge.org
Information on this title: www.cambridge.org/9781107673045
www.cambridge.org/9781107662919

© Cambridge University Press 2014

This publication is in copyright. Subject to statutory exception and to the provisions of relevant collective licensing agreements, no reproduction of any part may take place without the written permission of Cambridge University Press.

First published 2011
Second Edition 2014

Printed in India by Repromen Offset Printers Pvt. Ltd., Bangalore

A catalogue record for this publication is available from the British Library

ISBN 978-1-107-67304-5 Paperback
ISBN 978-1-107-66291-9 Paperback with CD-ROM

Cambridge University Press has no responsibility for the persistence or accuracy of URLs for external or third-party internet websites referred to in this publication, and does not guarantee that any content on such websites is, or will remain, accurate or appropriate. Information regarding prices, travel timetables, and other factual information given in this work is correct at the time of first printing but Cambridge University Press does not guarantee the accuracy of such information thereafter.

NOTICE TO TEACHERS IN THE UK
It is illegal to reproduce any part of this work in material form (including photocopying and electronic storage) except under the following circumstances:
(i) where you are abiding by a licence granted to your school or institution by the Copyright Licensing Agency;
(ii) where no such licence exists, or where you wish to exceed the terms of a licence, and you have gained the written permission of Cambridge University Press;
(iii) where you are allowed to reproduce without permission under the provisions of Chapter 3 of the Copyright, Designs and Patents Act 1988, which covers, for example, the reproduction of short passages within certain types of educational anthology and reproduction for the purposes of setting examination questions.

NOTICE TO TEACHERS
The photocopy masters in this publication may be photocopied or distributed [electronically] free of charge for classroom use within the school or institution that purchased the publication. Worksheets and copies of them remain in the copyright of Cambridge University Press, and such copies may not be distributed or used in any way outside the purchasing institution.

Every effort has been made to trace the owners of copyright material included in this book. The publishers would be grateful for any omissions brought to their notice for acknowledgement in future editions of the book.

CONTENTS

	Overview	*iv*
	Preface	*vi*
1.	Adobe Photoshop 7.0	1
2.	MS Access 2007	20
3.	Introduction to Visual Basic	48
4.	Toolbox and its Controls	61
5.	Operators and Functions	82
6.	Sequential Programming in VB	97
7.	Conditional Programming in VB	104
8.	Repetition Programming in VB	118
9.	Creating Menu in MDI Application	132
10.	Connecting VB with MS Access 2007	143
11.	Elementary C++	154
12.	Elementary Java	164
13.	Virus and Anti-virus	174
14.	Troubleshooting	185

Lesson Name	Contents	Objectives	Activities
1. Adobe Photoshop 7.0	• Adobe Photoshop features • Main components of Photoshop window • Opening and Importing images • Toolbox • Creating a new image • Layers and Layer Palette • Channels • The Filters Menu • Masks • Texts and Fonts	To make students learn about Adobe Photoshop version 7.0	• To list out the menus in Photoshop • To explore the toolbox • To save the manipulated file • To create two layers with Layer 1 in color mode, Layer 2 in grayscale mode • To create a new layer to give an embossed effect to the picture • To select layer with text to be edited, apply a bend and move the text • Lab work – Additional activities
2. MS Access 2007	• Some important terms related to database • Functions of DBMS • Database objects • MS Access • Creating new databases and modifying them in MS Access 2007 • Data Types • Primary Key • Creating and modifying tables in MS Access 2007 • Changing the view	To make students learn about databases and to work on it in MS Access 2007	• To gather more information on database and its concept from the Internet • To create tables following specific instructions and modify its content • To create a database in MS Access 2007 to specifications • Lab Work – Additional activities
3. Introduction to Visual Basic	• Visual Basic • Starting Visual Basic • Components of Visual Basic window • Executing Visual Basic program • Inserting controls in Visual Basic project • Saving a project and a form	To introduce the concept of Visual Basic	• To explore different options present in VB • To name and explain any five options and to match their effects in Visual Basic IDE • To create forms with labels following specific instructions and save them with specific names • Lab Work – Additional activities
4. Toolbox and its Controls	• Toolbox	To make students understand the tools used in VB	• To design a form with specified controls • To set the appropriate properties for the controls designed • To set appropriate properties for controls designed on the created form • To add details in an already existing form • To set properties for controls designed • To place on image at a specified place in an existing form using appropriate tools • To design a text box as specified • Lab Work – Additional activities
5. Operators and Functions	• Variables • Operators in Visual Basic • Built-in functions in VB • Some important functions used in VB	To make students know about various operators and functions used in VB	• To sort out valid and invalid names of variables • To declare an integer variable • To assign a value to a variable • To declare a string variable and to assign a value to it • To accept a decimal number and to create command buttons for calculation • To accept a sentence in a text box and to create command buttons • To accept two numbers using an Input Box on two different variables • Lab Work – Additional activities
6. Sequential Programming in VB	• Sequential programming in Visual Basic • Giving comments in Visual Basic • End Statements	To help students understand sequential type of programming in VB	• To accept dimensions in a text box and to calculate the area in a message box • To accept marks of three subjects in different boxes and to calculate the average scored in the fourth box • Lab Work – Additional activities
7. Conditional Programming in VB	• Conditional statements • Compound comparisons with the logical operators	To help students understand conditional type of programming in VB	• To accept the percentage of a student in a text box and to give a result • To accept data in a text box and to display appropriate messages • To accept a login name and to display a message • Lab Work – Additional activities

OVERVIEW

Lesson Name	Contents	Objectives	Activities
8. Repetition Programming in VB	• Repetition statements • FOR...NEXT Loop • DO...Loop • Nested Loops	To help students understand repetition programming in VB	• To accept data and to display it as specified • To accept a number from a user and print the table of the number using DO...WHILE Loop • To print the square of numbers from 1 to 10 using DO...Loop WHILE • To do the above activity using both ways of DO...Loop • To accept a number from a user and to generate the table for it • To generate the given pattern • To accept five numbers of user and to display the sum • Lab Work – Additional activities
9. Creating Menu in MDI Application	• SDI and MDI forms • Creating MDI application • Creating Menu Bar in MDI application	To make students learn about MDI applications in VB	• To create a file in MS Paint and to find out what message will be flashed if another file is created without closing the previous one • To find out whether MS Excel supports SDI or MDI • To add an element to an already existing project with a message • To change the MDI element property to false • To write Form 3 show in the load event of Form 2 • To execute the application to see how these three forms behave with respect to the parent form • To maximize, minimize and restore to normal size the 3 forms and to observe the difference • Lab Work – Additional activities
10. Connecting VB with MS Access 2007	• ADO data control • Inserting ADO data control • Connecting Visual Basic to MS Access 2007 • Connecting the text box to the fields of the table • Executing the form • Modifying MS Access table using ADO data control	To help students use the concept of MS Access 2007 in VB	• To create a table in MS Access 2007 • To design a VB Form • To connect the form with MS Access 2007 • Lab Work – Additional activities
11. Elementary C++	• Operators in C++ • Arithmetic Assignment operators in C++ • Operator precedence • Conditional constructs	To make students learn about operators and conditional statements in C++	• To accept value from the user and display result as per instructions given • Lab Work – Additional activities
12. Elementary Java	• Variables • Data types • Operators in Java • Simple programming structure in Java	To make students learn about variables, operators and programming structures in Java.	• To accept value from the user and display result as per instructions given. • Lab Work – Additional activities
13. Virus and Anti-virus	• Computer virus • What a virus cannot do • How does a computer virus spread • Symptoms of a computer viruses • Types of computer viruses • Protection against computer virus	To enable students to protect their computers against virus using anti-virus	• To be familiar with the characteristics of different viruses. • Lab Work – Additional activities
14. Troubleshooting	• Troubleshooting • Importance of computer maintenance • Areas to troubleshoot • Steps of troubleshooting • Some common problems and their troubleshooting	To make students solve common issues related to computer hardware and software	• To find out how data loss can be prevented when several files and applications are open and MS Word stops responding • To find out where one should check when hardware device attached to a computer does not respond • Lab Work – Additional activities

Click Start: Computer Science for Schools, Second Edition is the comprehensively updated version of the previous edition. The revised edition is primarily based on Windows 7 and Microsoft Office 2007 with updates from Windows 8 and Microsoft Office 2010.

Each level of the series has been designed keeping in mind the mental aptitude and learning ability of the learners as well as their interests. Efforts have been made to use examples from day-to-day life, which help the learners bridge the gap between the knowledge of the subject and the real world. The books are designed to offer a holistic approach and help in the overall development of the learners.

The special features of the book are:

- **Snap Recap** to recapitulate the concepts learnt earlier
- **Learning Objectives** to clearly define the aims and objectives of the chapter
- **Fact File** to enhance the knowledge of the students
- **Quick Key** and **Try This** to introduce shortcuts and alternative methodologies
- **Activities** interspersed within each chapter to promote application based learning
- **Exercises** to make tasks interactive and promote guided discussions
- **Glossary** and **Now You Know** to aid quick revision of the concepts learnt
- **Lab Work** to encourage learning by doing
- **Biographies** to inspire young learners
- **Teacher's Notes** provide creative suggestions to further strengthen learning
- **Teacher's Manual** to facilitate teaching

In addition to this, special icons, notes, shortcuts, troubleshooting tips, text related screen shots and illustrations have been used to support and strengthen the process of learning.

The Students' Books are available both with and without the CD-ROM.

The books, thus, will not only make learning fun but also help the learners achieve a certain level of expertise in this fast changing world of Computer Science.

Anjna Virmani
Shalini Harisukh

1 Adobe Photoshop 7.0

LEARNING OBJECTIVES

You will learn about:
1. important features of Adobe Photoshop
2. Startup Screen – Toolbox, Menu Bar, Option Bar, Palettes, Layers
3. opening and importing images
4. Toolbox
5. creating a new image
6. Color modes, Color Palette and Brush Palette
7. Layer, Layer Palette, Creating, Hiding, Deleting layer
8. Channels, Masks, Text and Fonts

Introduction

Adobe Photoshop, also known as **Photoshop**, is a graphics editing program developed and published by Adobe Systems. Photoshop allows all formats of images, such as GIF, JPG, PCX, BMP and many more, to be imported and edited, customised or changed into almost anything imaginable. Web designers, photographers and other graphics professionals use Photoshop to prepare images for web pages, to correct and retouch photographs, to customise images with special effects and text, to import and export images in a variety of file formats and much more. So far, 14 versions of Photoshop have been released by Adobe Systems. You will learn to use Adobe Photoshop 7.0 in this lesson. Higher versions such as CS, CS 2, CS 3, CS 4, CS 5 are also available. Photoshop is available in more than 20 languages.

Adobe Photoshop Features

Some of the important features of Adobe Photoshop 7.0 are discussed here.

Selection

You can select only that part of an image where you want changes to take effect.

Layering

Layering lets you work on different parts of a photo which can then be put together for a dramatic finish.

Image size alteration

This feature enlarges or reduces an image as needed.

Cropping

This feature lets you select the portion of the image you want to retain.

Sharpening and softening

Photoshop features the facility to render a sharper or blurred effect on images. This feature is mostly used in portraits to create a better focus on the subject or part of an image.

Merging images

This feature allows two or more separate images to be merged into one.

Removal of unwanted elements

This technique involves the use of clone tool to maintain the texture of the image. This is used to get rid of distracting objects in an image which gives more focus on the subject.

Selective Color Change

This feature lets you alter the color of certain parts of an image while the rest of the image retains the original color.

Slicing

This feature helps in slicing a whole image into parts. It is widely-used in creating mock-ups of websites.

There are several other features of Photoshop. All these features will help you to edit the image faster and more efficiently with professional looking results.

Starting Adobe Photoshop

Follow these steps to open Adobe Photoshop:

1. Click on **Start** button ⟹ **All Programs**.
2. Select **Adobe Photoshop 7.0** (Fig. 1.1).
3. The **Adobe Photoshop** window appears (Fig. 1.2).

The Adobe Photoshop work area includes the command menus at the top of the screen and a variety of tools and palettes for editing and adding elements to an image.

Fig. 1.1 *Adobe Photoshop 7.0*

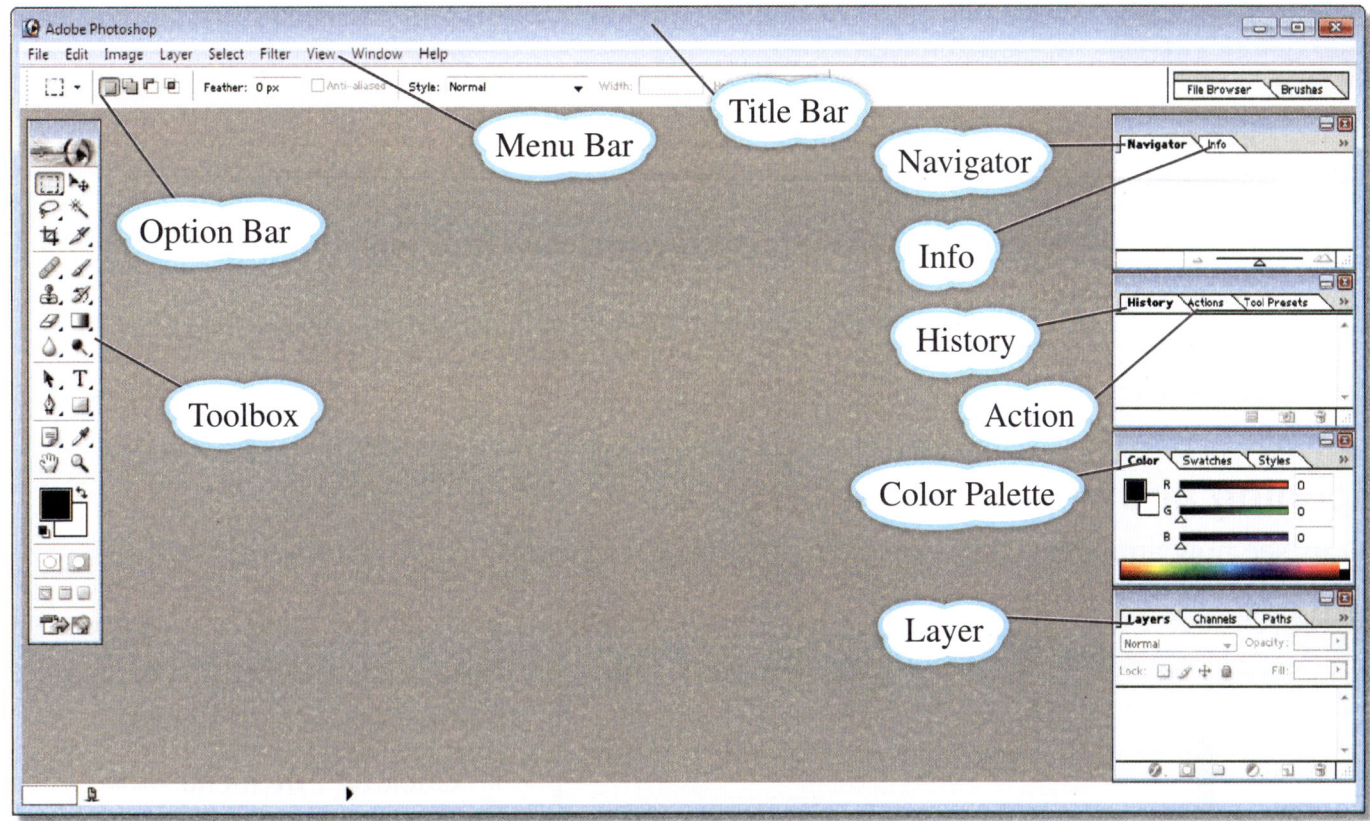

Fig. 1.2 *Adobe Photoshop window*

Main Components of Photoshop Window

The main components of Photoshop window are explained here.

Title Bar
Title Bar displays the name of the application in use.

Menu Bar
Menu Bar contains the main menu along with related options to work in the software.

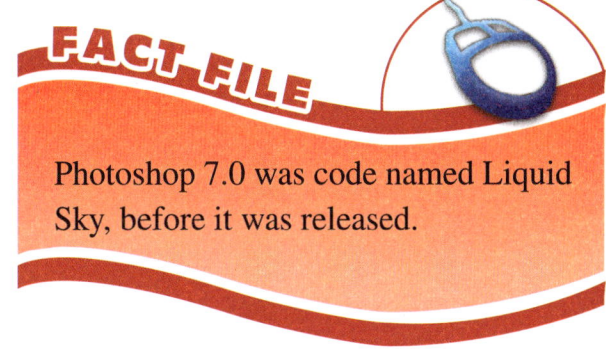

Photoshop 7.0 was code named Liquid Sky, before it was released.

Toolbox
Toolbox contains various tools used in Photoshop.

Option Bar
Option Bar contains different options to allow customisation of tools selected in the Toolbox.

Navigator/Info/Color Palette
These palettes allow zooming in and out, shows information about the cursor point and selection of colors.

History/Actions/Layers
These palettes allow multiple backward steps, automation of tasks and manipulation of layers.

ACTIVITY

A. Click on Start button ⟹ All Programs ⟹ Adobe Photoshop 7.0. Check on all the menus and make a list of it.

B. Check the Toolbox and place your mouse pointer on each tool. The name of the tool will be displayed. Make a list of it.

C. Check the palettes on the right side of the screen. Also, check each tab of the palettes.

Opening and Importing Images

Let us see how an image can be opened in Adobe Photoshop.

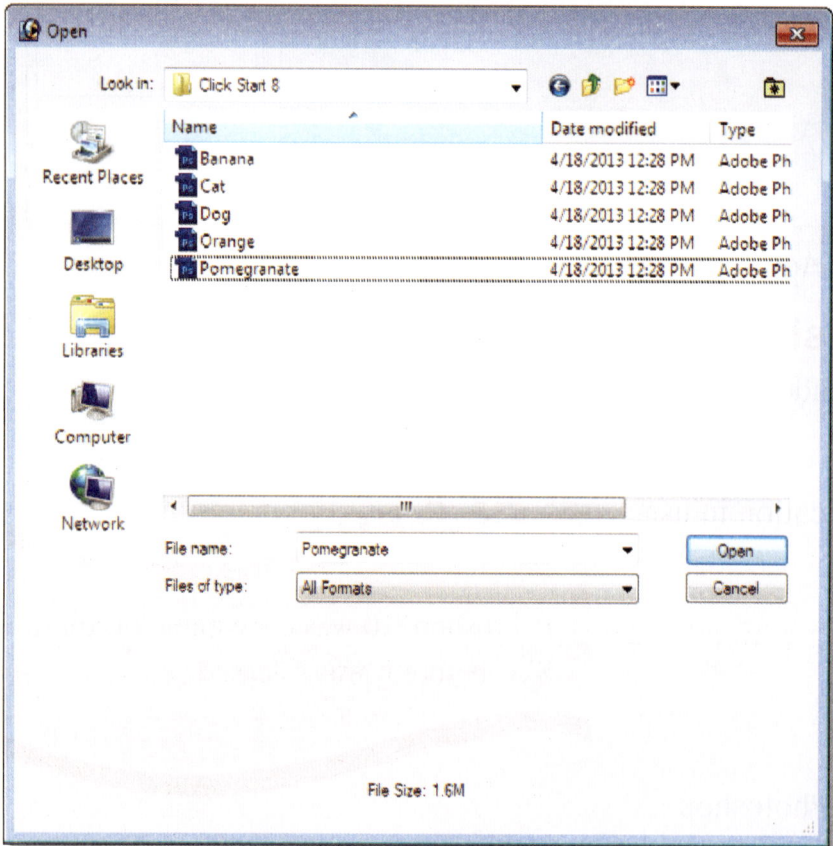

Fig. 1.3 *Open dialog box*

You can open and import images in various file formats. To open a file, follow the steps given here:

1. Click on **File** menu ⟹ **Open** option.
2. The **Open** dialog box appears (Fig. 1.3).

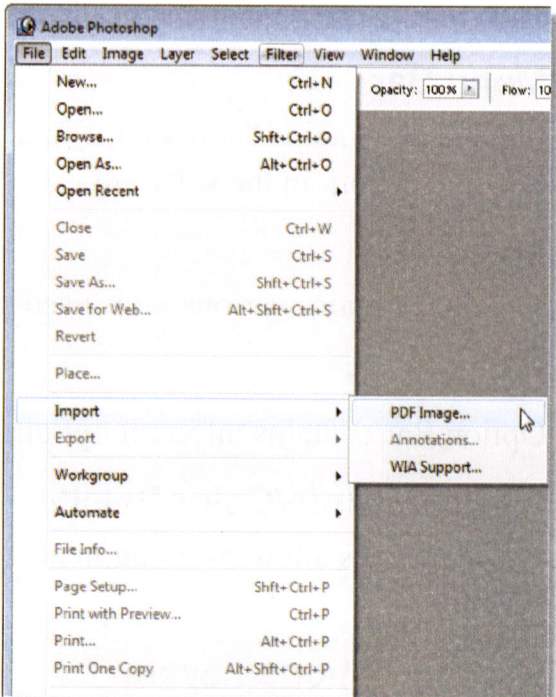

3. Select the desired file and click on the **Open** button.

1. You may also import an image. To do so, click on **File** menu ⟹ Select **Import** option (Fig. 1.4).

Fig. 1.4 *Importing an image*

2. Click on the required type in the submenu that appears. For example, on clicking the **PDF Image** option, the **Select PDF for Image Import** dialog box appears (Fig. 1.5).

3. Select the desired file and click on the **Open** button.

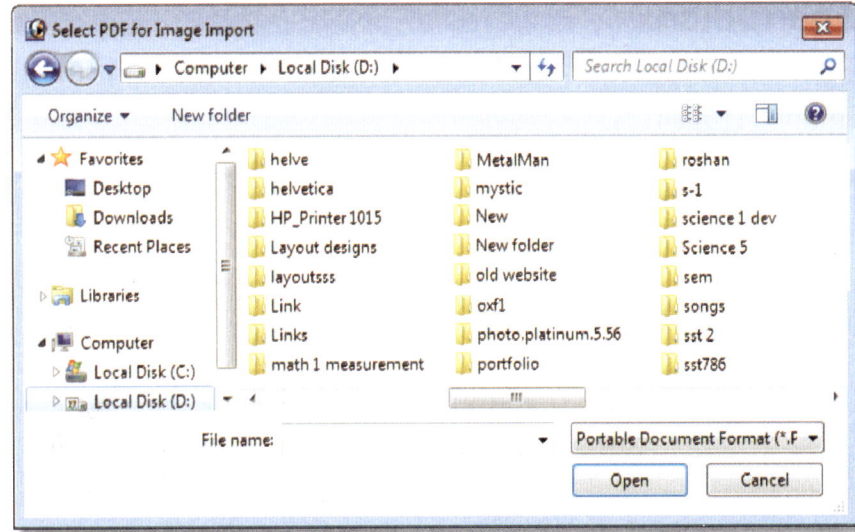

Fig. 1.5 *Select PDF for Image Import dialog box*

4. Once the image has been opened or imported the Image window appears on the main window (Fig. 1.6).

Fig. 1.6 *Image window appears*

FACT FILE

You can also import an image in the software by using a scanner.

The Toolbox

Photoshop provides various tools for selecting, painting, drawing, editing, erasing and viewing images (Fig. 1.7).

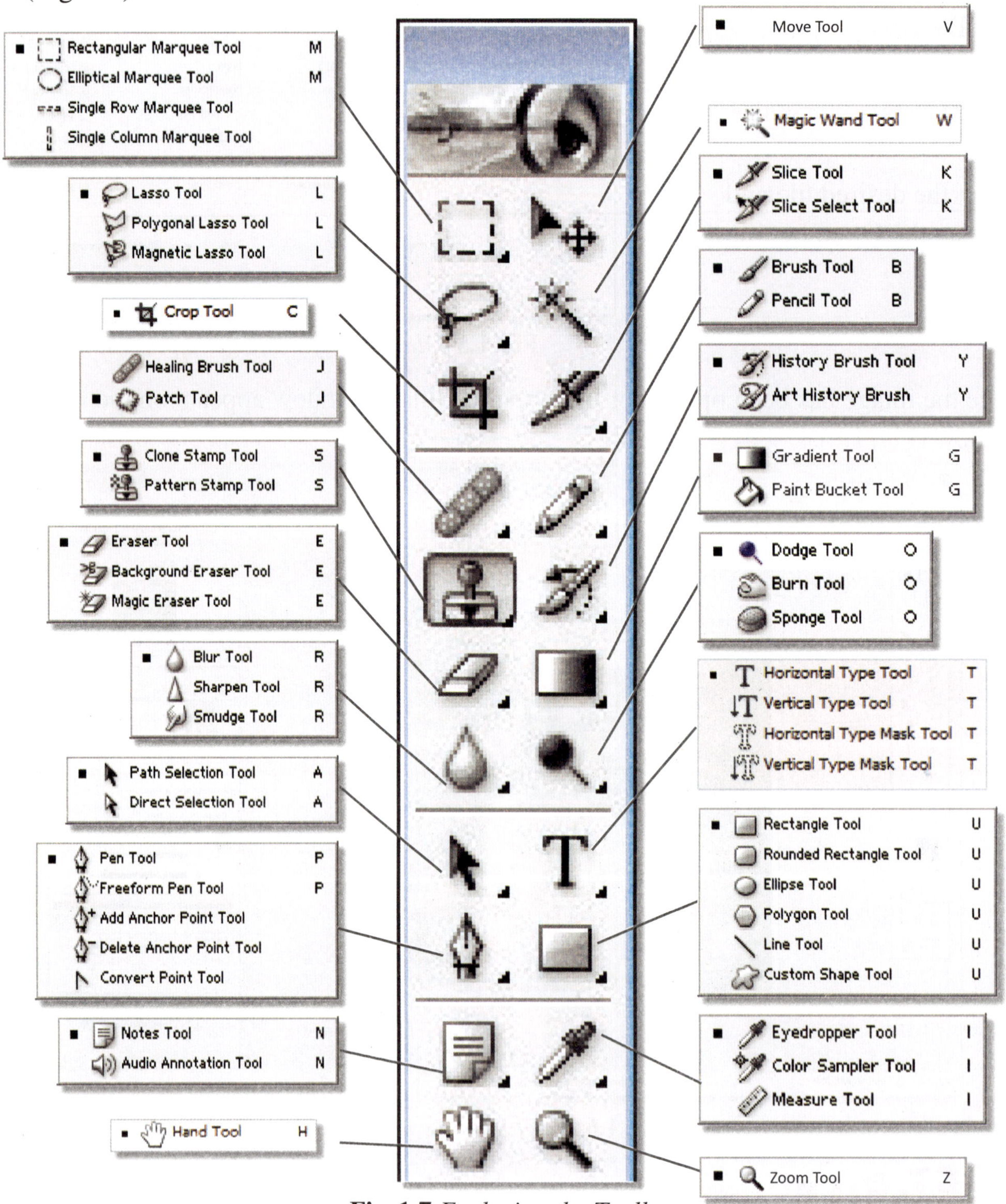

Fig. 1.7 *Exploring the Toolbox*

These tools can be classified into the following categories:

1. *Selection tools:* These are used to select an image or a part of it. For example, Marquee tools, Lasso tools, Magic Wand tool, Move tool and Crop tool.

2. *Painting Tools:* These tools are used to color an image. For example, Brush tool, Pencil tool, Gradient tool.
3. *Drawing Tools:* These tools are used to draw figures and shapes. For example, Custom Shape tool, Rectangle tool, etc.
4. *Retouching Tools:* These tools provide a finishing touch to an image. Such as removal of scars or acne marks from a photo using Spot Healing Brush tool, Healing Brush tool, Eraser tool, Clone Stamp tool, Blur tool, etc.

FACT FILE

The Hand tool, the Zoom tools, the Zoom commands and the Navigator Palette let you view different areas of an image at different magnifications. You can open additional windows to display several views at once (like different magnifications) of an image. You can also change the screen display mode to change the appearance of the Photoshop work area.

Let us learn about some of the tools used in Adobe Photoshop in detail (Table 1.1 on next page).

Using the tools

Follow these steps to select a tool from the Toolbox:

1. Click on the icon of the desired tool in the toolbox.
2. A small triangle at the lower right of a tool icon indicates hidden tools. Positioning the pointer over a tool displays a tool tip with the tool's name and keyboard shortcut.

TRY THIS!
Select a part of an image using **Marquee/Lasso** tool. Click **Edit** menu ⟹ **Copy** option. Open another image in the window. Click **Edit** menu ⟹ **Paste** option.

TRY THIS!
Select a part of an image using **Marquee/Lasso** tool ⟹ **Move** tool ⟹ Press **Alt** key and move the selection to a different location in the picture.

ACTIVITY

Complete the following activity.
1. Open any image.
2. Use different tools from the Toolbox to manipulate the image. Also, use various options given in the Option menu for each tool.
3. Save the file with some other name so that the changes are not made in the original image.

Table 1.1 *Tools and Their Description*

8

Some interesting features used along with the tools

Color modes and models: A color mode determines the color model used to display and print images. Photoshop can work with different color modes. The mode available in Photoshop includes HSB (Hue, Saturation, Brightness); RGB (Red, Green, Blue); CMYK (Cyan, Magenta, Yellow, Black); and CIE L*a*b*. To change the color mode, click on **Image** menu ⟹ **Mode** option (Fig. 1.8).

Color Palette: The Color Palette (Fig. 1.9) displays the current foreground and background colors. The foreground and background can be selected using the sliders or from the spectrum of colors displayed on the color ramp at the bottom of the palette. You can also select the Foreground and the Background color of an image using the Color Selection box on Toolbox.

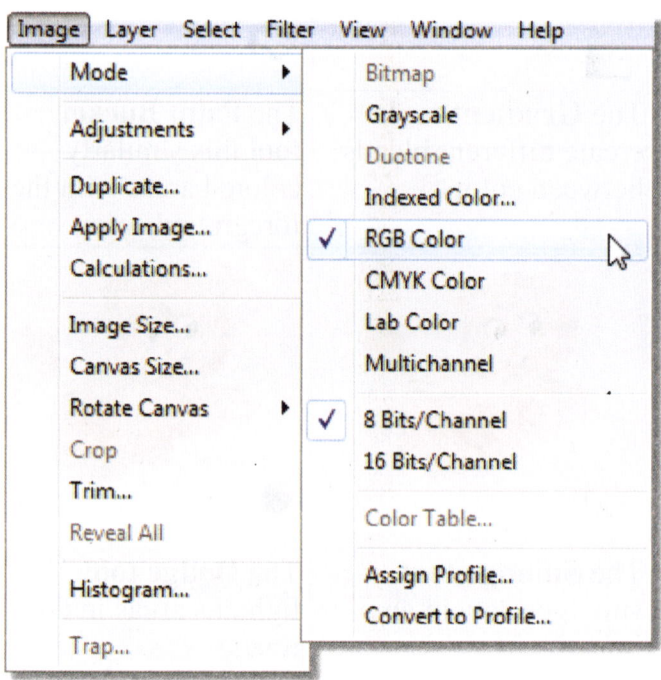

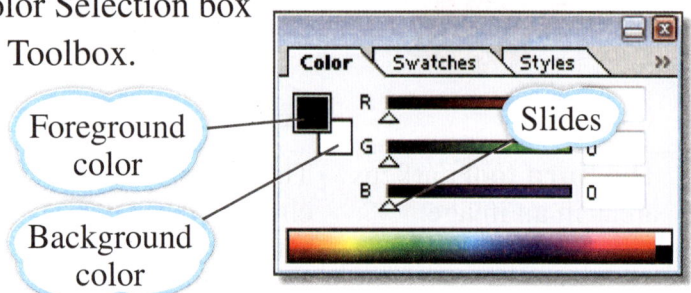

Fig. 1.9 *Color Palette*   **Fig. 1.8** *Selecting RGB color mode*

The Brushes Palette

The Brushes Palette in Photoshop 7 lets the user make thousands of different types of brushes by selecting preset brushes and designing custom brushes (Fig. 1.10). To see the Brushes Palette, click on the **Brush Palette** icon at the right end of the **Options bar** of any tool that uses a brush.

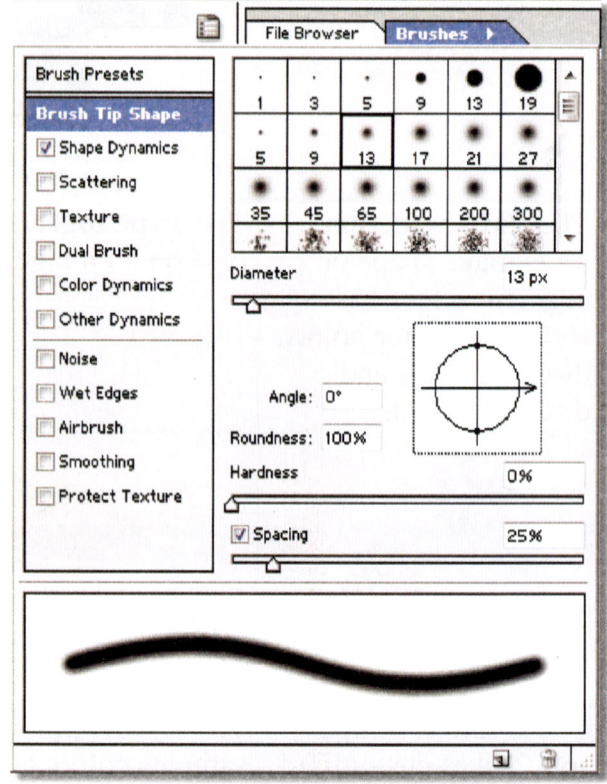

Fig. 1.10 *Brush Palette*

Creating a New Image

Follow these steps to create a new image:

1. Click on **File** menu ⟹ **New** option. The **New** dialog box appears (Fig. 1.11).

2. After selecting the various options, click on **OK** button. A **New** blank file will open.

   Note: Default name is Untitled-1.

3. Save the **New** file. Click on **File** menu ⟹ **Save As...** option.

4. Type the filename in the **Save As** dialog box that appears. Click on the **OK** button.

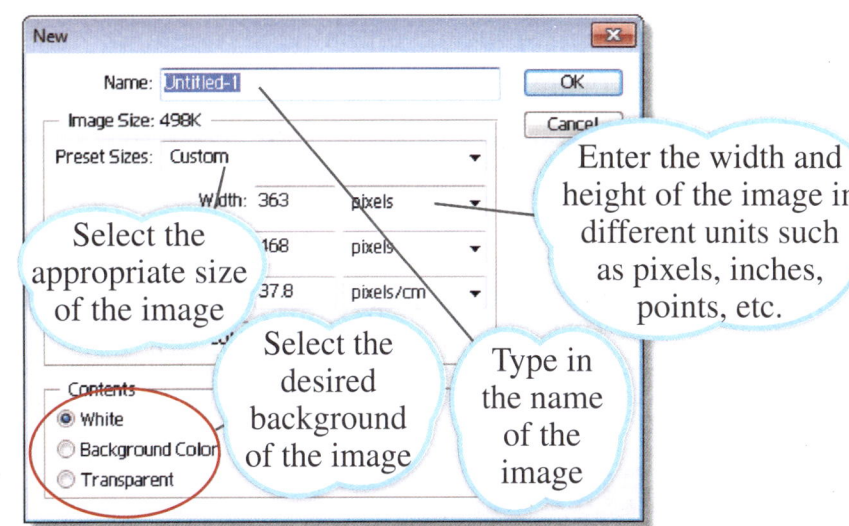

Fig. 1.11 *New dialog box*

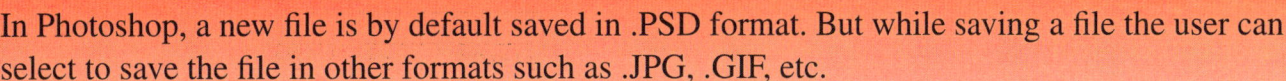

In Photoshop, a new file is by default saved in .PSD format. But while saving a file the user can select to save the file in other formats such as .JPG, .GIF, etc.

Layers

Layers provide a powerful method of working on one element of an image without disturbing the others. These layers can be grouped together to form layer sets.

Think of layers as cellophane sheets stacked one on top of the other (Fig. 1.12). You can see through a layer to the layers below.

Layers have the following features:

- Layers work as several images, layered on top of one another. Each layer has pixels that can be independently edited.

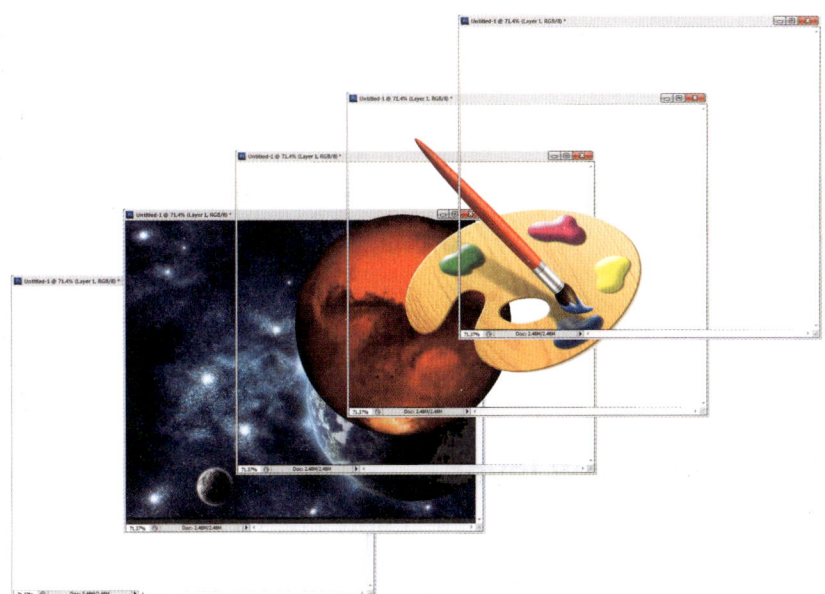

Fig. 1.12 *Stack of thin sheets depicting layers*

- Most Photoshop commands/tools work only on the layer that you select.
- You can combine, duplicate, and hide layers in an image. You can also shuffle the order in which the layers are stacked.
- Layers can have transparent areas, so that you can see the other layers underneath. When you cut or erase, the affected pixels become transparent. Also, you can change the opacity of a layer.

Note: You must save files with a .PSD or a .TIFF extension to continue to work with the images. These are large file formats. When you are finished with editing your image, you can flatten the layers into a single layer and save the file as a .JPG, .BMP and .GIF.

FACT FILE

Photoshop files may also have .PSB file extension. .PSB stands for **Photoshop Big**. While a PSD file has a maximum height and width of 30,000 pixels and a length limit of 3 Gigabytes; a PSB file has maximum height and width of 300,000 pixels and a length limit of around 4 Exabyte.

Layer Palette

The user can control the layers in an image by using the buttons in Layer Palette. This palette can accomplish many tasks such as creating, hiding, displaying, copying and deleting layers (Fig. 1.13).

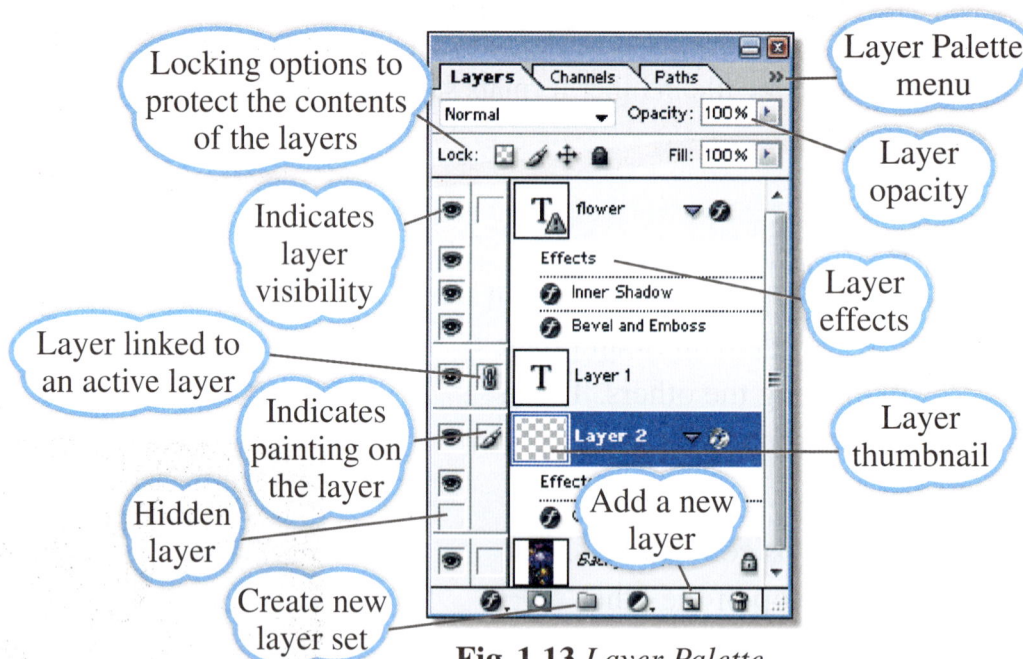

Fig. 1.13 *Layer Palette*

Creating a new layer

Follow these steps to create a new layer:

1. Display the **Layer Palette** by clicking on **Windows** menu ⇒ **Layers** option.
2. Select the layer above which you want to add the new layer.
3. Click on the **Create a New Layer** button.

FACT FILE

By default, a new image in Photoshop has a single layer called the **Background**. The user can add any number of additional layers above the background layer.

Hiding a layer

Follow these steps to hide a layer:

1. Select a layer from the **Layer Palette**. Click the **Eye** icon on the layer.
2. The layer will be hidden.

Double-click on the layer to type a new name for this layer.

Duplicating a layer

Follow these steps to create a duplicate layer:

1. Display the **Layer Palette** by clicking on **Windows** menu ⟶ **Layers** option. The **Layer Palette** is displayed.
2. Click on the Layer Palette menu. A drop-down list appears.
3. Select the **Duplicate** layer option to get a copy of the layer.

Deleting a layer

Follow these steps to delete a layer:

1. Display the Layer Palette by clicking on **Windows** menu ⟶ **Layers** option. The **Layer Palette** is displayed.
2. Click on the layer you want to delete.
3. Click on the **Delete Layer** button.

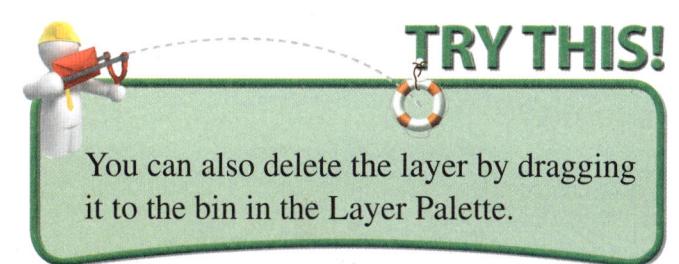

You can also delete the layer by dragging it to the bin in the Layer Palette.

ACTIVITY

Complete the following activity.

1. Create two layers. Layer 1 will display the image in color mode. Layer 2 will display the image in grayscale mode.
2. Create a new layer and give an embossed effect to the picture.

Channels

Photoshop uses channels for storing information about color elements in the image. The ability to edit individual channels gives the user control over the colors and details in an image. If an image has multiple layers, each layer has its own set of color channels (Fig. 1.14). The number of default color channels in an image depends on its color mode. For example, an image in RGB mode contains three channels, one each for Red, one for Green and one Blue. Similarly, for a CMYK image has at least four channels, one each for Cyan, Magenta, Yellow and Black information.

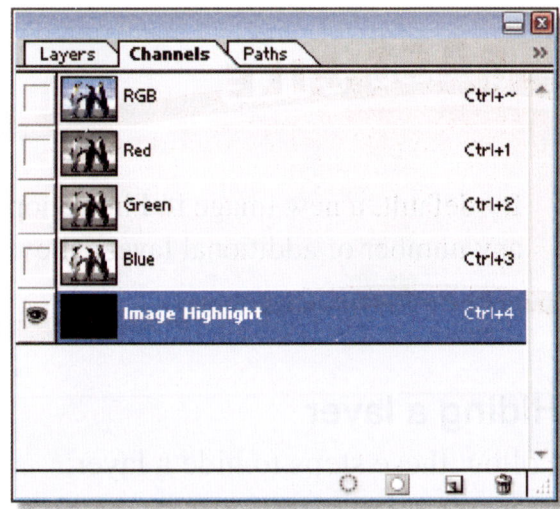

Fig. 1.14 *Channels in Photoshop*

 By default, Bitmap-mode, grayscale, duotone, and indexed-color images have one channel.

The Filters Menu

You can choose filters to add different types of special effects to an image. To apply a filter follow the steps given here:

1. Select the area to be filtered. You may also select a complete layer or a set of layers.
2. Click on the **Filter** menu.

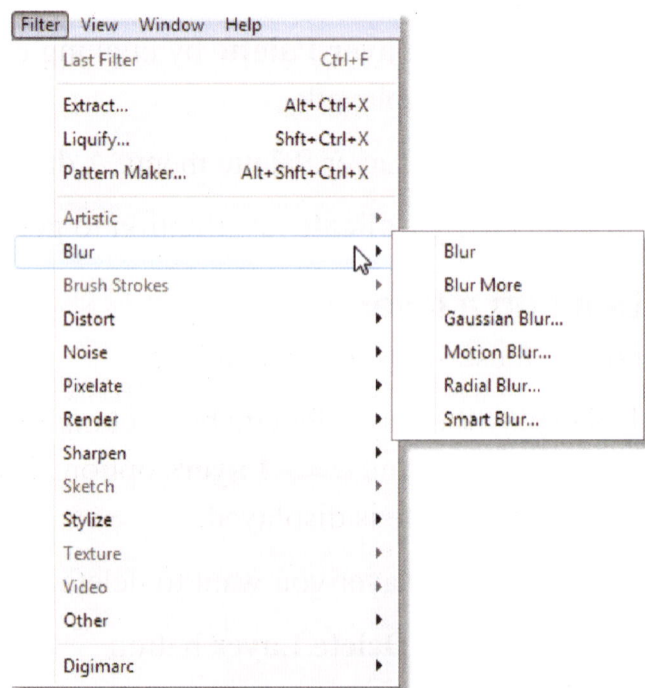

Fig. 1.15 *Filters*

3. Select any filter from the list of options. The corresponding dialog box appears to set the properties of the selected filter (Fig. 1.15).
4. Click on the **OK** button. Filter is set to the image (Fig. 1.16).

Fig. 1.16 *Filter applied to an image*

FACT FILE

The **Filter Gallery** allows you to apply many different filters to a layer. Click on Filter menu. Select Filter Gallery option. The Filter Gallery appears.

Masks

Masks are used to change one part of an image without affecting the rest of the image. When a part of an image is selected, changes affect only the selected area. The area that is not selected is masked, and hence protected from changes.

When a mask channel is selected in the Channels palette, foreground and background colors appear as grayscale values.

Quick Mask

Quick Mask mode lets the user create and view a temporary mask for an image. This mode lets the user see both the image and the mask at the same time. The advantage of editing a selection as a mask is that almost any Photoshop tool or Filter can be used to modify the mask.

Text and Fonts

Adding text

Text can be easily added and formatted on any picture in Photoshop.

1. Select the **Type** tool from the **Toolbox**.
2. Click on the part of the image where the text is to be inserted.
3. Select the font, font size, attributes and alignment required from the **Text Palette**.
4. Type the text and it will appear on the picture.

Moving text

Press the **Command** key and use the **Move** tool to drag the text to its new position.

Deleting text

The text is added as a layer. To delete the text, follow the steps given here:

1. Click on the layer containing the text from the **Layers Palette**.
2. Click on **Layer** menu ⇒ **Delete Layer** option.

FACT FILE

You can convert each letter into an artistic element. For example, you can use filters to twist the text element into different shapes or rotate the text into angles.

ACTIVITY

Complete the following activity.
1. Select the layer your text is on.
2. Select the text to be edited.
3. Change the color and font type of the text.
4. Apply a bend. Move the text.
5. Save the changes.

GLOSSARY

Adobe Photoshop: It is a graphics editing program.

Brush Palette: It lets the user make thousands of different types of brushes.

Channels: It is used for storing information about color elements in an image.

Color Mode: It determines the color model used to display and print images.

Color Palette: It displays the current foreground and background colors.

Filters: It is used to add different types of special effects to an image.

Layers: It provides a powerful method of working on one element of an image without disturbing the others.

Layer Sets: It is group of layers.

Layers Palette: It controls the layers in an image.

Masks: They are used to change one part of an image without affecting the rest of the image.

Quick Mask mode: It lets the user create and view a temporary mask for an image.

NOW YOU KNOW

1. Photoshop allows all formats of images, such as GIF, JPG, PCX, BMP and many more, to be imported and edited, customised or changed into almost anything imaginable.
2. The Adobe Photoshop work area includes the command menus at the top of the screen and a variety of tools and palettes for editing an image.
3. Photoshop provides various tools for selecting, painting, drawing, editing, erasing and viewing images.
4. You can open and import images in various file formats. The available formats appear in the Open dialog box.
5. At the time of creating a new image you can adjust the size, background and the resolution of the image file.
6. Photoshop can work with different color modes.
7. The ability to edit individual channels gives the user control over the colors and details in an image.
8. The text can be easily added and formatted in the Photoshop.

EXERCISE

A Fill in the blanks.

1. .... provides various tools for selecting, painting, drawing, editing, erasing and viewing images.
2. The features that allow two or more separate images to merge as one is ....
3. At the time of creating a new image you can adjust ...., ... and ....
4. A .... determines the color model used to display and print images.
5. .... provides a powerful method of working on one element of an image without disturbing the others.

B Give one word for:

1. The extension of Photoshop file.
2. Tool for writing a text.

3. Changing the color of the background and foreground.

4. The symbol on the layer that denotes that the layer is visible.

5. The mode that lets the user create and view a temporary mask for an image.

C. Identify the following tools and give its usage.

Tool	Name	Usage
🖉		
T		
💧		
⬛		
🖉		

D. Answer the following questions.

1. Why do we use Adobe Photoshop? Give any three features.

2. What is the use of a Toolbox? Explain the tools used for zooming an image.

3. What is a color mode in Photoshop?

4. What are layers? Give any three features of layers.

5. What are the steps of creating a new layer?

6. What is a mask and a quick mask?

7. How can you add a text in an image file?

LAB WORK

A. Create a new file with 120 resolution and 9.0 inch by 9.0 inch size with a white background.
B. Import any image file of your choice.
C. Change the foreground and the background color.
D. Use a Text tool to give a heading to your file.
E. Add a layer and place another picture on it.
F. Select Text tool and type your name in blue, in 30 pt font and position it at top left where it will be visible.
G. Use the Gradient tool on the image.
H. Select a portion of a picture and change the direction.
I. Save the file.

TEACHER'S NOTES

1. Help the students create a thumbnail image that they can place next to their name in the class list.
2. If possible, show the higher versions of Photoshop to the students. Explore their various latest features with them.

2 MS ACCESS 2007

LEARNING OBJECTIVES

You will learn about:

1. Some important terms related to database
2. functions of DBMS
3. MS Access 2007
4. starting MS Access 2007
5. creating new databases in MS Access 2007
6. creating tables in Design view
7. saving tables in MS Access 2007
8. viewing tables in MS Access 2007

Introduction

Database is the arrangement of data in a manner where it can be retrieved easily. Microsoft Access is a database program that is used for storing all kinds of information in the form of tables, queries, forms, reports, etc. It has many built-in features to assist you in constructing and viewing the information stored in the database. Once information is stored in Microsoft Access database, it is easy to find, analyse, and print.

Some Important Terms Related to Database

Let us learn about a few terms related to database here.

Database: It is an integrated collection of logically-related records in the form of tables that offers an organised mechanism for storing, managing and retrieving information. It stores and manages information related to a particular subject or purpose. For example, school, libraries, banks, etc.

Database Management System (DBMS): It is a set of computer programs that controls the creation, maintenance and the use of the database in the computer by the user. For example, MS Access, FoxPro and FoxBASE.

Table: It is a collection of related information in the form of rows and columns. For example, in a school database a few tables which feature are students, library, teachers, admin staff and admission details (Fig. 2.1).

Record: It is complete information arranged horizontally in a table. For example, the complete information of a student may contain student's name, address, city, phone number, class and section in the database.

Field: It is a column arranged vertically in a table that stores the information of the same type. For example, Admission No. is a field that stores only admission number and Student Name stores only the names of the students.

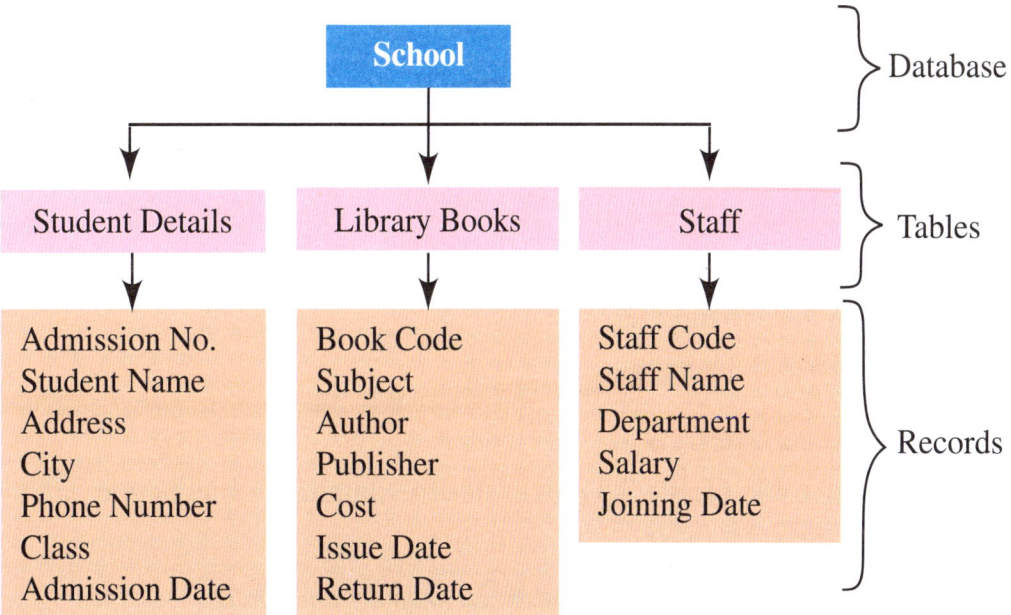

Fig. 2.1 *Structure of a database*

Functions of DBMS

DBMS is useful in several aspects. These are discussed here.

1. *Reduces data redundancy:* Data redundancy means duplication of data. For example, in a library the name of a book may occur under the author's name and its ISBN number. However, with the help of DBMS the redundant data can be removed.

2. *Facilitates sharing of data:* Different users can access and use the same database as the format of the files stored remain the same.

3. *Controls data inconsistency:* In DBMS, the change in any one file is automatically updated in all the related files. For example, in a library if there are two records for a single book, one under the author's name and another under new stock it might happen that the details are changed under one record. This may lead to inconsistency as both the records for the same book would comprise of different information. Such problems are easily dealt with the help of DBMS.

4. *Enforces standards:* In DBMS, certain standards can be applied in data representation.

5. *Ensures data security:* The access to any record can be made protected in DBMS. The files can be accessed only by those who are authorised to do so.

6. *Maintains integrity:* DBMS maintains integrity by keeping some constraints when the data is entered. These constraints are the rules that are designed to keep data consistent and correct. They act like a check on the incoming data.

FACT FILE

Relational Database Management System (RDBMS) proposed by E.F. Codd in 1970. It is a type of database where data is organised as related tables. These databases are more powerful as relevant data can be extracted, tables can be extended and modified from these without having to reorganise the existing tables.

Database Objects

The following table (Table 2.1) identifies the database objects you can use while creating a Microsoft Access database.

Table 2.1 *Objects and Their Description*

Name of the Object	Description
Table	It stores information in the form of rows (records) and columns (fields). For example, one table could store a list of friends along with their details, while another table could store their marks.
Queries	There are used for sorting, grouping or filtering data in MS Access. For example, a query might only display a list of students in class 7 out of all school students.
Forms	Customised screens to provide an easy way to enter and view data in a table or query.
Reports	These present data from a table or query in printed format.

ACTIVITY

A. **Gather more information on database and its concepts from the Internet. Also, find out the following:**
   1. Its key features
   2. Version history
   3. Real-life usage

B. **Make a list of at least five types of databases available in the computer world.**

MS Access

MS Access makes use of tables and records to store information. It is a database management system from Microsoft. It can also import data stored in other applications and databases. Now, let us learn how MS Access 2007 application can be used.

Starting MS Access 2007

Follow these steps to open MS Access 2007 application:

1. Click on **Start** button ⇒ **All Programs** ⇒ **Microsoft Office** ⇒ **Microsoft Office Access 2007** (Fig. 2.2).

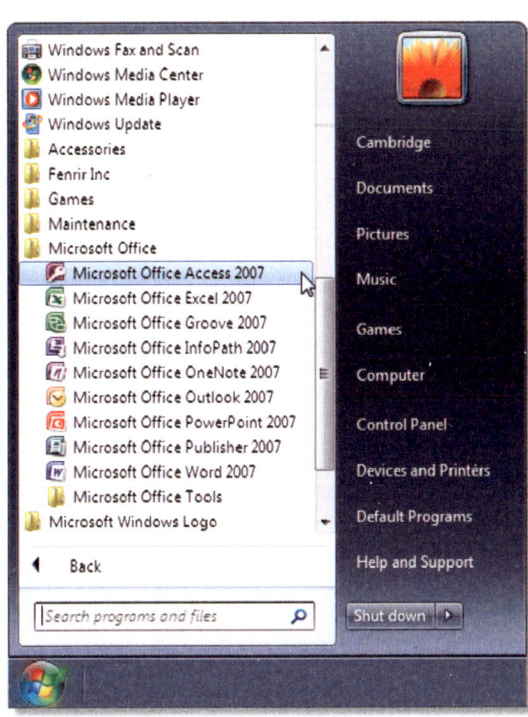

Fig. 2.2 *Opening MS Access 2007*

2. MS Access 2007 window appears (Fig. 2.3).

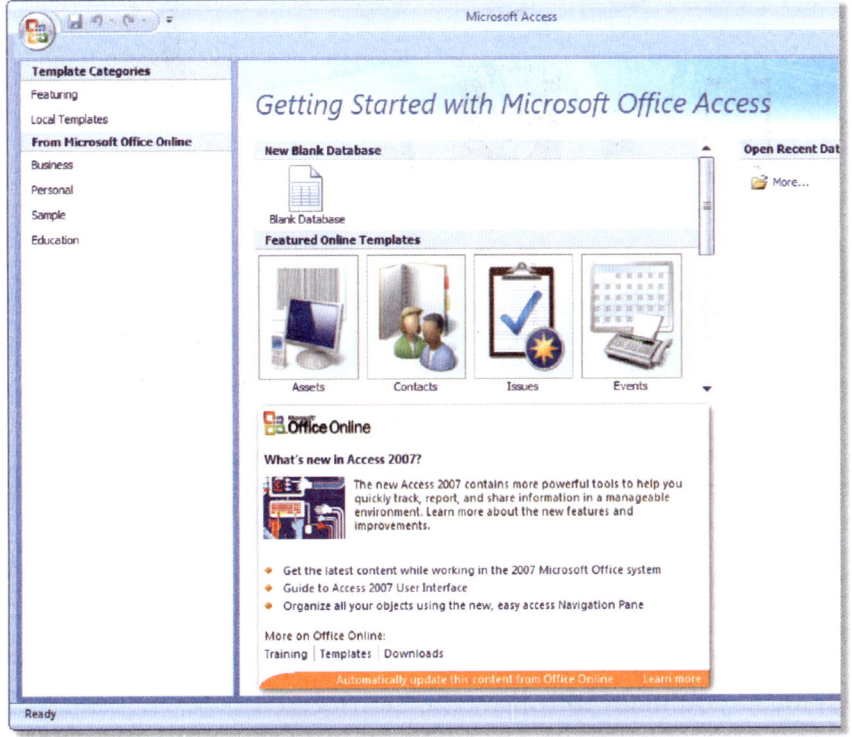

Fig. 2.3 *MS Access 2007 window*

Creating Databases in MS Access 2007

Microsoft Access Database is made up of several components. These components are called **database objects**. One or more of these objects are found when a database is created. These components are stored in a single database file.

Using a Template

1. Click on the **Local Templates** in the **Template Categories** in the left pane of the MS Access 2007 window (Fig. 2.4).

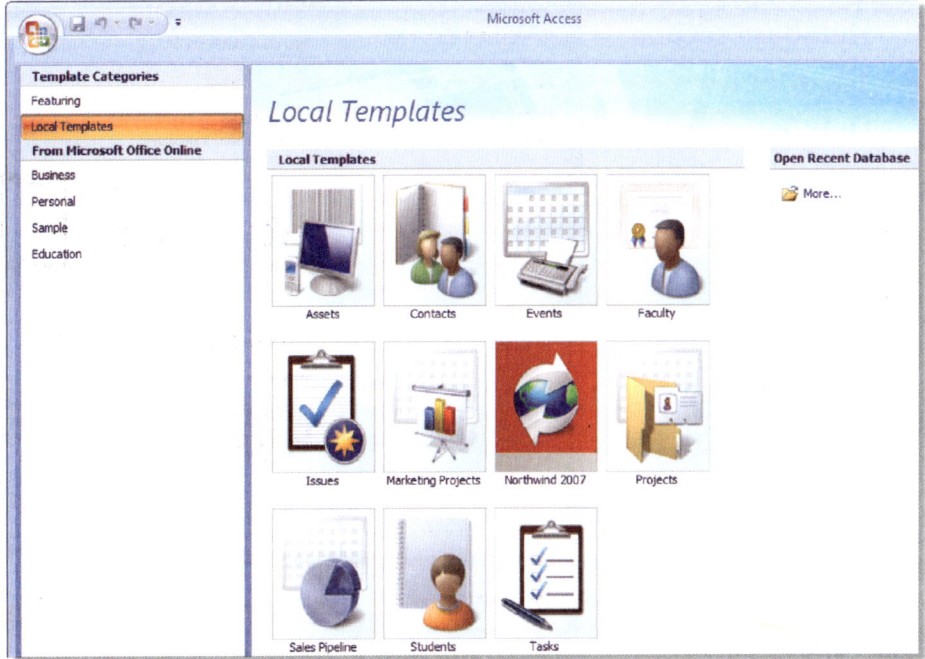

Fig. 2.4 *Local Templates in the MS Access 2007 window*

23

2. Select the template of your choice from the Local Templates section in the middle.

3. A pane appears on the right. Change the name of the file in the **File Name:** box and change the location of the database using the Browse button (Fig. 2.5).

4. Click on **Create** in the right pane of the MS Access 2007 window.

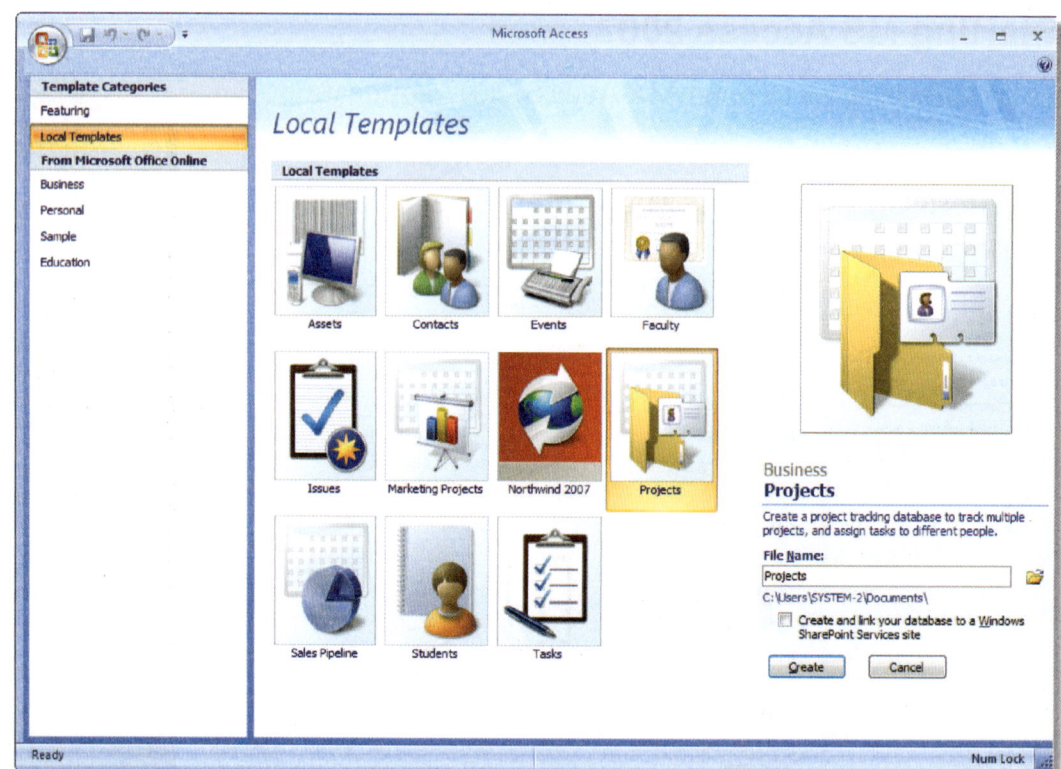

Fig. 2.5 *Creating a database using a template*

Using a Blank Database

To create a new database using a blank database you need to follow the steps given below:

1. Click on **Blank Database** in the **New Blank Database** section. The **Blank Database** pane appears on the right.

2. Type a name for the file in the **File Name:** box.

3. You can also change the location of the database by clicking on the **Browse** icon in the right pane (Fig. 2.6).

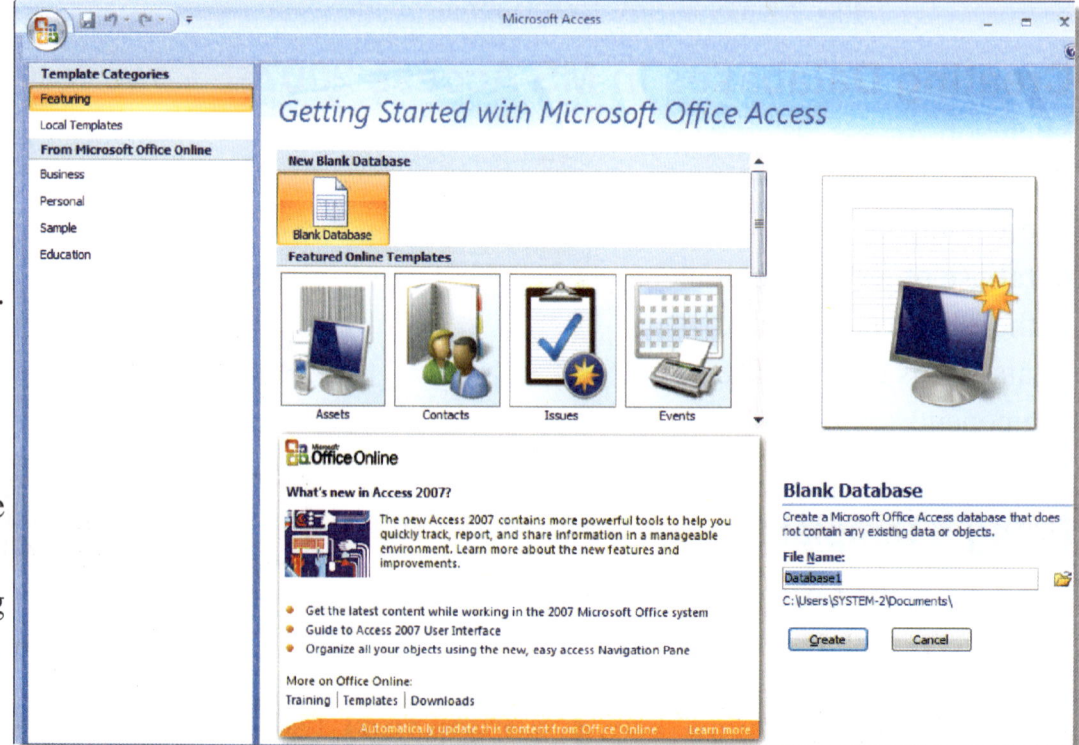

Fig. 2.6 *Creating a new Blank database*

24

The **File New Database** dialog box appears. Select the desired location and click on **OK** (Fig. 2.7).

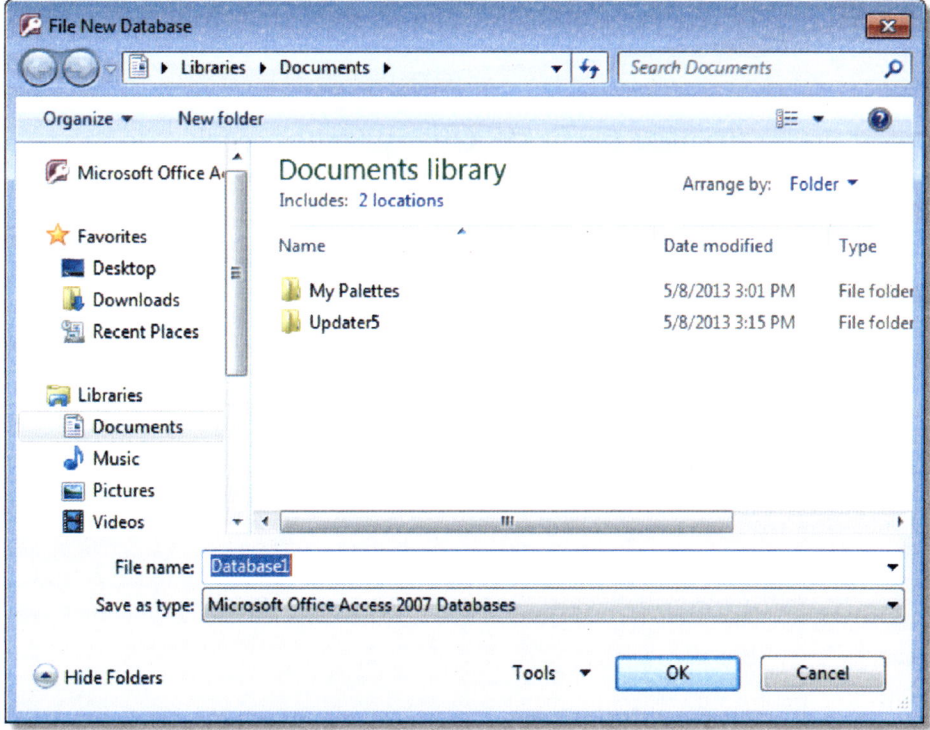

Fig. 2.7 *File New Database dialog box*

4. Click on the **Create** button. A new database titled **Table1** will be created seen in **Datasheet** tab.
5. The table has a field labelled as **ID**, it is a primary key. The header fields can be changed or added by double-clicking on it (Fig. 2.8).

We will learn to create databases in blank database sheets in this chapter.

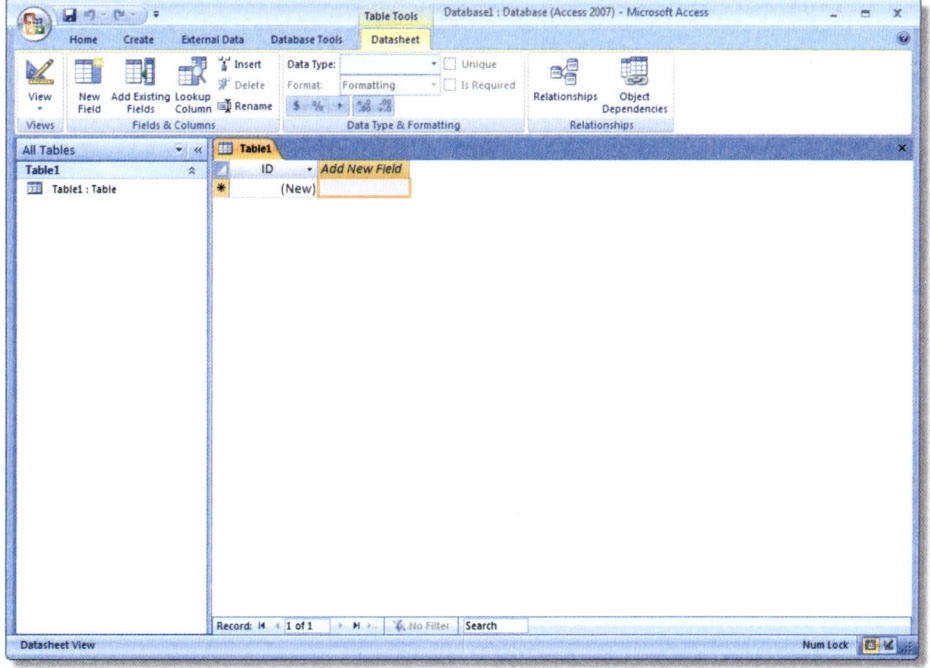

Fig. 2.8 *A new database using a blank database*

FACT FILE

The extension of an access database file in MS Office 2007 is .accdb.

The Database window

The Database window has the following components (Fig. 2.9):

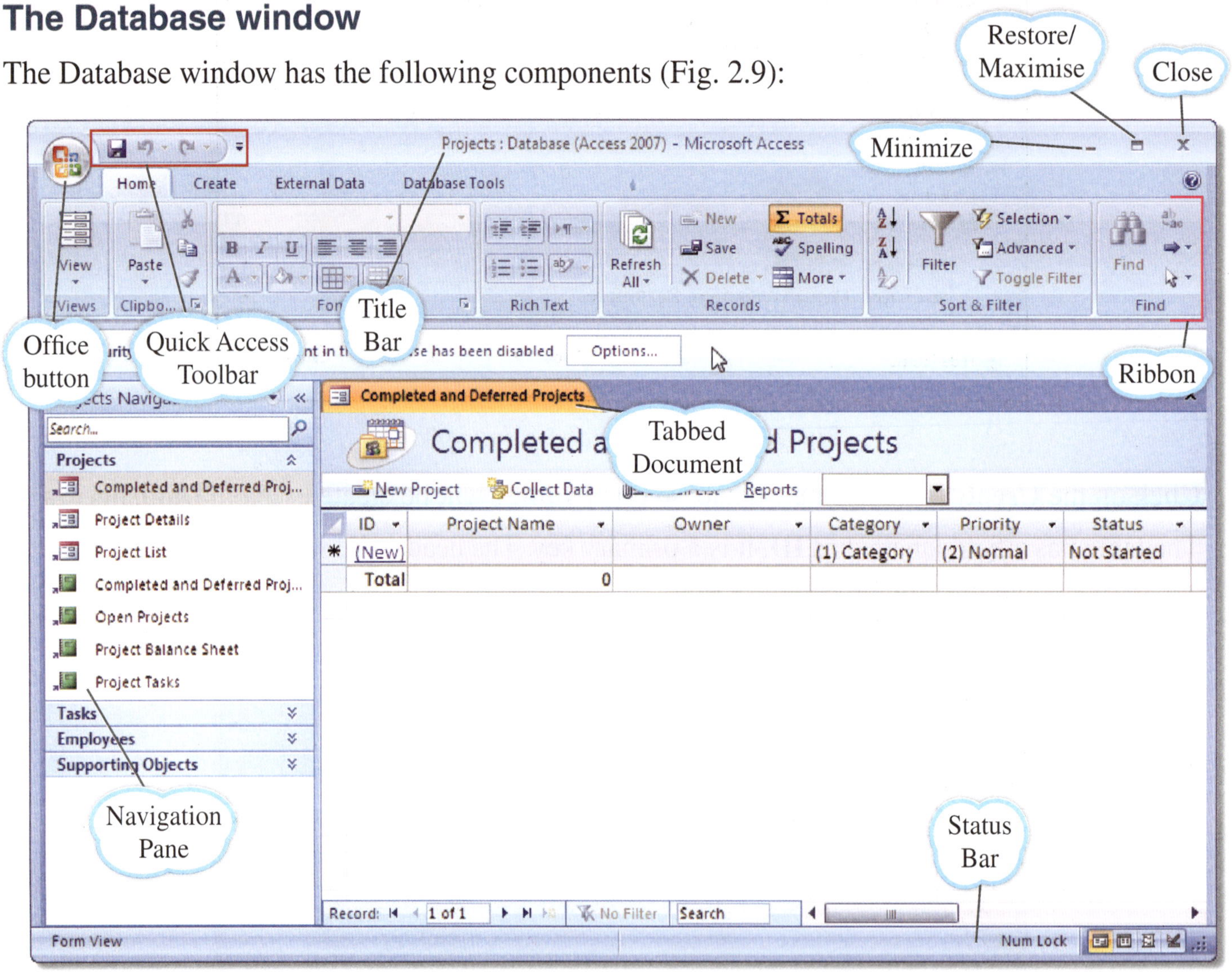

Fig. 2.9 *Components of a database window*

Title Bar: It shows the name of the database created. The **Minimise, Maximise/Restore** and **Close** buttons are also present in this area.

Microsoft Office Button: It is the button on the left of the Title Bar. It contains commands like New, Open, Save, Save As, Print, etc.

Quick Access Toolbar: It has some of the most frequently used commands in MS Access like Save, Undo and Redo. The toolbar can be shifted below the Ribbon also and more commands can be added to it.

Ribbon: It contains the commands that can be performed against different database objects. These commands are classified under groups in different tabs.

Navigation Pane: It is the left pane of the window. Here, database objects in the currently opened or freshly created databases are displayed.

Tabbed Document: The database objects appear in tabs unlike the overlapping windows in the earlier versions.

Status Bar: It is present at the bottom window and displays the status and buttons to change the page views.

FACT FILE

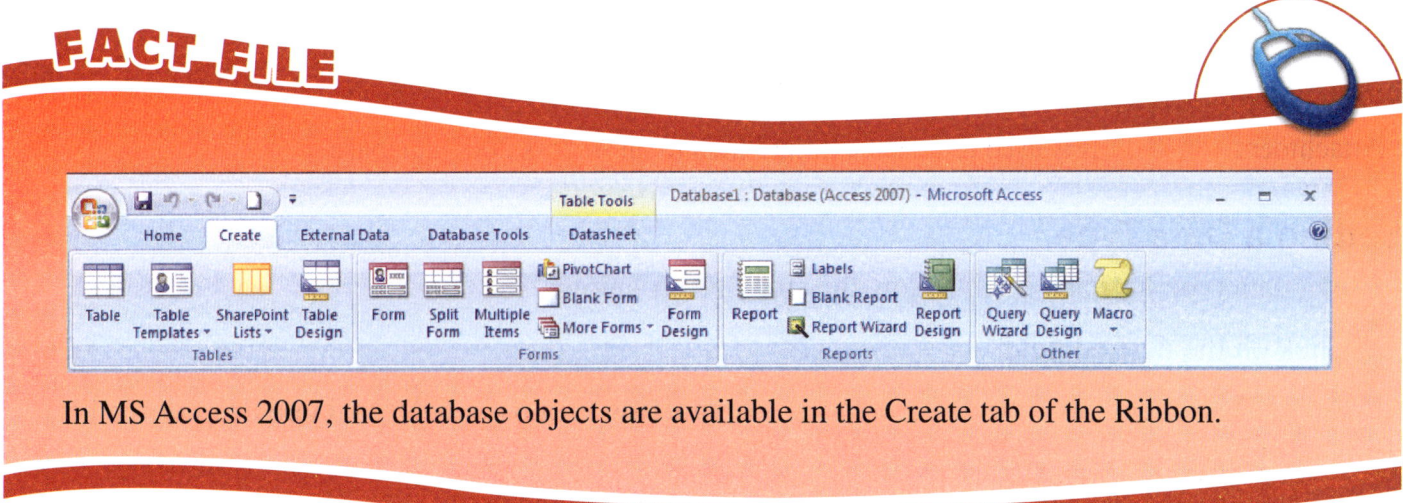

In MS Access 2007, the database objects are available in the Create tab of the Ribbon.

Data Types

The Data Type for every Field Name describes the form in which the data is accepted. Descriptions of some of the commonly used Data Type values that appear in the drop-down list are shown in Table 2.2.

Table 2.2 *Commonly Used Data Types in MS Access 2007*

Data Type	Description
Text	It stores alphanumeric values, that is, both numbers and letters. Maximum 255 characters can be stored. For example, a product ID or an address.
AutoNumber	It is an integer that automatically generates an increasing or decreasing order of numbers when records are added or deleted. If there is no primary key in the table then AutoNumber uniquely identifies the records.
Memo	It is used for lengthy text and numbers such as definitions or descriptive notes. A maximum of 65536 characters are allowed.
Number	It holds numeric data that is used for calculations. Both decimals and without decimal digits are allowed.

Date/Time	It stores the date and time values in different formats.
Currency	It specifies different currencies and displays them in different formats. It stores an integer that increments or decrements automatically as you add or delete records.
Yes/No	This can have only one of the two values, that is, True/False, Yes/No or On/Off.
OLE Object	It stands for Object Linking and Embedding. Data from some other software like MS Excel, PowerPoint, MS Word, etc. can be brought and stored in a table as an OLE object column.
Hyperlink	It is a link to an Internet resource.
Attachment	It is used to attach external files to an Access 2007 database.

Setting a Data Type

To set a data type for each field, follow the steps given below:

1. Click on the desired field.
2. Select **Datasheet** tab ⟹ **Data Type & Formatting** group ⟹ **Data Type** drop-down list (Fig. 2.10).

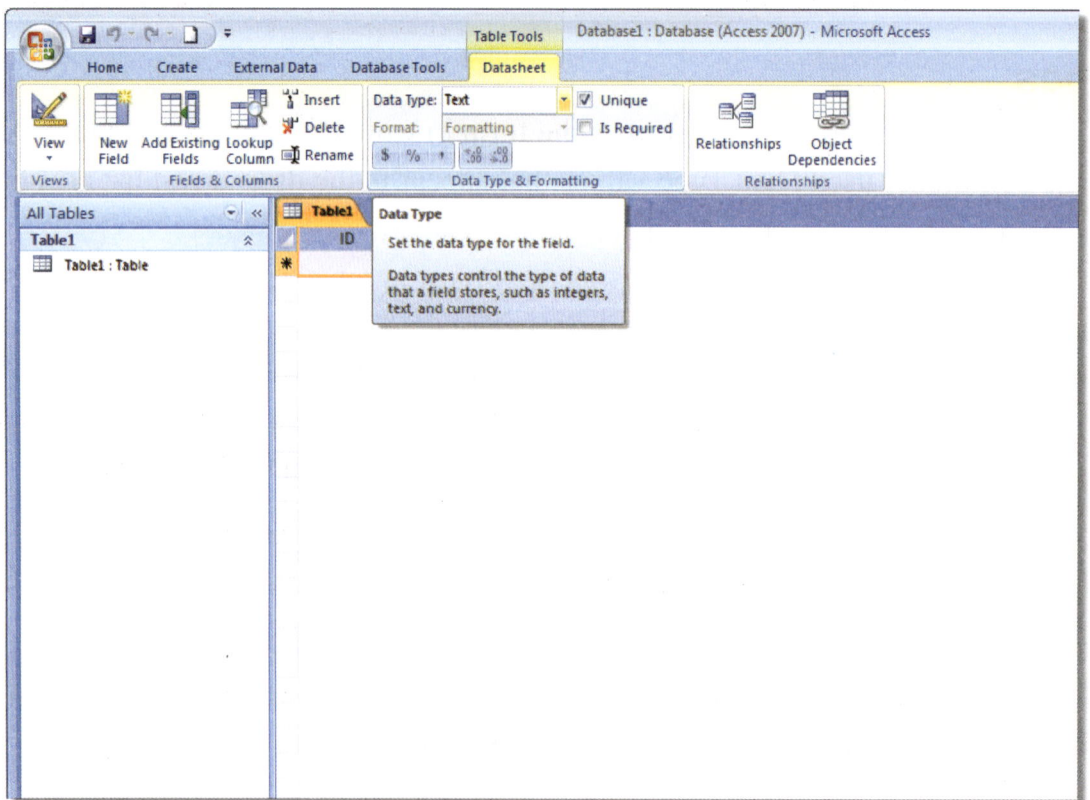

Fig. 2.10 *Setting Data Type*

3. Click on the desired data type in the list.

Primary Key

Every table in Microsoft Access must have at least one field that uniquely identifies each record in the table. This field is known as a primary key. This primary key should always have a value that is not repeated for any other record. For example, in any table for students, it is possible that there are two students with the same name. It becomes difficult to distinguish two records without a unique value. Here, you can assign admission number as the primary key because this remains unique for each student.

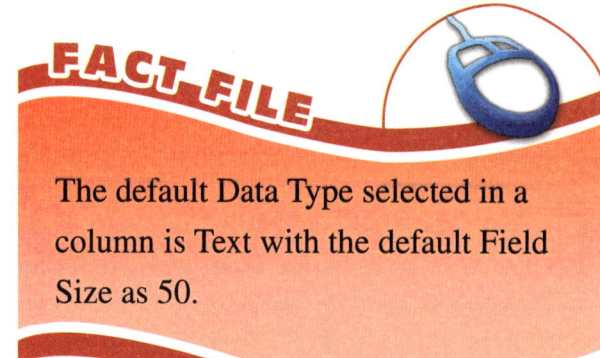

FACT FILE

The default Data Type selected in a column is Text with the default Field Size as 50.

Note: If the primary key is not assigned it is automatically added as an ID at the time of saving the table.

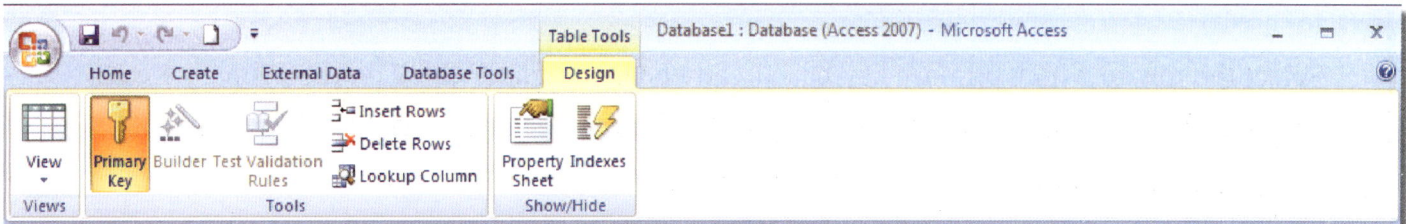

FACT FILE

You can even have multiple primary keys for a table. However, these should be unique values. To do so you must hold down the Ctrl key and then select the row selector for each field.

Assigning a Primary Key

To assign a primary key to the table fields you should select the required field. For example, select ADM NO, click on **Design** tab ⟹ **Tools** group ⟹ **Primary Key** option (Fig. 2.11).

Fig. 2.11 *Setting the Primary Key*

 OR

Select the required field and right-click on it. A shortcut menu opens. Select the Primary Key option (Fig. 2.12).

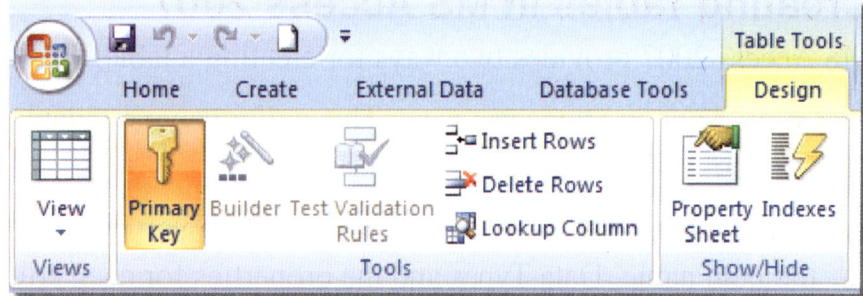

Fig. 2.12 *Setting a primary key using shortcut menu*

A key will be displayed in front of the column name to show that the column is now working as a primary key in the table (Fig. 2.13).

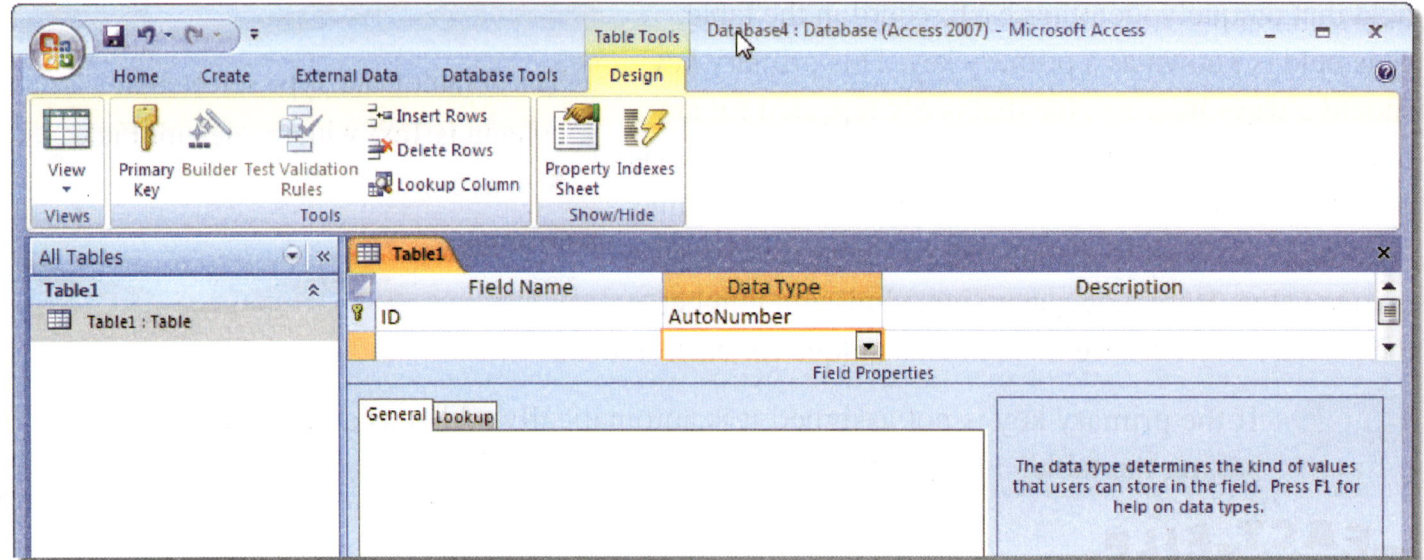

Fig. 2.13 *A column working as primary key*

Removing a Primary Key

To remove a primary key, select the required field and select the **Primary Key** option in the Tools group of the **Design** tab. You can also select the field, right-click on it and then select **Primary Key** from the shortcut menu.

The key symbol appearing next to the respective field will disappear.

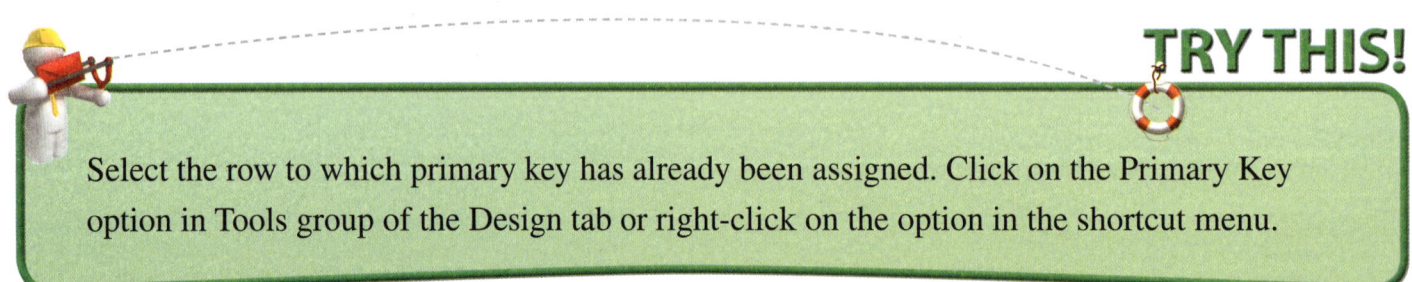

Select the row to which primary key has already been assigned. Click on the Primary Key option in Tools group of the Design tab or right-click on the option in the shortcut menu.

Creating Tables in MS Access 2007

MS Access 2007 provides two ways for creating a table. These are:

1. *Create table in Datasheet view:* This will give you a blank datasheet with unlabelled columns that looks much like an Excel worksheet.

2. *Create table in Design view:* With this option you define the structure of the table by specifying the field name, Data Types and the properties for each column. This is the most common way of creating a table.

In Datasheet View

Follow these steps to create a table in the datasheet view:

1. Open the database.
2. Select **Datasheet** tab ⟹ **Views** group ⟹ **View** drop-down list ⟹ **Datasheet View** option (Fig. 2.14).

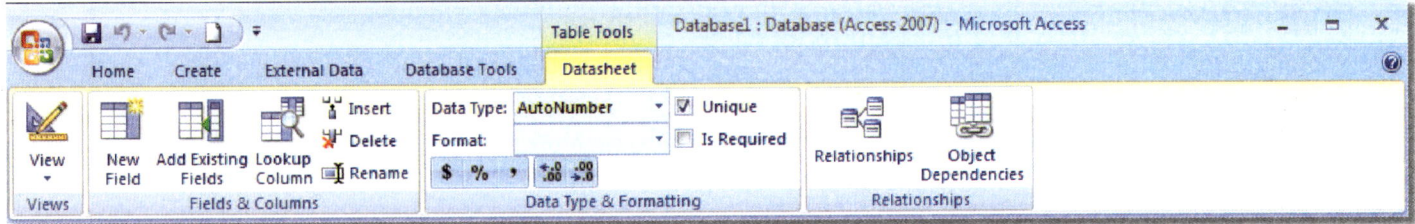

Fig. 2.14 *Datasheet View option*

3. Click on the **Tables** group in the **Create** tab.
4. A new tabbed document will be formed. Add **New Field** header will be seen next to the ID field.
5. Click on the column and select the data type. Add the data to the fields (Fig. 2.15).

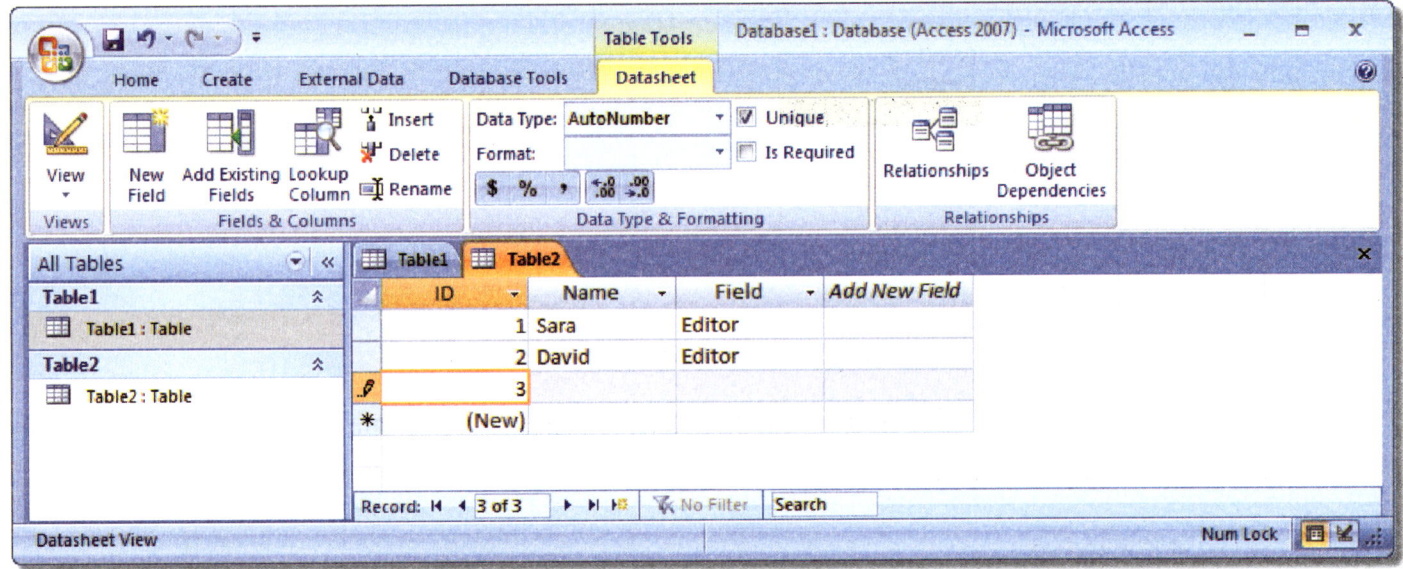

Fig. 2.15 *Creating a table in Datasheet View*

In Design View

Follow these steps to create a table in the Design view:

1. Open the database.
2. Select **Datasheet** tab ⟹ **Views** group ⟹ **View** drop-down list ⟹ **Design View** option (Fig. 2.16).
3. The Design View window is divided into two parts: **Field Grid pane** and **Field Properties pane**. These are discussed here.

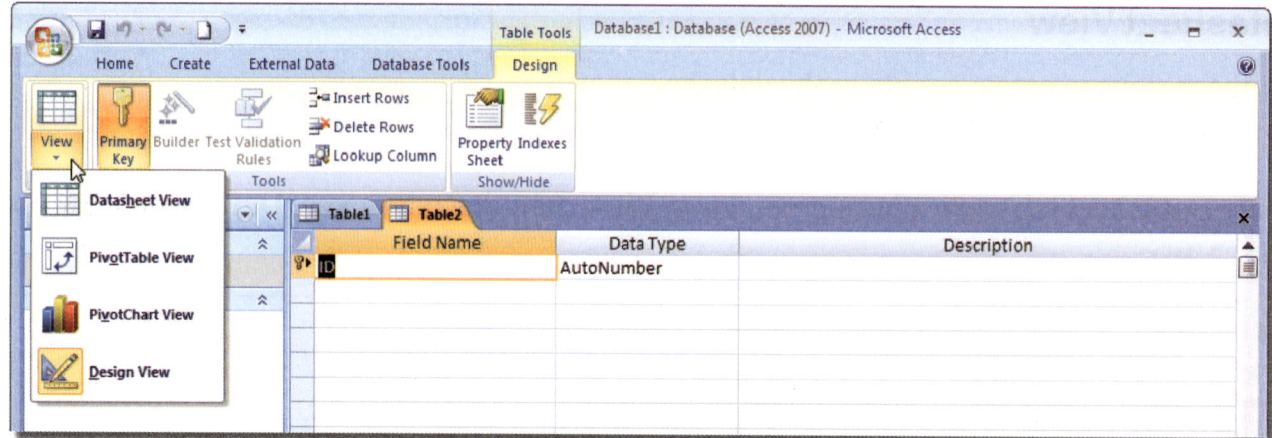

Fig. 2.16 *Design View option*

Field Grid pane: Field grid pane is used to define the fields in the tables along with their data types and an optional description of the field (Fig. 2.17). You can change the data type of the field in this view.

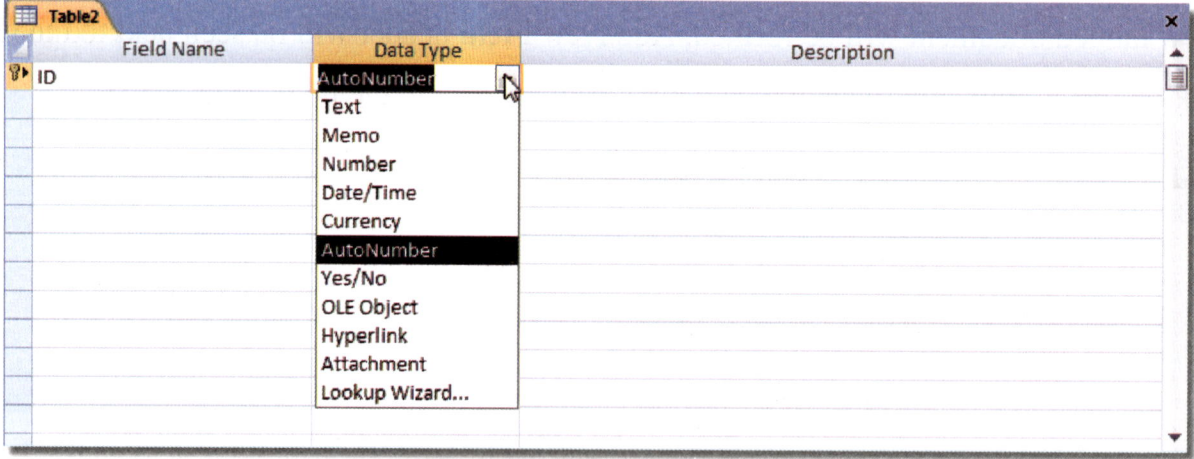

Fig. 2.17 *Field Grid pane*

Field Properties pane: You can give additional properties to the Field Name using Field Properties pane (Fig. 2.18). It is used to specify the field properties in detail such as field size, validation, etc.

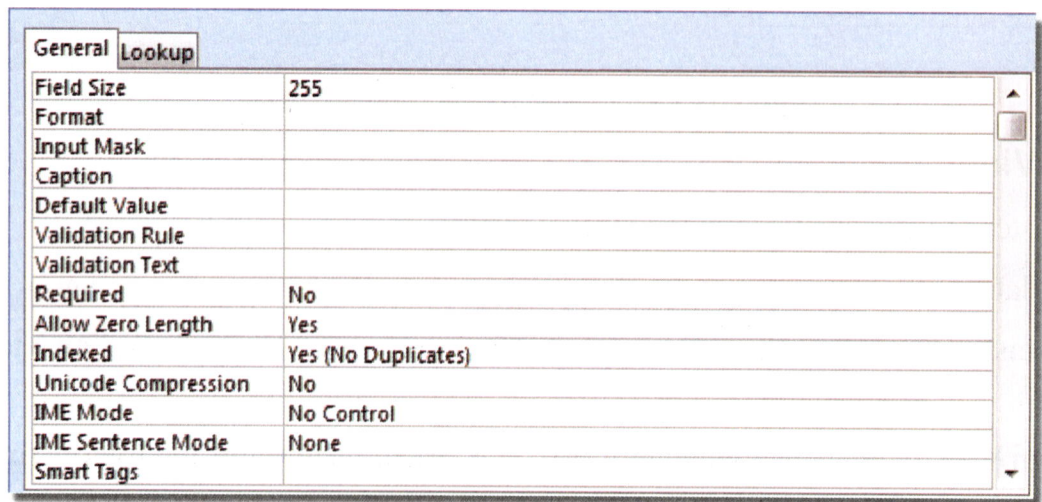

Fig. 2.18 *Field Properties pane*

Some of the commonly used options that can be filled in the Field Properties pane are explained in Table 2.3.

Table 2.3 *Some of the Field Properties Used in MS Access 2007*

Property	Description
Field Size	It is used to set the maximum size for data stored in the field set to the Text or Number data type.
New Values	It is used to set the order of numbers in the fields either in an increment or random order.
Format	It allows you to display data in a format which is different from the way it is actually stored. For example, you can choose a predefined format or other symbols for creating a custom format to define a currency.
Input Mask	It stores the condition to be followed at the time of accepting data in Datasheet view.
Caption	It is used to display an alternate name for the field to make it more explanatory.
Default Value	It sets a value that is displayed automatically for the field when a new record is added.
Validation Rule	It sets constraints to the values that can be accepted into a field.
Validation Text	It shows error messages that appear when the user violates the set validation rule.
Required	It helps to set whether the data is compulsory in a column or not.
Allow Zero Length	In combination with the required property, it can be used to define whether a blank value means the user has no data on it or whether the value itself has no data.
Indexed	It speeds up sorting but may slow down the database.
Smart Tags	It is used to add tags like date, telephone number, financial symbol or person name in the field. Each tags is associated with an action or a list of actions.
Text Align	It is used for the alignment of the text entered in the field.

4. Enter the required information in the Field Grid and Field Properties panes in the Design View window (Fig. 2.19). Use the Tab key or the Enter key to move through the different fields.

5. Assign one of the fields in the Field Grid Pane as the Primary Key. A key will be displayed in front of the column name to show that the column is now working as a primary key in the table (Fig. 2.20).

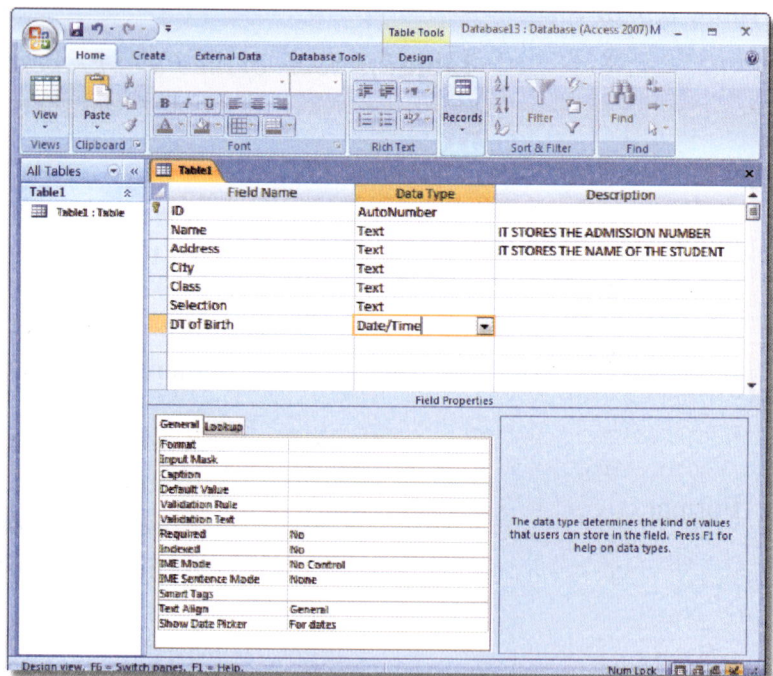

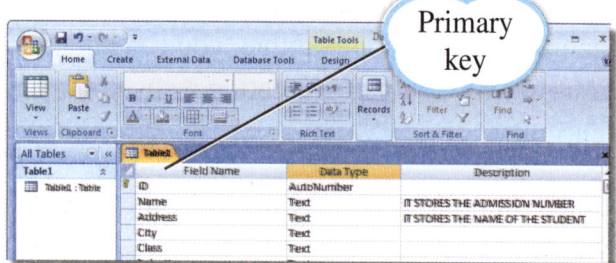

Fig. 2.20 *A column working as a primary key*

Fig. 2.19 *Filling the field information*

FACT FILE

A field name in the database can have a maximum of 64 characters in upper, lower or mixed case, and letters, numbers and some special characters can be used. However, it cannot have brackets and a period and it cannot start with a blank space.

Changing the View

MS Access 2007 provides different viewing options for working on the data. Given in Figure 2.21 are the four views in which a user can view their data:

1. Datasheet View
2. PivotTable View
3. PivotChart View
4. Design View

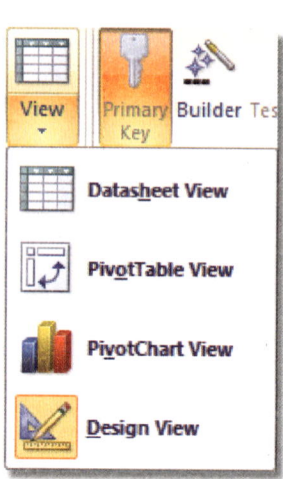

Fig. 2.21 *Options for changing the view*

Datasheet View and Design View are the two most commonly used views in MS Access. The row and column format is seen in the Datasheet view where the data can be added. Descriptions like field names, data types etc. can be added in the Design view.

It is possible to switch from one view to another using the **View** drop-down list in the **Views** group of the:

- **Datasheet** tab while switching from Datasheet view to Design view.
- **Design** tab while switching from the Design view to Datasheet view.

Modifying Tables and their Content

Tables created in Access 2007 can be modified in the Datasheet view. Data types can be changed and columns/fields can be added, deleted, moved and renamed.

The different groups in the **Datasheet** tab can be used to modify the table and its contents (Fig. 2.22).

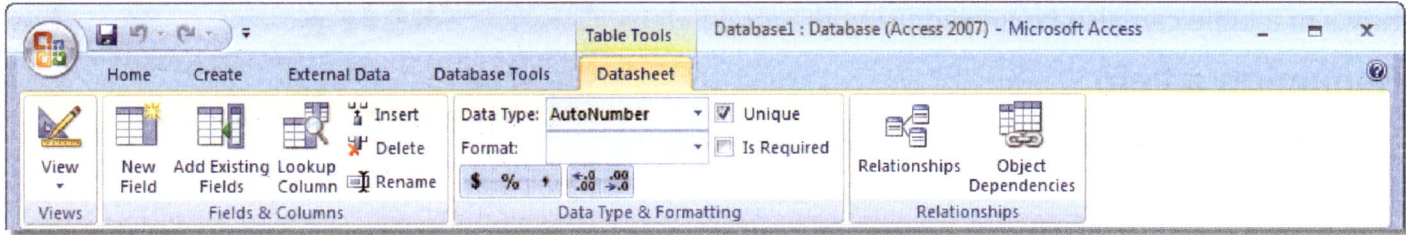

Fig. 2.22 *Datasheet tab*

Changing data types

1. Select the desired column header.
2. Click on the drop-down list next to the **Data Type** option in the **Data Type & Formatting** group and select the desired option.

Inserting a new field

1. Select the column header, on whose left you wish to insert a field.
2. Click on the **Insert** option in the **Fields & Columns** group of the **Datasheet** tab.

Deleting a field

1. Select the column header of the field you wish to delete.
2. Click on the **Delete** option in the **Fields & Columns** group of the **Datasheet** tab.
3. Click on **Yes** in the **Microsoft Office Access** dialog box.

Moving a field

1. Select the field to be moved (Fig. 2.23). A thick blue line appears along the left edge of the field.

ID	Monthly Incom	Bonus	Add New Field
Sara	5000	500	
David	1500	150	
Rita	6500	650	
Sehar	0	0	
Rashmi	4500	450	
Chris	1000	100	
Venkat	7000	700	
Total	2500	2550	

Fig. 2.23 *Selecting the field*

2. Hold the left mouse button till the cursor changes to .
3. Drag and drop the field in the desired location.

Rows in a table can also be moved using the above steps.

Renaming a field

1. Select the column header whose heading you want to change.
2. Click on the **Rename** option in the **Fields & Columns** group of the **Datasheet** tab.

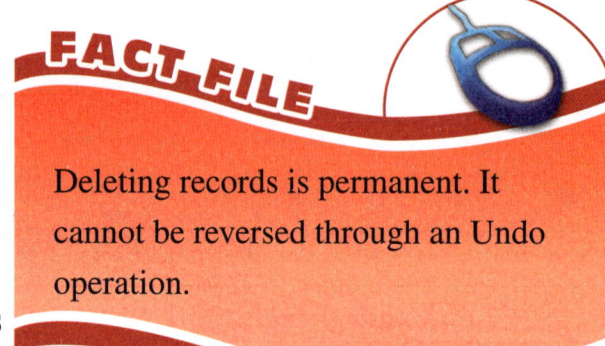

Deleting records is permanent. It cannot be reversed through an Undo operation.

TRY THIS!

Select a column/field. Click on the drop-down arrow next to the column header. Sort the data in the column as per your requirements.

ACTIVITY

Complete the following activity.

1. Prepare a table in MS Access 2007 listing the names and taste of your ten favourite food items.
2. Switch to Design View.
3. Explore the options for inserting and deleting rows in the Tools group of the Design tab.

4. Delete the rows in which the names of junk food items have been listed.
5. Insert new rows and complete the list with healthy foods.

Saving Databases in MS Access 2007

The databases created at the start are saved in a specific location which can be selected using the **Browse** button. The subsequent changes made to the database can be saved by clicking the **Save** button in the **Quick Access Toolbar**.

However in MS Access 2007, it is also possible to save the database in a different location and using the file format of your choice from the given list of options.

Follow these steps to save a table in MS Access 2007:

1. Click on the **Office** button.
2. Select **Save As** option from the drop-down list and select the file format. In this case, it is **Access 2007 Database** (Fig. 2.24).

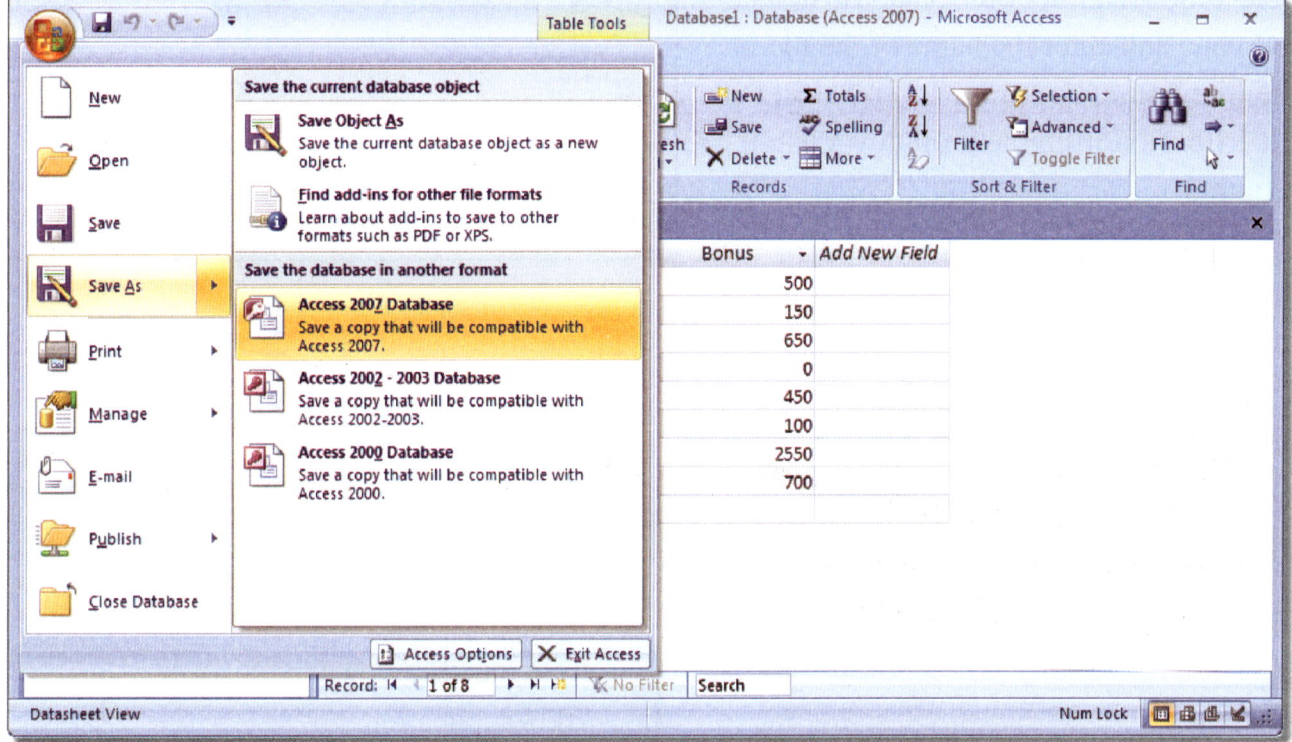

Fig. 2.24 *Selecting the Save As option*

3. The **Microsoft Office Access** dialog box appears. It seeks permission to save all the opened objects before saving the file. Click **Yes** (Fig. 2.25).

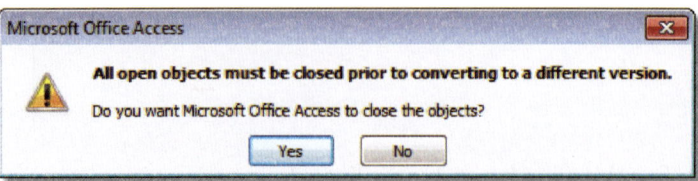

Fig. 2.25 *Microsoft Office Access dialog box*

4. The **Save As** dialog box appears.
5. Select the desired location for saving the file and enter the file name in the **File name:** box.
6. Click **Save** option (Fig. 2.26).

Opening an Existing Database

A database saved in MS Access 2007 can be opened by following these steps:

1. Open a database.
2. Click on the **Office** button and select **Open** from the drop-down list.
3. The **Open** dialog box appears.
4. Select the location of the database in the left pane and enter the name of the file in the **File name:** box (Fig. 2.27). Select the file extension from the drop-down list, if required.
5. Click on **Open**.

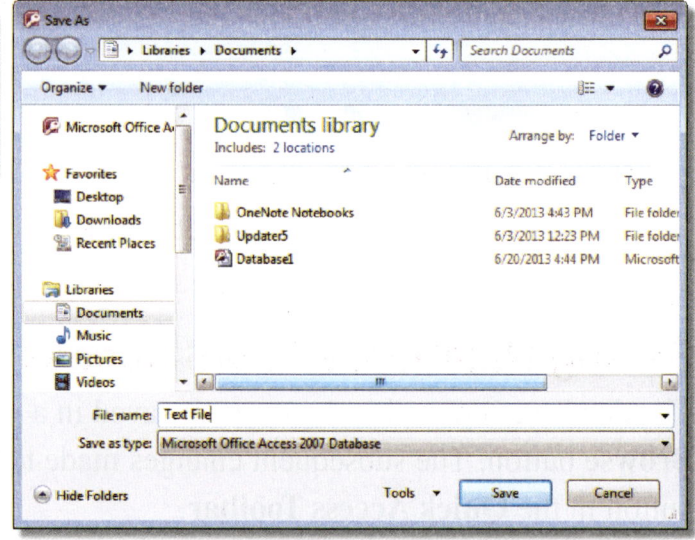

Fig. 2.26 *Save As dialog box*

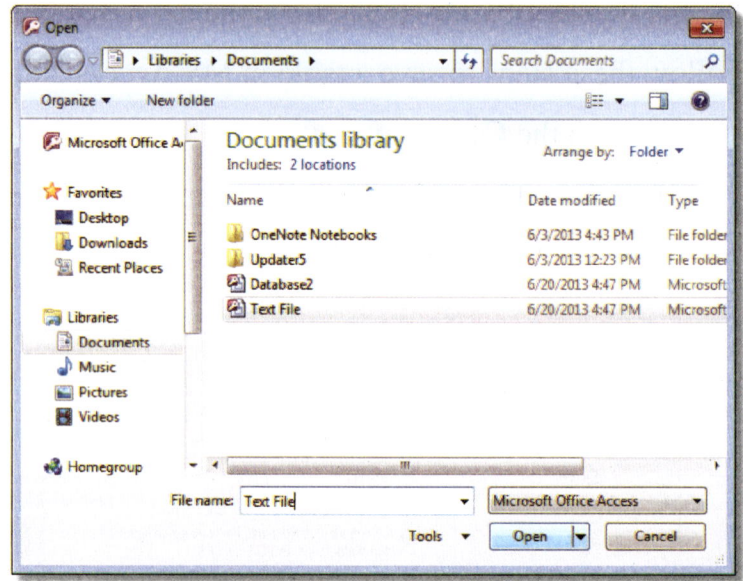

Fig. 2.27 *Open dialog box*

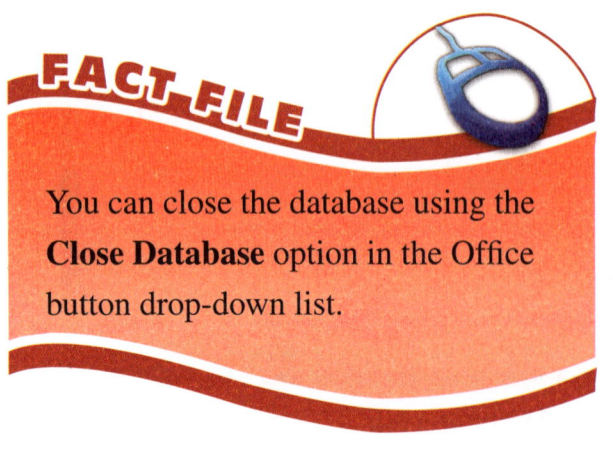

You can close the database using the **Close Database** option in the Office button drop-down list.

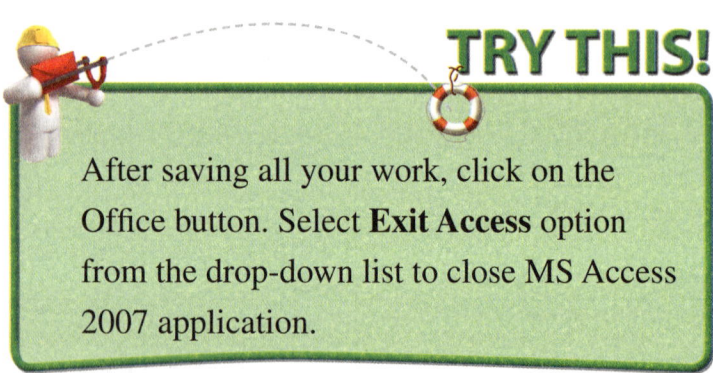

After saving all your work, click on the Office button. Select **Exit Access** option from the drop-down list to close MS Access 2007 application.

Queries in MS Access 2007

A query is a question pertaining to the data with a specific answer to it. Thus, it is a way of retrieving specific information from single or multiple tables of the database.

Follow these steps to raise a query in MS Access 2007:

1. Open the database.
2. Click on the **Create** tab in the MS Access 2007 Ribbon.
3. Select the **Query Design** option in the **Other** group (Fig. 2.28).

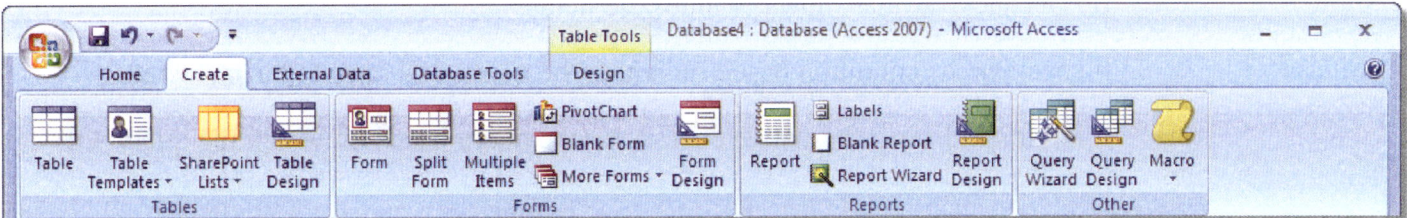

Fig. 2.28 *Other group in the Create tab*

4. The **Show Table** dialog box appears (Fig. 2.29).
5. In the **Tables** tab, select the table from the list of tables created and click **Add**.
6. Repeat the same step to add more tables. Click on **Close** after the required tables have been added.
7. The **Query** tab opens. The upper pane displays the tables selected. The lower pane represents the **Design grid** (Fig. 2.30).

Design grid pane: It is the portion of the Query tab where fields and criteria for the query are added.

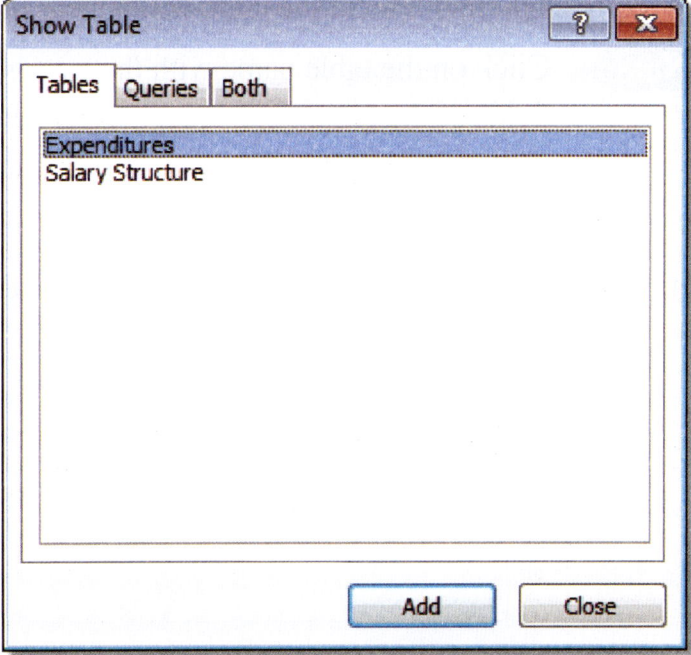

Fig. 2.29 *Show Table dialog box*

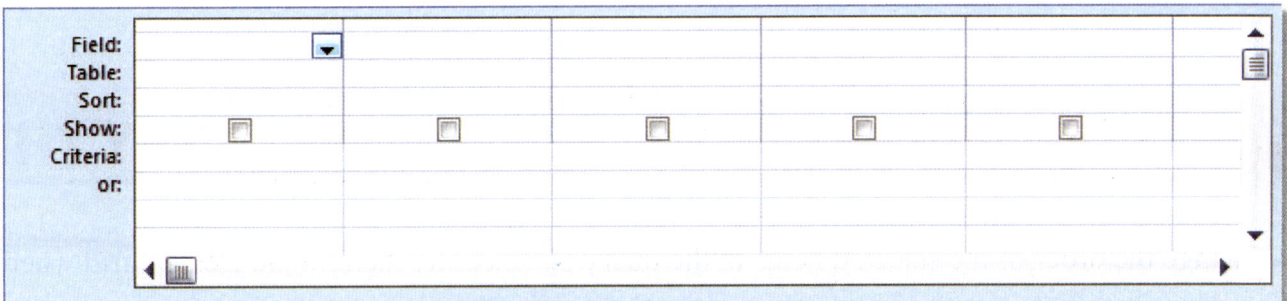

Fig. 2.30 *Design grid pane*

Some of the commonly used options that can be filled in this pane are explained in Table 2.4.

Table 2.4 *Design grid properties*

Property	Description
Field	It shows the fields in the selected table to be included in the query.
Table	It displays the name of the table from which the field has been added.
Sort	It determines the sorting order of the data in the datasheet produced by the query.
Show	It is a checkbox that shows or hides the fields.
Criteria	It specifies the condition based on which the query will have to be answered.
or	It is for specifying alternative criteria for the query based on which the query will be resolved.

8. Click on the down arrow in the **Field** property boxes and add the fields in the desired order. The corresponding name of the table will appear in the **Table** property.

Note: Click on the table name with the asterisk (*) symbol in the drop-down list, to add all the fields of the table to the query. You can also double-click on a field name in the upper pane or drag it to the desired box to add it to the Field property in the Design grid.

9. Sort the data in the selected field based on your preference using Sort property.

10. Specify the criterion for the query in the **Criteria** property box. Add multiple criteria in the **or** property box (Fig. 2.31).

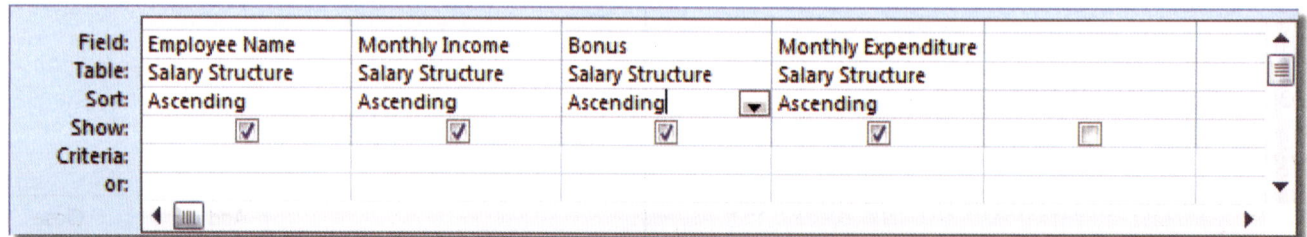

Fig. 2.31 *Design grid filled for the query*

11. If required, click on the **Save As** option in the **Office** button drop-down list to save the query.

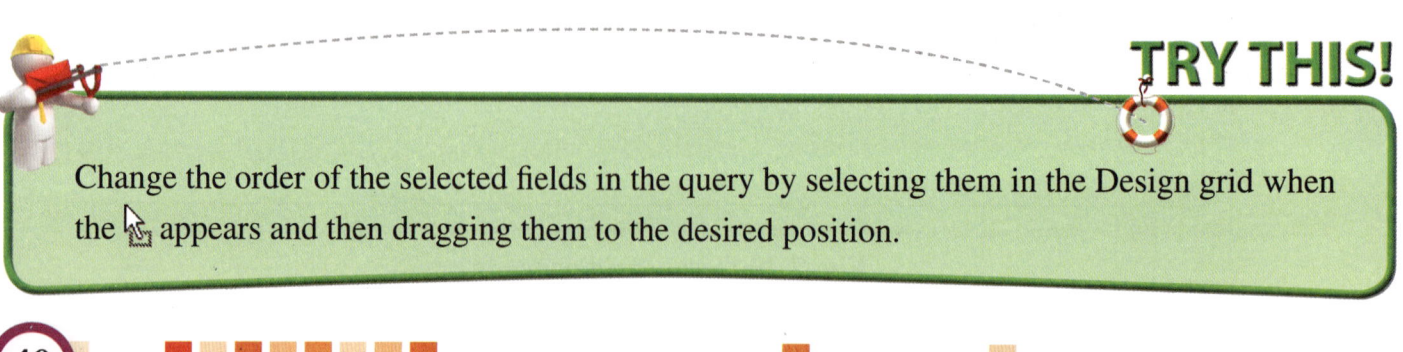

TRY THIS!

Change the order of the selected fields in the query by selecting them in the Design grid when the  appears and then dragging them to the desired position.

To Run a Query

Follow these steps to run a query:

1. Click on **Design** tab ⟹ **Results** group ⟹ **Run** option (Fig. 2.32).

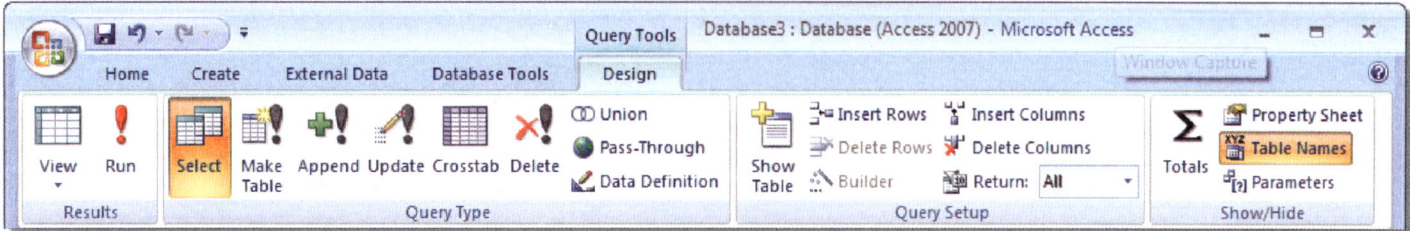

Fig. 2.32 *Run option*

2. The result for the query appears in the **Query** window in the Datasheet view (Fig. 2.33).

Fig. 2.33 *Result to the query raised*

> **FACT FILE**
>
> When two or more criteria are written in the Criteria property line, the result will show only those entries where all the specified criteria are met. However, when the criteria is specified in the Criteria and 'or' property line, then the result will show entries where either of the criteria is met.

Forms in MS Access 2007

Forms are customised screens for viewing, entering, modifying and deleting data in a table or a query.

Create a form using the following steps:

1. Open a database.
2. Click on **Create** tab ⟹ **Forms** group ⟹ **Form** option (Fig. 2.34).

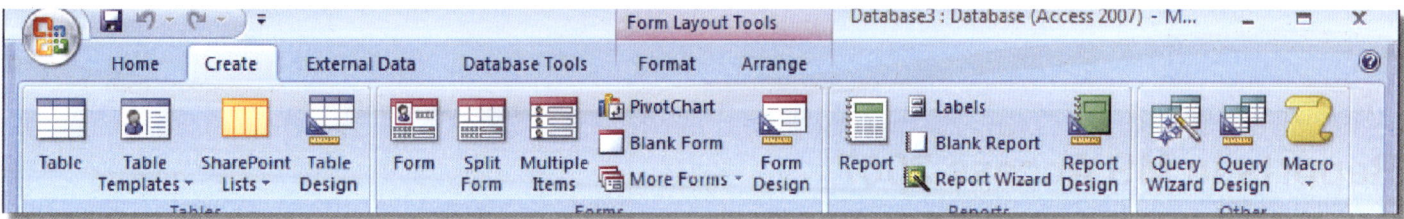

Fig. 2.34 *Form option in the Create tab*

3. The form is titled the same as the table chosen. It opens in the **Form View**.

4. Move through the different pages of the form using the Navigation box in the **Status Bar** (Fig. 2.35).

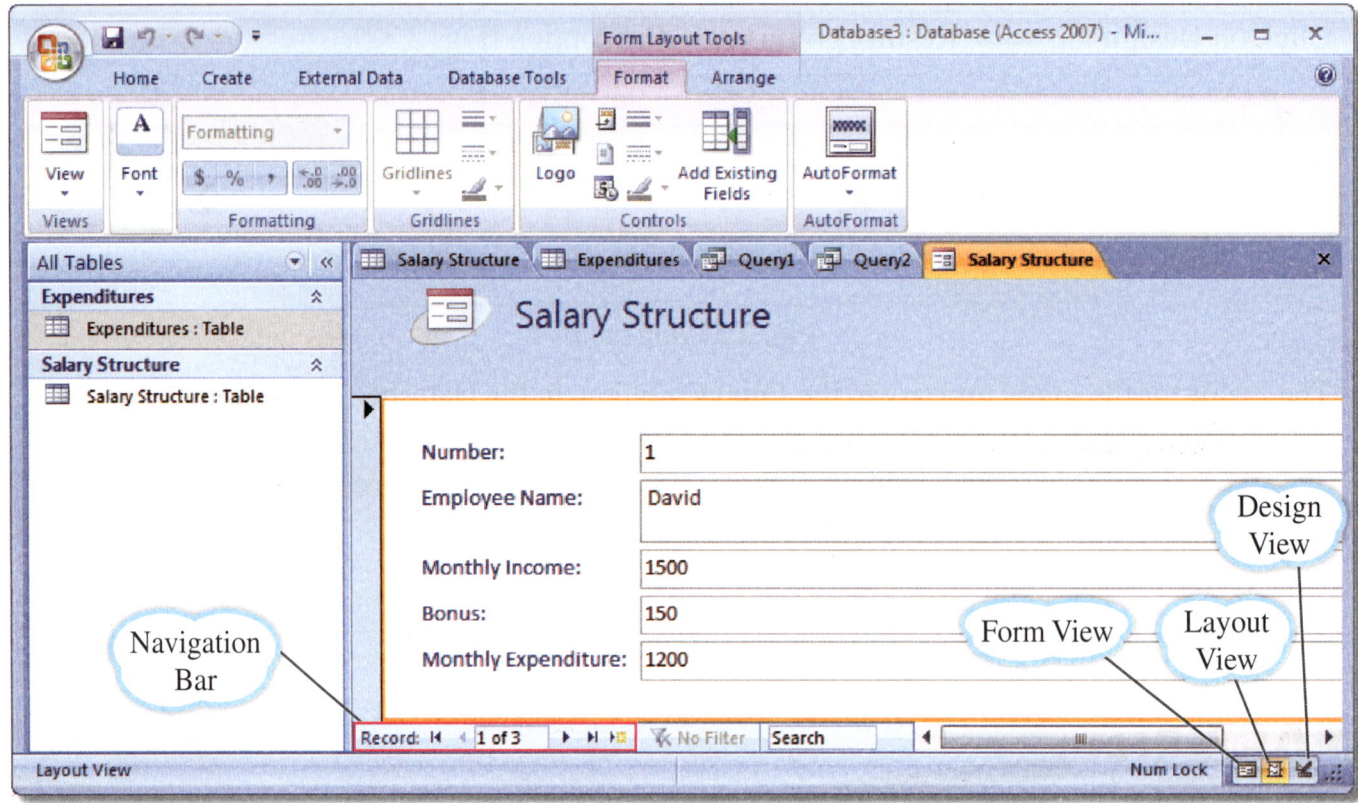

Fig. 2.35 *Creating a Form*

5. Save the form using the **Save As** option in the **Office** button drop-down list.

6. You can change the view of your form using the icons given in the Status Bar. **Layout View** can be used to change the layout of the form, just select a style from the **AutoFormat** group of the **Format** tab. The **Design View** can help in changing the design of the form.

FACT FILE

You can make changes to the content of the form. Right-click on the logo or the title of the table and select Properties from the shortcut menu.

Make the required changes in the Property Sheet pane on the right-side of the screen.

Reports in MS Access 2007

Reports are the representation of data in a printed format. The size, appearance and layout of the print can be customised based on the requirements.

Follow these steps to create a report in MS Access 2007:

1. Open the database. Select the table or the query for which a report has to be created.
2. Click on **Create** tab ⟹ **Reports** group ⟹ **Report** option (Fig. 2.36).

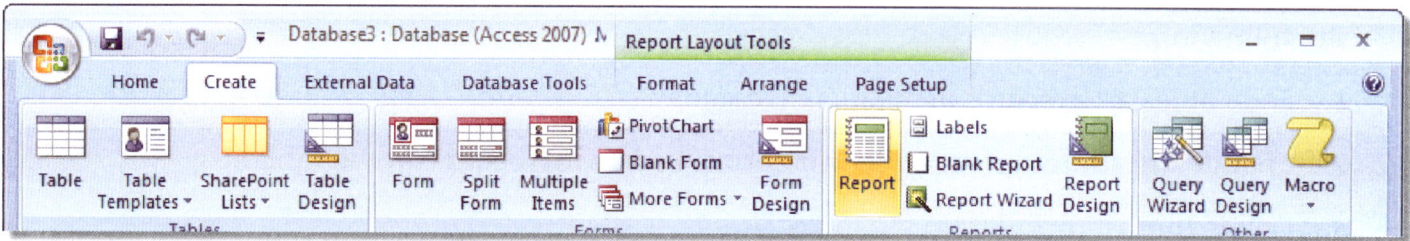

Fig. 2.36 *Report option in the Create tab*

3. A report is created by Access and it will appear on the screen (Fig. 2.37).
4. Use the **Layout View** in the Status Bar to format the report.
5. Use **Print Preview** to see how the report will look on paper when printed (Fig. 2.38).
6. Print the report using the **Print** option in the **Office** button drop-down list.

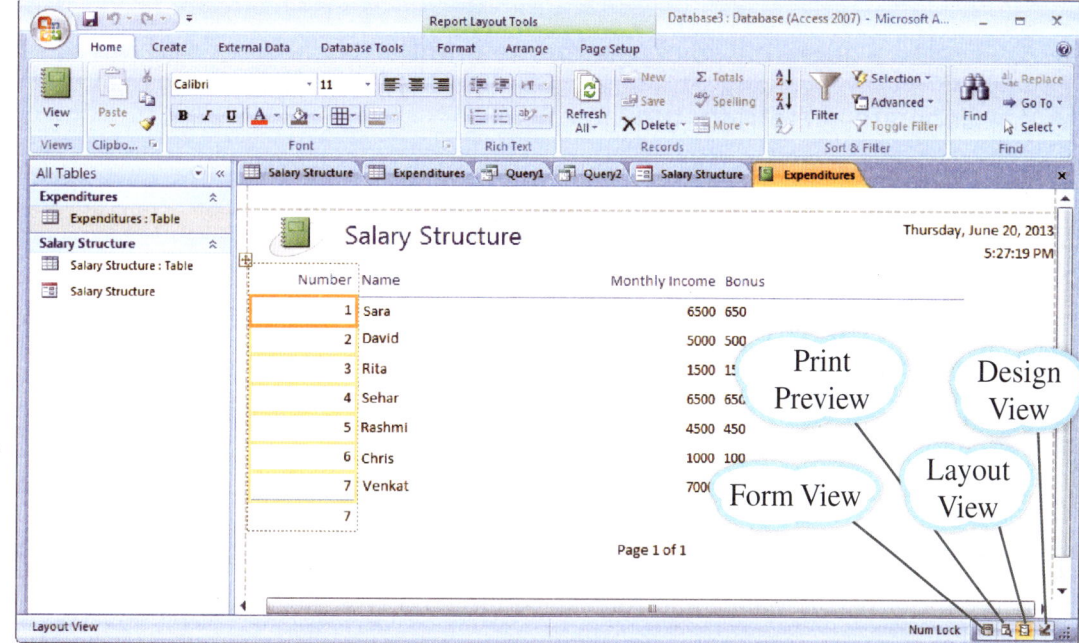

Fig. 2.37 *Report created for the selected table*

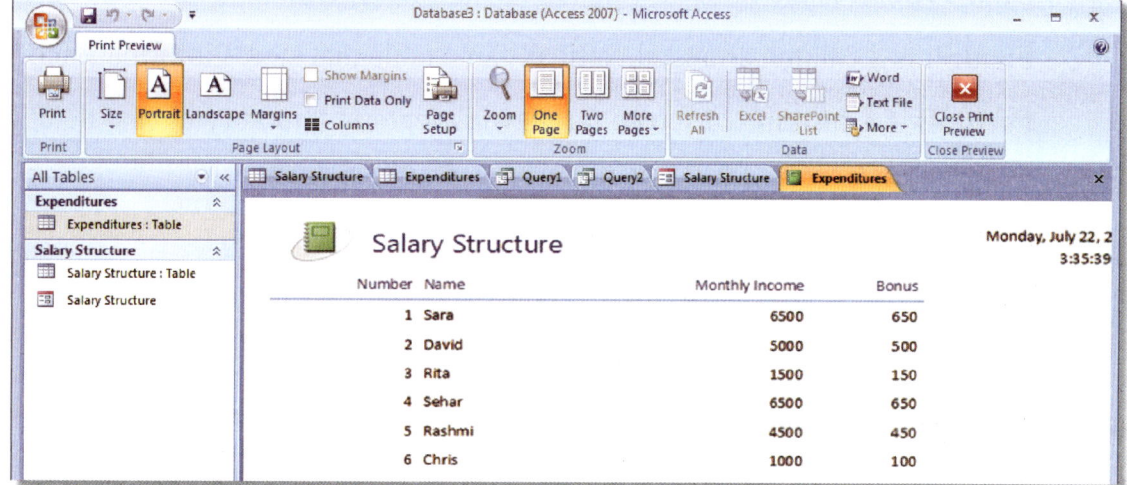

Fig. 2.38 *Print Preview of the Report*

ACTIVITY

Create a table with the records of animal lovers in your housing society. Use different descriptive fields to separate the data. Give a unique ID to each. After doing so practice the following:

1. Enter at least 10 records in the table created.
2. Change the address of record 3 and phone number of record 6 in the table.
3. Delete the last record from the table.
4. Add other fields for suggestions and activities to save animals.
5. Save all the changes made to the table.
6. Create a query based on the phone number of contacts and run it.
7. Generate a report for the table.
8. Close the table.
9. Close the database.

GLOSSARY

Database: It is the integrated collection of logically-related records in the form of tables.

Database Management System (DBMS): It is a set of computer program that controls the creation, maintenance and the use of the database in the computer by the user.

Database Objects: They are various components of MS Access.

Data Type: It is the form in which the data is accepted.

Field: It is a column arranged vertically in a table that stores information of the same type.

Form: It is a customised screen for viewing, entering, modifying and deleting data in a table or a query.

Primary Key: It uniquely identifies each record in the table.

Query: It is a question pertaining to the data with a specific answer to it

Record: It is complete information arranged horizontally in a table.

Report: It is the representation of data in a printed format.

Table: It is a collection of related information in the form of rows and columns.

NOW YOU KNOW

1. Microsoft Access is a database program used for sorting information in the form of tables, queries, forms, reports, etc.
2. DBMS is useful in the following aspects: reduces data redundancy, facilitates file sharing, controls data inconsistency, enforces standards, etc.
3. A new database can be created either using a blank database or a template.
4. Tables can be created either in Datasheet view or Design view in MS Access 2007.
5. Design view consists of two panes: Field Grid pane and Field Properties pane.
6. Queries are raised to retrieve specific information from a table or tables.
7. Forms provide different views for adding, deleting, formatting and designing the data.
8. Queries, forms and reports created for a table or tables can be saved in the database.

EXERCISE

A Fill in the blanks.

1. ……………………… is a collection of logically related records in the form of tables.
2. Lengthy text and numbers such as definitions or descriptive notes are represented by ……………………. data type.
3. The Run option in the ………………… group of the Design tab is used to run a query.
4. Datasheet, PivotTable,………………………..and Design are the four views used to view the database in MS Access 2007.
5. …………………………is the extension given to a database saved in MS Access 2007.

B Give one word for:

1. The tab in MS Access 2007 Ribbon for creating queries, forms and reports.
2. The option for exiting MS Access 2007 application.
3. The pane while creating a query where the different properties and criteria are set.
4. The view in which contents of the table can be edited and modified.
5. The panes visible in the Design View while creating a table.

C. Give the difference between:

1. Datasheet view and Design view
2. Table and Form database objects
3. Number and AutoNumber data type
4. Field pane and Property pane

D. Answer the following questions.

1. What is DBMS? Give example.
2. Suggest two ways to assign a primary key to a field in a table.
3. What are database objects? Name any four.
4. Write the steps for inserting and deleting fields in a table.
5. What are data types? Name all possible data types that can be used in MS Access 2007.
6. A query has been generated for a group of related tables in a database. Is it possible to get a hardcopy of the query? If yes, suggest how.

LAB WORK

Design a database of a shopping mart with the following tables. Enter at least 10 records in each table.

	Item	Data Type	Order	Data Type	Customer	Data Type
1.	Item		Order		Customer	
2.	Quantity in Stock	Number	Item Ordered	Number	Order No.	Number
3.	Rate per Item	Currency	Customer No.	Text	Amount	Currency

DANIEL S. BRICKLIN

Daniel S. Bricklin was born on 16 July 1951 in Philadelphia, Pennsylvania, USA.

In 1979, Bricklin with Bob Frankston, a native of Brooklyn, New York co-founded Software Arts Inc. and co-created the software program VisiCalc, the first electronic spreadsheet. Bricklin received the Grace Murray Hopper Award in 1981 for VisiCalc.

MS Office 2010 Updates

MS Access 2010:

1. It allows the users to share a database on the web. A database is created using Access 2010 and published through Access Services in the Microsoft SharePoint 2010 server. This allows other users, who do not have Access 2010 on their system, to view the data.

2. It provides enhanced levels of security to the user's data. This has been made possible with the help of Microsoft SharePoint Foundation 2010. This ensures recovery of deleted files, setting access permissions and audit revision history.

3. It has a new functionality **Screenshot** which allows the user to take a snapshot of any active document.

4. **Smart Tags** allow additional information to be added to a database which otherwise would require the support of the web. It is in the Design View of the report, from or data access page. It can also be used to schedule meetings, add contacts of instant messaging, etc.

TEACHER'S NOTES

1. Use the Internet to learn more about how MS Access 2007 is used in the corporate world.
2. Prepare a class list of students in alphabetical order and give them their attendance record of last three months. Give each student a copy of it and ask them to prepare a table in MS Access 2007 based on it. Also, ask the students to generate a report.

3 Introduction to Visual Basic

LEARNING OBJECTIVES

You will learn about:
1. Visual Basic
2. starting Visual Basic
3. components of Visual Basic window
4. inserting controls in a Visual Basic project
5. executing a Visual Basic program
6. saving a project and a form

Introduction

Visual Basic is a programming system created by Microsoft. The basic aim of creating this system was to give a user-friendly environment that supports Graphical User Interface (GUI). It is derived from an earlier language, BASIC, which means Beginners All Purpose Symbolic Instruction Code. BASIC is a simple language with simple programming constructs and is used in text based environment, that is, it supports Character User Interface (CUI). It enables Rapid Application Development (RAD) of GUI applications.

Visual Basic was one of the first systems that made it practical for writing programs for the Windows operating system. These software tools not only create Windows programs, but also take full advantage of its Graphical User Interface by letting programmers draw their systems with a mouse on the computer. This is why it is called Visual Basic (VB).

FACT FILE

The final release of Visual Basic was version 6 in 1998. Microsoft's extended support ended in March 2008 and the designated successor was Visual Basic.Net (now known simply as Visual Basic)

Visual Basic is an event-driven programming language

Event-driven programming is a way of programming in which the flow of the program is determined by an event. An event is any action performed either by using the mouse click, double-click, etc. or by pressing keys on the keyboard.

Visual Basic is an event driven programming language, that is, the programs that you create in it are based on the events performed by the user on different objects created in a form.

Visual Basic Integrated Development Environment

Integrated Development Environment (IDE) is a term commonly used in programming world to describe the interface and the environment that you use to create your own applications. It is called integrated because it has many features like designing, editing, compiling and debugging within a common environment.

The Visual Basic IDE is made up of following the components:

- Menu Bar
- Tool Bar
- Tool Box
- Project Explorer
- Property Window
- Form Design Window
- Form Layout Window
- Code Window

You will learn about these later in this chapter.

Uses of Visual Basic

With Visual Basic you can create:

- An educational program for teaching any module to school or college level students.
- For businessmen, it can create business programs such as inventory management system, payroll system, financial program as well as accounting program to help manage businesses and increase productivity.
- It can create programs for programmers who create games.

Starting Visual Basic

The following steps are followed to open the Visual Basic screen:

1. Click on **Start** button ⟹ **All Programs** ⟹ **Microsoft Visual Basic 6.0** folder ⟹ **Microsoft Visual Basic 6.0** (Fig. 3.1).

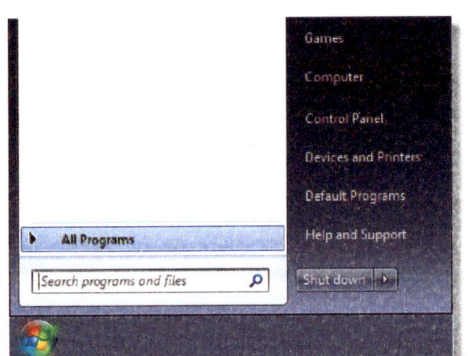
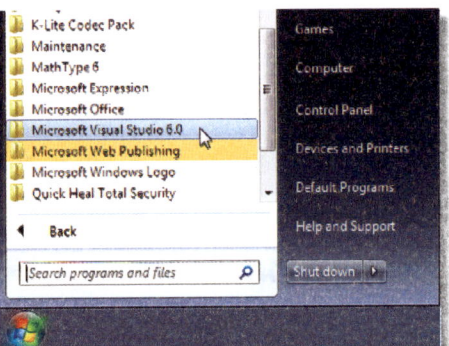

Fig. 3.1 *Opening Visual Basic*

2. The Visual Basic window appears (Fig. 3.2).

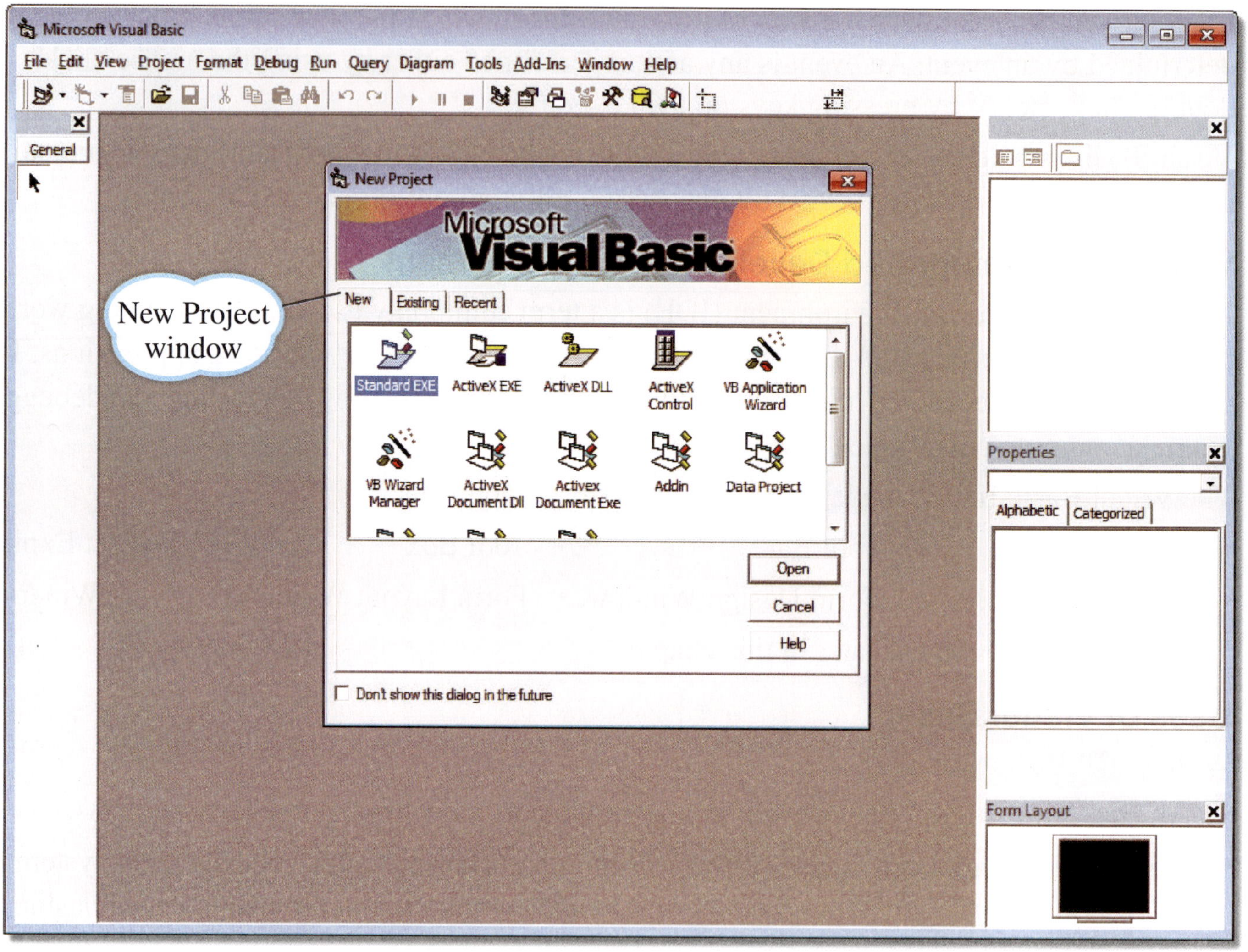

Fig. 3.2 *Opening Visual Basic*

3. Visual Basic window shows a start up window known as a **New Project** window.

Note: A project in Visual Basic is a collection of different objects like forms. It is another name of an application. A project is saved with an extension of .vbp.

The New Project window has three tabs. These are given below.

- *New:* This is the default tab with Standard EXE option selected. It helps you to create a new project.
- *Existing:* This tab displays the list of the projects created earlier and stored in the system.
- *Recent:* This tab displays the list of the most recently created projects.

4. Select the **New** option and click on the **Open** button.
5. The Integrated Development Environment (IDE) of Visual Basic appears (Fig. 3.3).

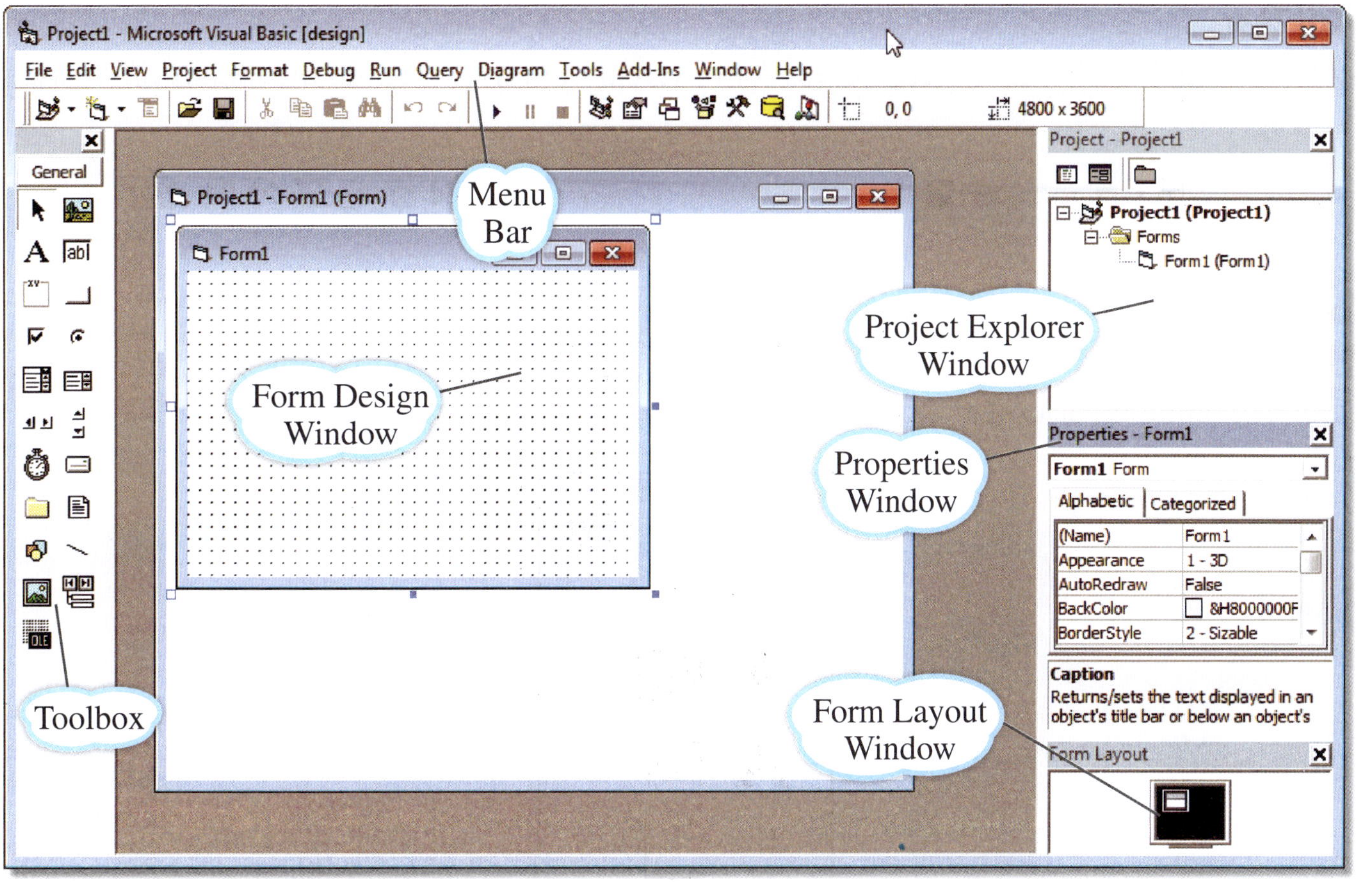

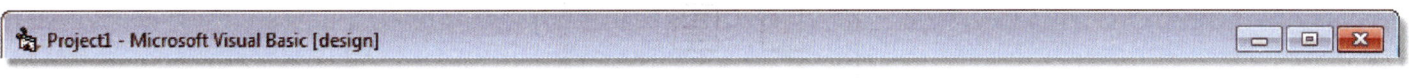

Fig. 3.3 *The Integrated Development Environment (IDE)*

Components of Visual Basic Window

Let us study the components of Visual Basic Window in detail.

Title Bar

The Title Bar displays the name of the project along with the mode you are currently viewing. For example, in Figure 3.4 the name of the project is Project1 and it is in the Design Mode.

Fig. 3.4 *Title Bar*

Note: The default name of the project in Visual Basic is Project1, Project2, Project3 and so on.

Menu Bar

The Menu Bar is present below the Title Bar (Fig. 3.5). It contains different menus like File, Edit, View, Project, etc.

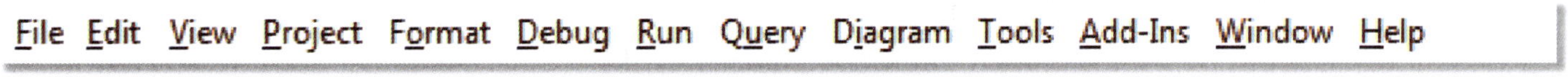

Fig. 3.5 *Menu Bar*

Tool Bar

Tool Bar contains tools as a quick access for different options present in the menus of the Menu Bar (Fig. 3.6).

Fig. 3.6 *Tool Bar*

Toolbox

The Toolbox contains a set of controls that are used to place on a form while designing it, thereby creating the user interface area (Fig. 3.7).

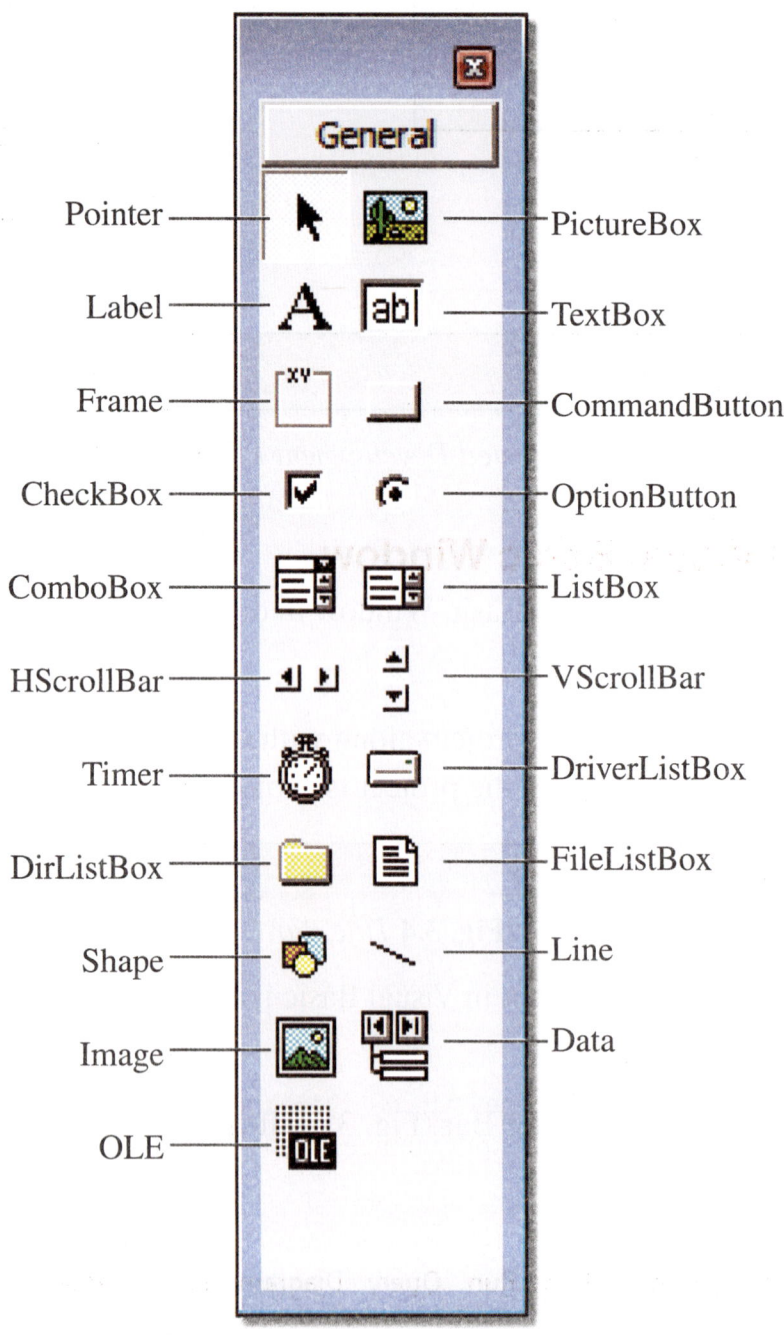

Fig. 3.7 *Toolbox*

The various tools from the Toolbox are explained here (Table 3.1). You will learn about some of these in detail in the next chapter.

Table 3.1 *Various Tools of Toolbox*

Tools in VB	Icons	Uses
Pointer		It helps in resizing and moving an object.
PictureBox		It displays icons/bitmap files. **Note:** It displays text or acts as a visual container for other controls.
Label		It displays a text that the user cannot modify or interact with.
TextBox		It creates a text box to display message or accept data.
Frame		It contains other controls/tools which act and control as group.
CommandButton		It is used to carry out the specified action when the user chooses it.
CheckBox		It displays a True/False or Yes/No option.
OptionButton		It creates Radio buttons so the user can select only one option from the given multiple options.
ComboBox		It provides a drop-down list and allows the user to select an item from it.
ListBox		It displays a list of items from which a user can select one.
HScrollBar		It allows the user to select a value within the specified range of values.
VScrollBar		It allows the user to select a value within the specified range of values.
Timer		It executes the timer events at specified intervals of time.
DriveListBox		It displays valid disk drives and allows the user to select one of them.
DirListBox		It allows the user to select the directories and paths which are displayed.
FileListBox		It displays the file of the current folder.
Shape		It is used to add shape to a form.
Line		It is used to draw straight lines in a form.
Image		It is used to display images as icons, bitmaps, etc.
Data		It enables the user to connect to an existing database and display information from it.
OLE		It is used to ole link or embed objects from other applications.

Project Explorer window

The Project Explorer window displays a list of all the forms in a project (Fig. 3.8). It is present on the right side of the screen. The Project Explorer window gives you a tree-structured view of all the files inserted into an application. You can expand these and collapse branches of the views.

The various components of a Project Explorer window are given below.

- *View Code:* It is used to view the coding of the selected form or a project.

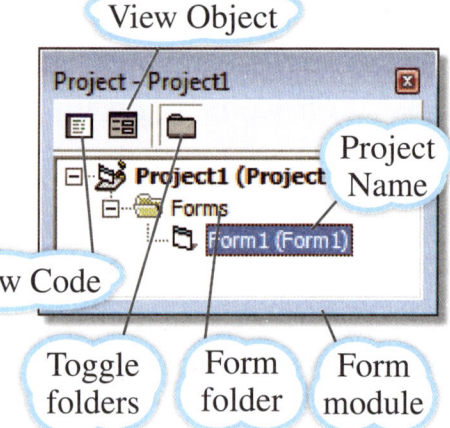

Fig. 3.8 *Project Explorer window*

- *View Object:* It is used to view the objects used in a specific form or a project.
- *Toggle folders:* It is used for switching between various folders.
- *Project name:* It displays the name of the project.
- *Forms folder:* It comprises of all the forms for the selected project.
- *Form module:* It contains forms developed or being developed under the selected project name.

Properties window

The Properties window is also present at the right side of the Visual Basic window. The Properties window displays the various properties of the objects selected on the form (Fig. 3.9). Each form in an application is also considered as an **object**. Thus, a form has properties and any controls placed on it will have properties too. All of these properties are displayed in the Properties window with the default values but these values can be changed by the programmer.

Form Layout window

Form Layout window determines the starting position of the form relative to the screen (Fig. 3.10).

Fig. 3.10 *Form Layout window*

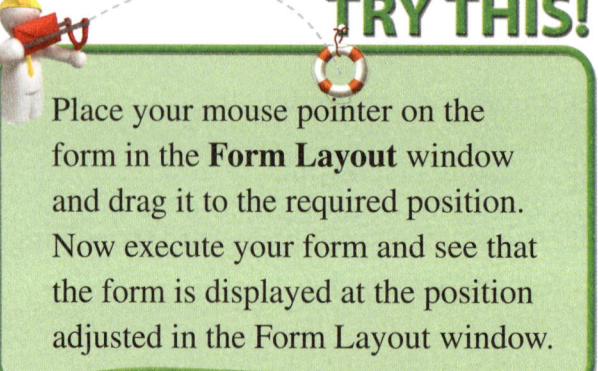

TRY THIS!

Place your mouse pointer on the form in the **Form Layout** window and drag it to the required position. Now execute your form and see that the form is displayed at the position adjusted in the Form Layout window.

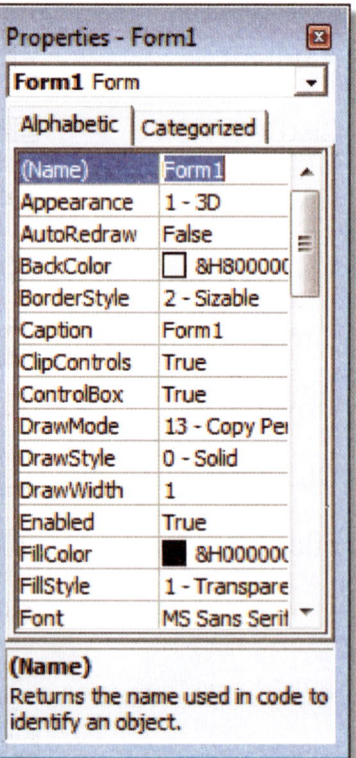

Fig. 3.9 *Properties window*

Form Design window

Form Design window is placed in the form of a grid used to design a form (Fig. 3.11). A form in Visual Basic displays various controls that provide the user interface. Some of the controls are Labels, Textbox, Command buttons, etc. A form is saved with an extension of .frm (Form files).

A form could be an introduction screen, a dialog box giving the user options, a box containing a warning, etc. All these forms can be designed in the Form Design window using the tools present in the Toolbox.

Fig. 3.11 *Form Design window*

FACT FILE

You can switch between the Form Design window and the Code window either by clicking on the tools present in the Project Explorer or by selecting either of the first two options in the View menu.

Code window

The Code window is used for event-driven programming for different objects created on the form. It is used for writing, displaying and editing code. You may get the Code window by either of the following methods:

1. Click on **View** menu ⟹ **Code** option.
2. The Code window appears (Fig. 3.12). Notice the change in name of the form in the Title Bar. It changes from (Design) to (Code).

You can also get the Code window by double-clicking anywhere on the form in the Design mode.

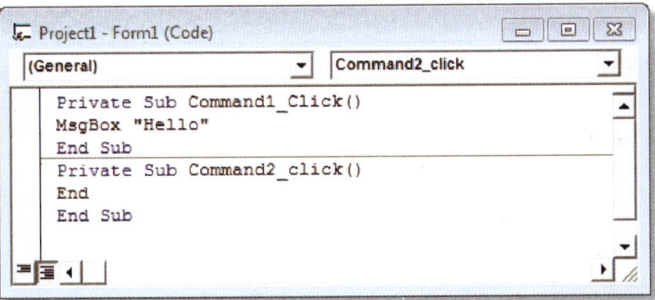

Fig. 3.12 *Code window*

TRY THIS!

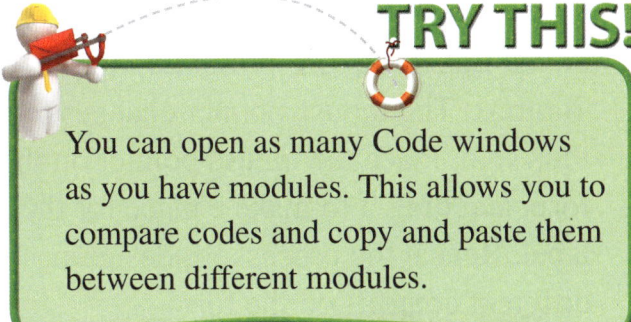

You can open as many Code windows as you have modules. This allows you to compare codes and copy and paste them between different modules.

ACTIVITY

A. Start Visual Basic and select View menu. Explore the different options present in it.
B. Name and explain at least five options present in the View menu. Click on them to see the effect in Visual Basic IDE.

Executing Visual Basic Program

You need to execute the Visual Basic program to view the results of the design and coding. To do so you need to follow the steps given below:

1. Click on **Run** menu ⟹ **Start** option.

   Click on **Start** button ▶ on the Toolbar.

2. The **Output** window appears (Fig. 3.13).

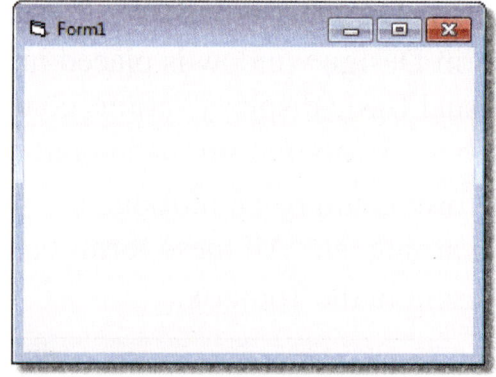

Fig. 3.13 *Output window of Visual Basic project*

Inserting Controls in Visual Basic Project

Let us see how an application can be created in VB. Follow these steps to insert controls in the Visual Basic Project.

1. Click on **Start** button ⟹ **Visual Basic 6.0** folder ⟹ **Visual Basic 6.0 application**.

2. In the **New Project** window, select the **Standard EXE** option.

3. Click on **Create** button.

4. A new window with the default name Project1 and with a default form Form1 appears (Fig. 3.14).

5. Use the objects present on the Toolbox to design the controls on the form as shown in (Fig. 3.15). For example, click on the Label tool **A** present on the Toolbox. The mouse pointer changes to a Plus sign. Place the mouse pointer on the form and drag it to make a place for the label. Repeat the process for designing different controls on the form.

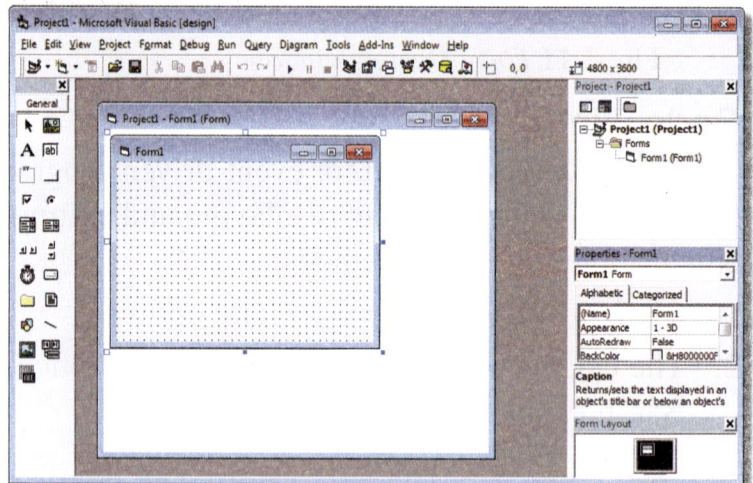

Fig. 3.14 *Visual Basic form in IDE*

 You can also add other application objects and ActiveX controls to a form.

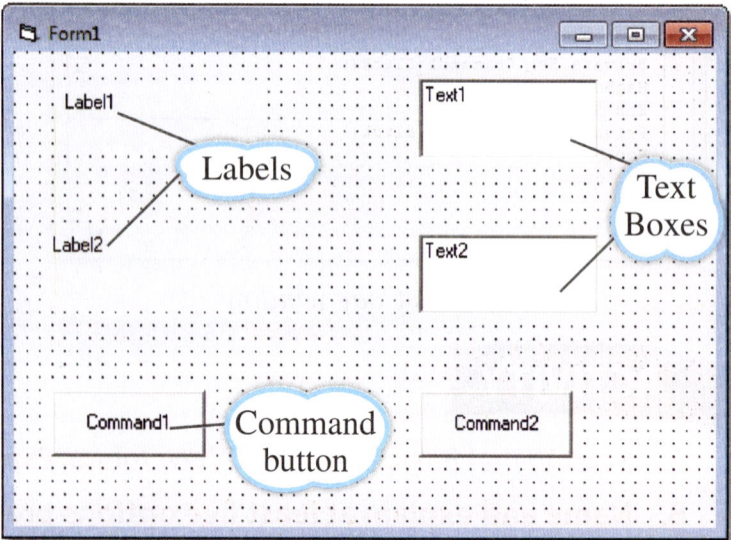

Fig. 3.15 *Designing different controls on the form*

6. Go to the Properties window and change the property as given below:

   a. Caption of Label1 as ENTER NAME.
   b. Caption of Label2 as ENTER CLASS.
   c. Caption of Command1 as DISPLAY HELLO.
   d. Caption of Command2 as EXIT.
   e. Text of Text1 as blank.
   f. Text of Text2 as blank.

7. After doing the above changes the Form Design window will appear as shown in Figure 3.16.

8. To execute the form to see the presentation of the form (Fig. 3.17), click on **Start** button present on the Toolbar.

   OR

   Click on **Run** menu ⟹ **Start** option.

9. To stop the execution of the form, click on **Stop** tool present on the Toolbar.

   OR

   Click on **Run** menu ⟹ **End** option.

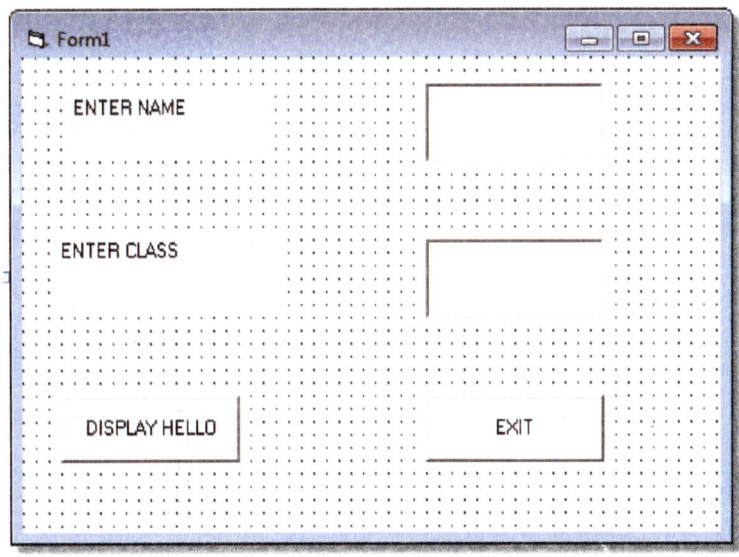

Fig. 3.16 *Form in the design mode*

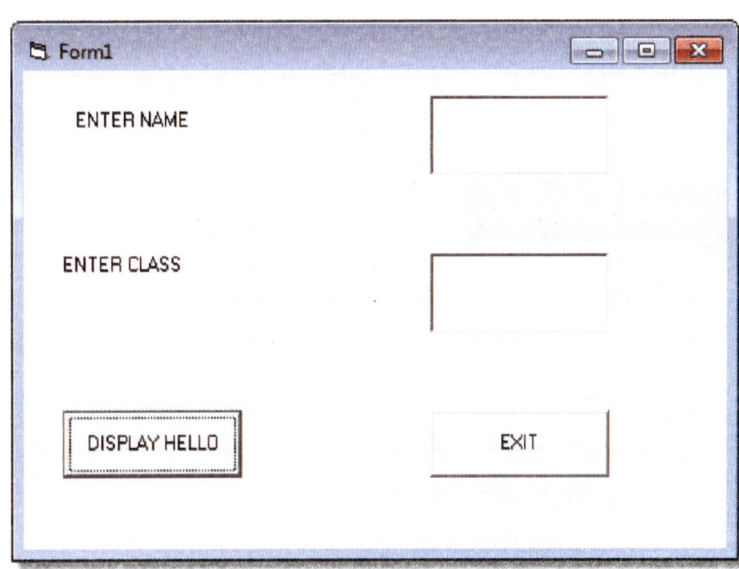

Fig. 3.17 *Form after execution*

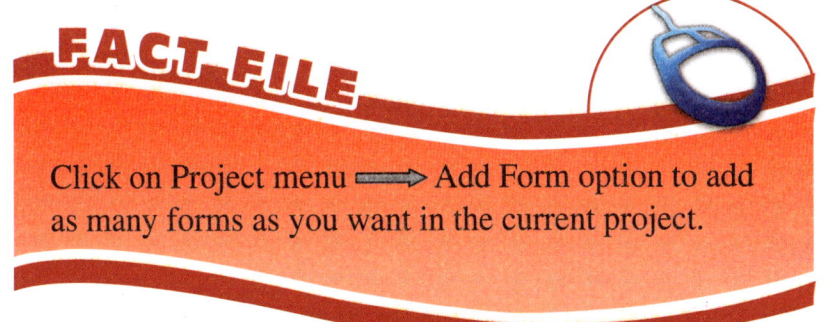

Click on Project menu ⟹ Add Form option to add as many forms as you want in the current project.

Saving a Project and a Form

You can save any project in Visual Basic by following the steps given here:

1. Click on **File** menu ⟹ **Save Project As**… option (Fig. 3.18).

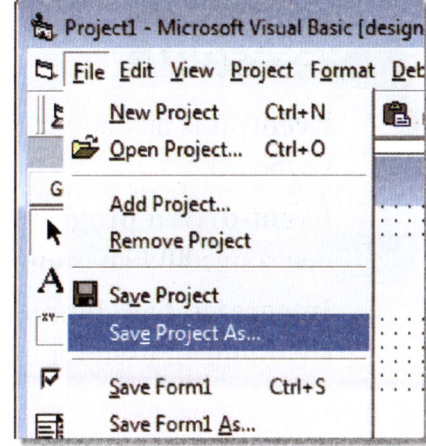

Fig. 3.18 *Saving a project*

2. The **Save File As** dialog box appears (Fig. 3.19). Enter the name of the form here. Click on the **Save** button.
3. The **Save Project As** dialog box appears (Fig. 3.20). Enter the name of the project here. Click on the **Save** button.
4. The newly created form and project will be saved with the specified name.

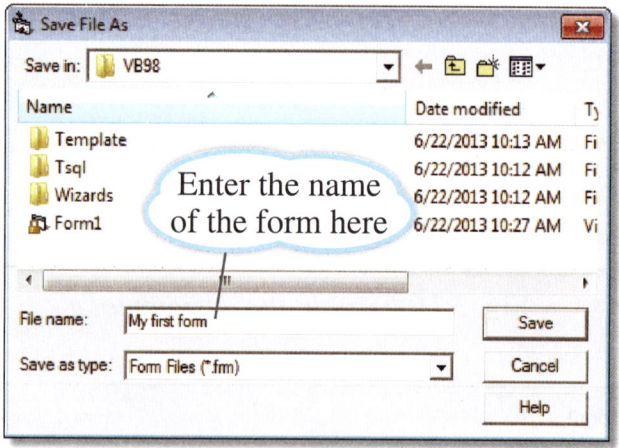

Fig. 3.19 *Save File As dialog box*

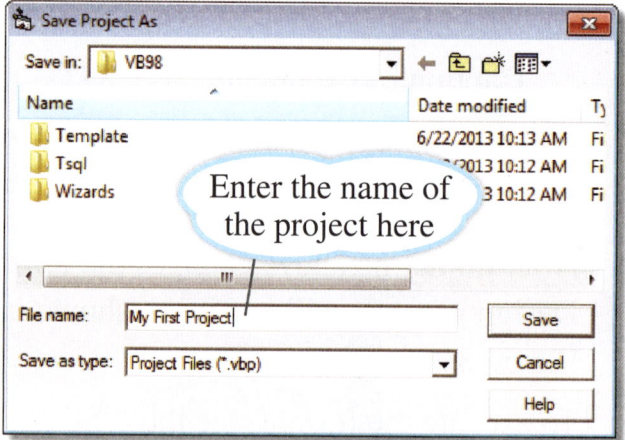

Fig. 3.20 *Save Project As dialog box*

ACTIVITY

Complete the following activity.

1. Create a new form with one label in the middle to display a welcome message.
2. Create another form in the same project with a text box to display, Hello World.
3. Create another form in the same project with 2 labels and 2 text boxes to enter names of the first and second friend, respectively. Enter the friends' name after you run your form by pressing the Start option in the Run menu.
4. Save the project and all three forms with specific names in your computer.

GLOSSARY

Event: It is any action performed either by using the mouse or by pressing keys on the keyboard.

Event-driven programming: It is a way of programming in which the flow of the program is determined by an event.

Integrated Development Environment (IDE): It describes the interface and the environment used for creating applications.

NOW YOU KNOW

1. Visual Basic is a programming system created to give a user friendly environment that supports Graphical User Interface.
2. The Toolbox contains a set of controls that are used to place on a form while designing it, thereby creating the user interface area.
3. All of the objects that make up the application are packed in a Project Explorer window.
4. The Properties window displays the various properties of the objects selected on the form. Each and every form in an application is also considered an object.
5. Form Layout window determines the starting position of the form relative to the screen.
6. Form Design window is placed in the form of grid used to design a form.
7. The Code window is used in event-driven programming for different objects created on the form.

EXERCISE

A Fill in the blanks.

1. Visual Basic is an .... programming language.
2. IDE stands for ....
3. .... displays the controls that can be used to design a form.
4. Visual Basic is derived from ....
5. .... is an action performed either by using the mouse or the keyboard.

B Give the difference between:

1. Visual Basic and BASIC
2. Form Design window and Form Layout window
3. Toolbox and Tool Bar
4. Project Explorer window and Properties window
5. Project and Form

C. Label the following:

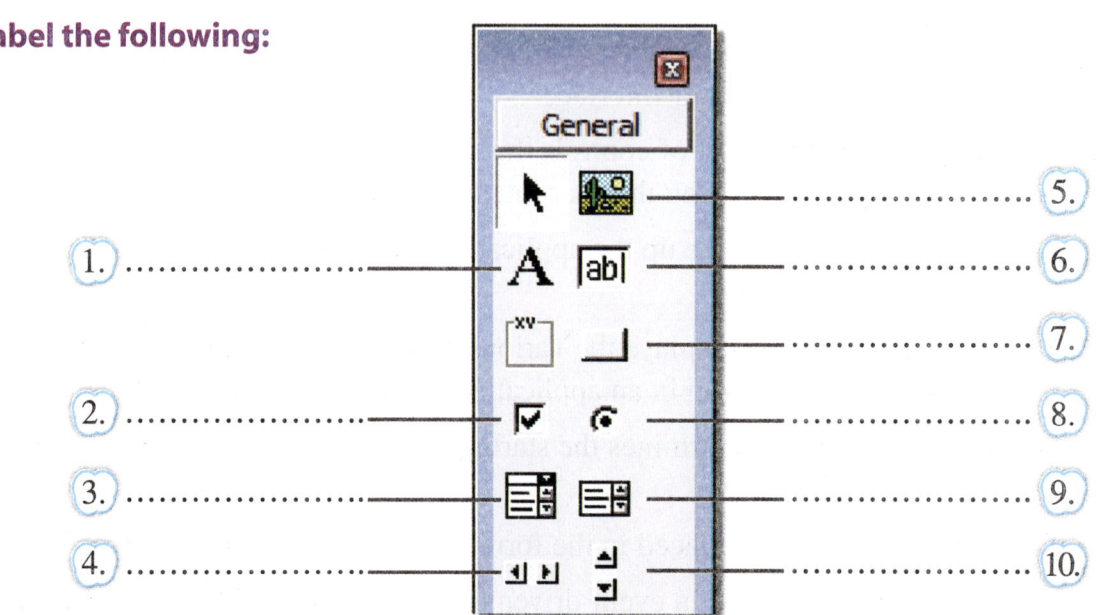

1. ....
2. ....
3. ....
4. ....
5. ....
6. ....
7. ....
8. ....
9. ....
10. ....

D. Answer the following questions.

1. Why do we use Visual Basic? Give at least three reasons.
2. What is an event and an event-driven programming language?
3. What is VB IDE? Name all the components of Visual Basic IDE.
4. How do you save a project and a form in Visual Basic?
5. What are the three different ways of executing a form?
6. Explain the three tabs of the New Project window.

LAB WORK

A. Imagine that your school music club is organising auditions for its various music bands. Create forms for students' registration with these bands. Think of some interesting names for these bands and create options for students to select.

b. Add interesting information in the project. Also, use different controls to enter student information such as Name, Class, Age, etc.

TEACHER'S NOTES

1. Talk to the students about Visual Basic.Net. Explain to them the transition from Visual Basic 6.0 to VB.net.

4 Toolbox and its Control

SNAP RECAP

The toolbox contains a set of controls that are used to place on a form while designing it, thereby creating the user interface area.

LEARNING OBJECTIVES

You will learn about:

- the various tools in Toolbox and their functions

Toolbox

Follow these steps to design the user interface:

1. Create a form.
2. Choose the object you want to draw from the Toolbox.
3. Draw the object on the form.
4. Change its properties in the Property window.

Let us now learn about some commonly used controls that can be inserted in the form to make it interactive.

Pointer tool

The Pointer tool is used to select an object. Whenever any tool is selected then the mouse pointer changes to a + sign. Using the Pointer tool, you can draw an object on the form. To get the mouse pointer back, click on the Pointer tool.

Note: Pointer tool is also the default tool of the Toolbox.

Label tool A

Label tool is used to display text on the form (Fig. 4.1). It is generally used to give the title in the form, an output after some calculations, or some message for the user. User cannot edit or change the text written in a label.

Some of the commonly used properties of the Label tool are given in Table 4.1.

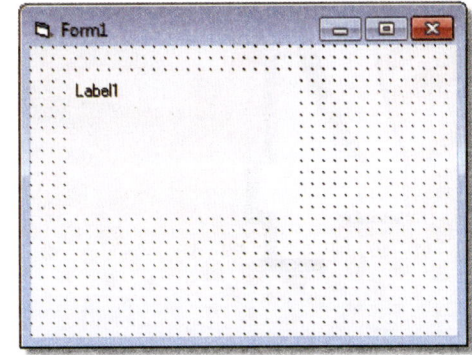

Fig. 4.1 *Using a Label Tool*

Table 4.1 *Properties of Label Tool*

Property Name	Property Function	Property Task Pane
Name	It returns the name of the label that identifies it in a form. The default name is Label1, Label2 and so on but the programmer can give any name to it at the time of designing the form.	(Name) Label1
Alignment	It sets the alignment of the label text with respect to the area covered on the form.	Alignment 2 - Center / 0 - Left Justify / 1 - Right Justify / 2 - Center / 1 - Opaque
Autosize	It displays whether a label can be automatically resized to display its entire contents or not.	AutoSize False / True / False / 0 - None
Backcolor	It sets the background color used to display text or graphic in a label.	BackColor &H8000000F& (Palette/System)
Caption	It displays the text that appears on the face of the object.	Caption Label1
Enabled	It sets the value that determines whether a label can respond to the user generated events or not.	Enabled True
Font	It opens a Font dialog box where the programmer can apply font settings to the text that appears on the label.	Font MS Sans Serif
ForeColor	It sets the forecolor of the object or text in a label.	ForeColor &H80000012& (Palette/System)
Mouse Pointer	It sets the cursor that is displayed when the mouse is over a label	MousePointer 0 - Default

ToolTipText	It sets the text that will appear when the mouse is moved over the label.	
Visible	It sets a value of True or False that determines whether a control will be visible or hidden during run time (that is, at the time when the project is run or started).	

Let us see an example of a Label control here. This is drawn using the Label tool and setting the properties for the same (Fig. 4.2).

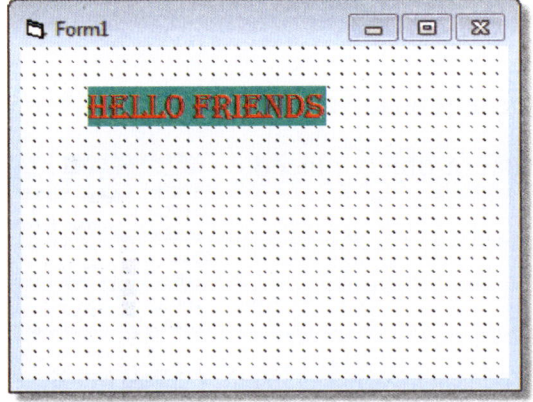

Property	Value
Name	Label1
Caption	HELLO FRIENDS
Enabled	True
Visible	True
Font	Algerian Size = 16
ForeColor	Red
BackColor	Aqua
Alignment	Center
AutoSize	True

Fig. 4.2 *Drawing a label using Label tool and setting its properties*

TextBox

TextBox tool draws a rectangular box on the form where the cursor blinks. It is different from Label tool as it accepts the input from the user (Fig. 4.3).

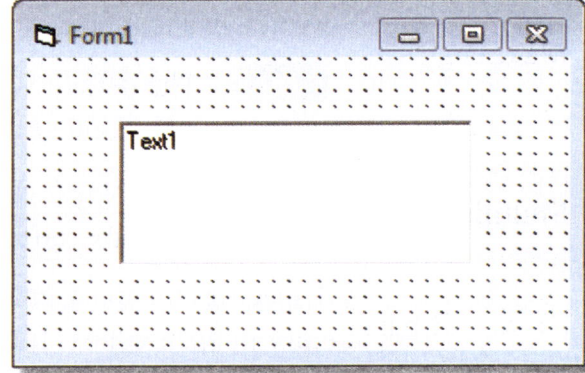

Fig. 4.3 *Using a TextBox tool*

Some of the commonly used properties of the TextBox tool are given in Table 4.2.

Table 4.2 *Properties of TextBox Tool*

Property Name	Property Function	Property Task Pane
Name	It specifies the name of the text box as it will be identified by in the memory. By default, it is named as Text1, Text2, and so on.	
Alignment	It is used to specify the alignment of the data entered in a text box.	

Property	Description	Example
BackColor	This specifies the background color of a text box.	
Enabled	It sets the value of True or False that determines whether the text box will be available for user generated events or not.	
Font	It sets the font attributes of the data in the text box.	
ForeColor	It specifies the foreground color of the text or object placed in a text box.	
MaxLength	It sets the maximum number of characters that can be written in a text box. **Note:** The default value is O, that is, the user can write any number of characters.	
Multiline	It contains the logical value of True or False that determines whether a text box can accept multiple lines of data.	
PasswordChar	It specifies the mask character to be displayed during data entry in the text box. It is generally used to enter passwords.	
ScrollBars	It is used to specify whether to include a horizontal or a vertical scrollbar in the text box. It is applicable only if multiline property of the textbox is set to True.	
Text	The default property of the text box that specifies the content of the text box.	
Mouse Pointer	It sets the shape of cursor when mouse hovers over a text box	
ToolTipText	It sets the text to be displayed when the mouse is paused over the text box.	
Visible	It is used to set the value of True and False that determines whether the text box will be visible or not during run time.	

FACT FILE

- Password Char property takes precedence over the Text property of the text box.
- Scrollbar property of a text box can only be used if Multiline is True, otherwise any change in the Scrollbar property will have no effect in the text box.

Let us see an example of a text box control here. This is drawn using the TextBox tool and setting the properties for the same (Fig. 4.4).

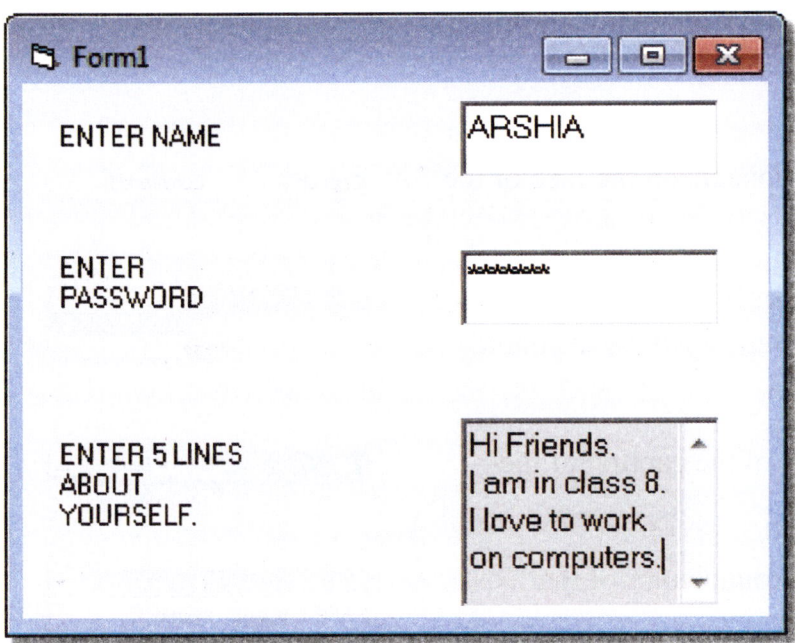

Fig. 4.4 *Drawing a text box using TextBox tool and setting its properties*

Property	Value
Text1	
Name	Text1
Text	(Blank)
Font	Size = 10
Text2	
Name	Text2
Text	(Blank)
Font	Size = 10
PasswordChar	*
MaxLength	10
Text3	
Name	Text3
Text	(Blank)
Font	Size = 10
MultiLine	True
Scrollbar	2 - Vertical
BackColor	Grey

ACTIVITY

A. Design a form with the following controls:
1. One label with the heading 'Student Club Membership Form'.
2. Two labels – Enter user name, Enter password.
3. Two text boxes for accepting user name and password. The password text box should display the password in asterisk (*).

B. Set the appropriate properties for the controls designed on the form.

Command button ⏎

Command button works when the user clicks on it (Fig. 4.5). This supports the concept of event driven programming in Visual Basic. The most commonly used event is Command_click( ). You can also use Form_load( ) to execute the statements when the form is loaded on the computer when you execute a form.

Some of the commonly used properties of the Command tool are given in Table 4.3.

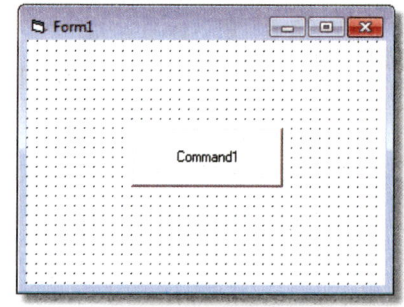

Fig. 4.5 *Using Command button*

Table 4.3 *Properties of Text Tool Command*

Property Name	Property Function	Property Task Pane
Name	It specifies the name of the Command button. The default name is Command1, Command2, and so on.	
Caption	It displays the text that appears on the face of the Command button.	
Enabled	It sets the value of True or False that determines whether the Command button will be available for user-generated events.	
Font	It sets the font attributes of the caption of the Command button.	
BackColor	This specifies the background color of the Command button.	
Style	It enables the user to display images when state changes.	
ToolTipText	It is used to specify what text will appear when the mouse hovers over a Command button.	
Visible	It specifies whether a Command button will be displayed on the form or not during run time.	

Let us see an example of a Command control here. This is drawn using the Command tool and setting the properties for the same (Fig. 4.6).

Property	Value
Name	Command1
Caption	Color Change
Font	Size = 13 style = bold, Name = Arial
ToolTipText	It changes the backcolor of the form

Fig. 4.6 *Drawing a command button using Command tool and setting its properties*

Msg command: Once you have drawn the Command control you can try the Msgbox command. This command can be used to display a message in a separate window when an event is occurring, such as, when the command_click() event happens. The message could be any warning, any error or simply a welcome message.

To do so follow the steps given below:

1. Create a new form with a Command button.
2. Give the caption name as 'Start the project'.
3. Double-click on the Command button to view the Code window and under the Command1_Click() event write the code as shown in Figure 4.7.

TRY THIS!

Use the Print command instead of the Msgbox command in the code for command_click() event.

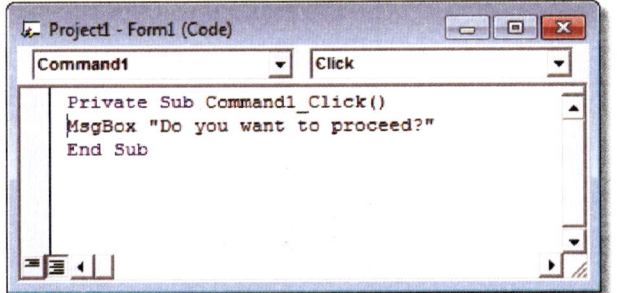

Fig. 4.7 *Writing a Msgbox command*

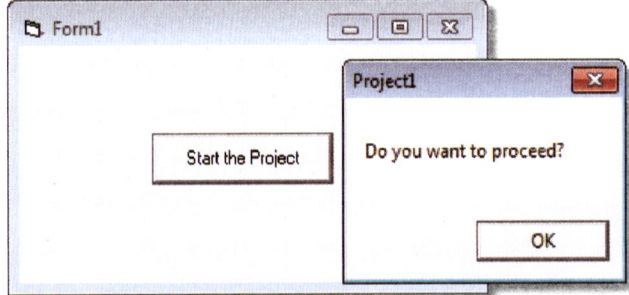

Fig. 4.8 *Message box pops up on clicking the Command button*

4. Run the Project. The message box pops up when the Command button is clicked (Fig. 4.8).

Some more events that can be used with the Command button are given here:

a. Text_Click(): This event is invoked when the user clicks once inside the text box.
b. Text_Dblclick(): This event is invoked when the user double clicks inside the text box.
c. Text_Change(): This event is invoked when the value inside the text box changes.

ACTIVITY

A. In the student membership form created in earlier activity, create the following:
  1. 1 command button – Accept Details
  2. 1 command button – Reset Details

B. Set the appropriate properties for the controls designed on the form.

Checkbox tool

Checkbox is used when the user has got the choice to select from one or more options (Fig. 4.9). Some of the commonly used properties of the Checkbox tool are given in Table 4.4.

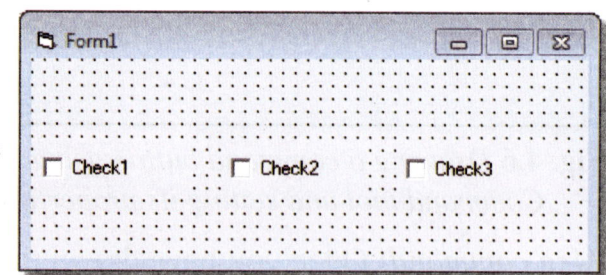

Fig. 4.9 *Using CheckBox tool*

Table 4.4 *Properties of CheckBox Tool*

Property Name	Property Function	Property Task Pane
Name	It specifies the name of the checkboxes. The default name is check1, check2 and so on.	(Name) Check1 / Reading
Alignment	It sets the alignment of the text on the face of the check box.	Alignment 0 - Left Justify / 0 - Left Justify / 1 - Right Justify
BackColor	This specifies the background color of the checkbox.	BackColor &H8000000F8 (Palette/System with Button Face, Button Shadow, Disabled Text, Button Text, Inactive Title Bar Text, Button Highlight, Button Dark Shadow, Button Light Shadow, ToolTip Text)
Caption	It displays the text that appears on the face of the checkbox.	Caption Reading / Reading
Enabled	It sets the value of True or False that determines whether the checkbox will be available for user-generated events.	Enabled True / True / False
Font	It sets the font attributes of the caption of the checkbox.	Font Arial

ForeColor	It sets the foreground color of the checkbox.	
ToolTipText	It is used to specify the text that will appear when the mouse hovers over a checkbox.	
Visible	It specifies whether a checkbox will be displayed on the form or not during run time.	

Let us see an example of a Checkbox control here. This is drawn using the CheckBox tool and setting the properties for the same (Fig. 4.10).

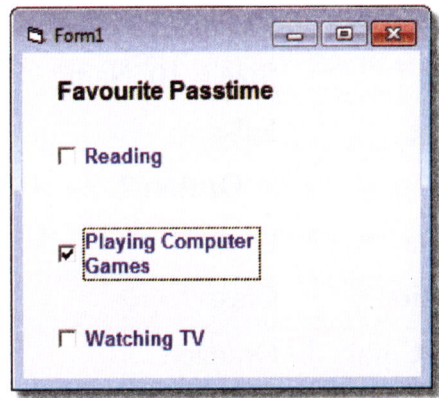

Fig. 4.10 *Drawing check box using CheckBox tool and setting its properties*

Property	Value
Check1	
Name	Check1
Caption	Reading
ForeColor	Blue
Font	Size = 10, Style = Bold, Name = "Arial"
Value	False
Check2	
Name	Check2
Caption	Playing Computer Games
ForeColor	Blue
Font	Size = 10, style = Bold, Name = "Arial"
Value	True
Check3	
Name	Check3
Caption	Watching TV
ForeColor	Blue
Font	Size = 10, style = Bold, Name = "Arial"
Value	False

Option button

Option button is also known as **Radio button**. They are used to display options from which the user is allowed to select only one (Fig. 4.11).

Some of the commonly used properties of the Option button tool are given in Table 4.5.

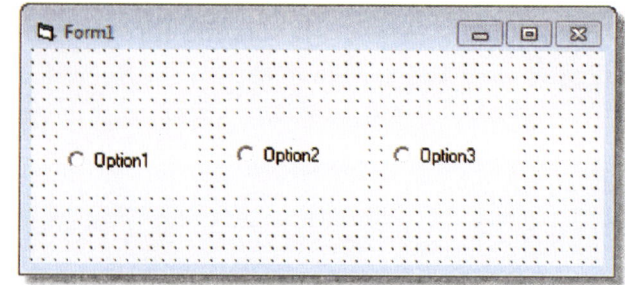

Fig. 4.11 *Using Option button*

Table 4.5 *Properties of Option Button Tool*

Property Name	Property Function	Property Task Pane
Name	It specifies the name of the radio buttons. The default name is Option1, Option2 and so on.	(Name) Option1 / Option1
Alignment	It sets the alignment of the text on the face of the Option button.	Alignment 0 - Left Justify / 0 - Left Justify / 1 - Right Justify

Let us see an example of an Option button Control here. This is drawn using the Option button tool and setting the properties for the same (Fig. 4.12).

Property	Value
Option 1	
Name	Option1
Caption	Class 6
ForeColor	Orange
Font	Size = 10, Name = "Arial"
Value	False
Option 2	
Name	Option1
Caption	Class 7
ForeColor	Orange
Font	Size = 10, Name = "Arial"
Value	False
Option 3	
Name	Option1
Caption	Class 8
ForeColor	Orange
Font	Size = 10, Name = "Arial"
Value	True

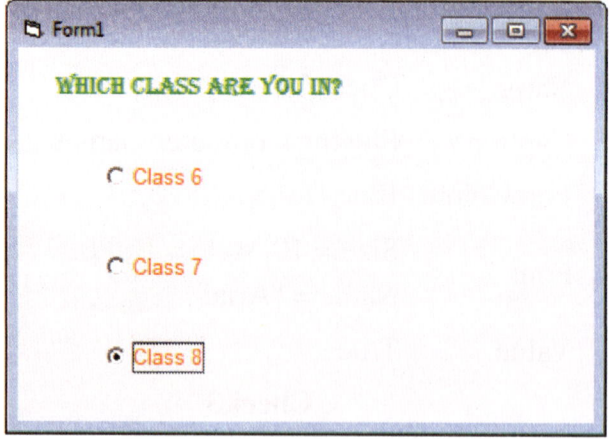

Fig. 4.12 *Drawing Option button using Option button tool and setting its properties*

Frame tool

Frame tool is used to group the controls together. It is generally used when a group of choices are given in the form of a CheckBox or an Option button (Fig. 4.13). For example, a group of hobbies for creating a checkbox or a group of class as in the above created form.

Note: Controls that are grouped together in frame control are called **child control**.

Some of the commonly used properties of the Frame tool are given in Table 4.6.

Fig. 4.13 *Using Frame tool*

Table 4.6 *Properties of Frame Tool*

Property Name	Property Function	Property Task Pane
Name	It specifies the name of the frame.	
BackColor	This specifies the background color of the frame.	
Caption	It specifies the text to be displayed on the frame.	
Border Style	It sets the value of True or False that determines whether a frame will have a border or not.	
Enabled	It sets the value of True or False that determines whether the frame will be available for the user-generated events.	
Font	It sets the font attributes of the caption of the frame.	

Let us see an example of a Frame control here. This is drawn using the Frame tool and setting the properties for the same (Fig. 4.14). To do so, follow the steps given here.

1. Add a Frame control using the Frame tool.
2. Insert the Radio buttons using the Radio button tool. Set the properties of the Radio buttons.
3. Set the properties of Frame control.

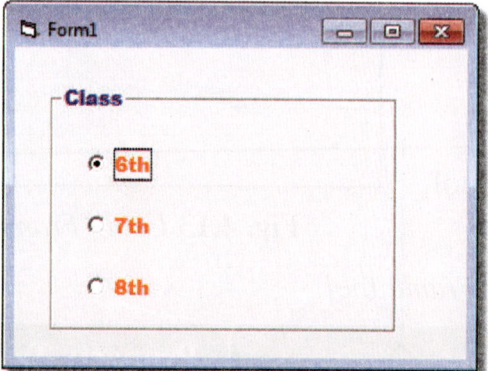

Property	Value
Name	Frame1
Caption	Class
Font	Size = 10, Name = "Arial"
ForeColor	Blue

Fig. 4.14 *Drawing Frame control using Frame tool and setting its properties*

ACTIVITY

A. In the club membership form create the following:

1. One frame for grouping membership period with radio buttons for 6 months, 1 year, 2 years.
2. One frame for grouping member's favourite picnic spots with checkboxes for amusement parks, historical monuments, botanical gardens and others.

B. Set the appropriate properties for the controls designed on the form.

ListBox tool

ListBox permits the programmer to load as many number of choices as the programmer wants in a text box, allows the user to make a selection and then proceed accordingly (Fig. 4.15). List boxes are ideal controls for presenting a list of choices to the user.

 If the number of choices exceed the value selected, then the scroll bars will automatically appear on the control.

Some of the commonly used properties of the ListBox tool are given in Table 4.7.

Fig. 4.15 *Using a ListBox tool*

Table 4.7 *Properties of ListBox Tool*

Property Name	Property Function	Property Task Pane
Name	It specifies the name of the list box. The default name is List1, List2, and so on.	(Name) List1
Alignment	It sets the alignment of the text on the face of the list box.	Alignment 0 - Left Justify / 0 - Left Justify / 1 - Right Justify
List	It sets the items contained in a list box.	List (List)
Sorted	It sorts the list items automatically.	Sorted False
Multiselect	It allows the user to make multiple selections in a list box. *0–None:* It is a single selection list box. *1–Simple:* A mouse click or pressing the spacebar selects or deselects an item in the list. *2–Extended:* If the user selects an item in the list box, presses and holds the Shift key down, and then selects another item in the list box, everything in between is selected as well.	MultiSelect 0 - None / 0 - None / 1 - Simple / 2 - Extended
Style	It sets the style of appearance of the list box.	Style 0 - Standard / 0 - Standard / 1 - Checkbox

Let us see an example of a ListBox control here. This is drawn using the ListBox tool and setting the properties for the same (Fig. 4.16).

To do so follow the steps given here:

1. Draw a label on the form and set its properties.
2. Draw a ListBox control and set its properties.

Property	Value
Name	List1
List	America
	Australia
	London
	Spain
	Singapore
Sorted	True
Font	Size = 10, Name = "Arial"
ForeColor	Light Blue

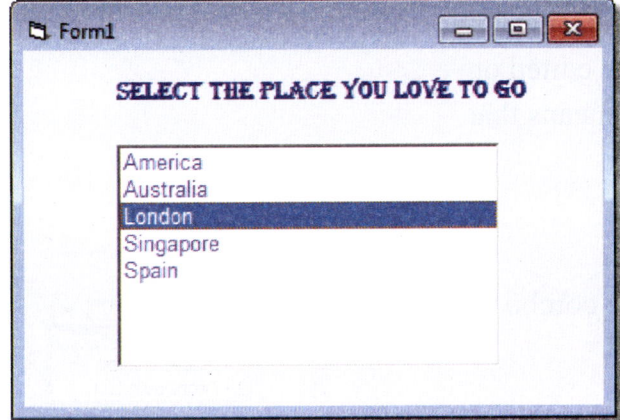

Fig. 4.16 *Drawing ListBox control using ListBox tool and setting its properties*

ComboBox tool

The function of the combo box (Fig. 4.17) is also to present a list of items where the user can click and select the items from the list. However, the user needs to click on the small arrowhead on the right of the combo box to see the items which are presented in the drop-down list. The major difference between a list box and combo box is that list box occupies more space in a form as compared to combo box. Also, by default editing is allowed only in a combo box.

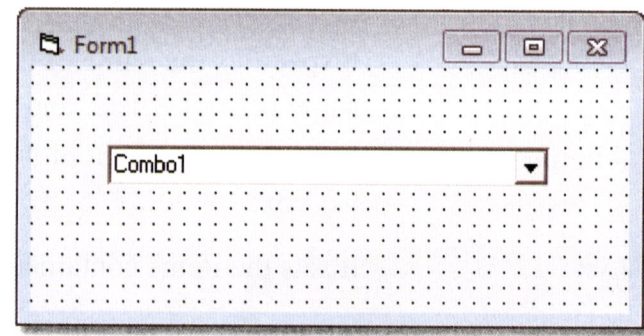

Fig. 4.17 *Using the ComboBox tool*

Note: Combo Box combines the features of Text Box and List Box. You can either select an option from the list or type in your own option.

Some of the commonly used properties of the ComboBox tool are given in Table 4.8.

Table 4.8 *Properties of ComboBox Tool*

Property Name	Property Function	Property Task Pane
Name	It specifies the name of the combo box. The default name is Combo1, Combo2, and so on.	(Name) Combo1 / Combo1
Alignment	It sets the alignment of the text on the face of the combo box.	Alignment 0 - Left Justify / 0 - Left Justify / 1 - Right Justify
List	It adds an item in the combo box.	List (List)
Text	It sets the text contained in the control.	Text chinese
Locked	It sets the value of True or False that determines whether a control can be edited or not. By default, Locked is False. It means that editing is allowed in a combo box.	Locked False
Sorted	It sorts the list items automatically.	Sorted False
Style	It sets the style of appearance of the combo box. *0*–Dropdown Combo *1*–Simple Combo *2*–Dropdown List	Style Dropdown Combo / 0 - Dropdown Combo / 1 - Simple Combo / 2 - Dropdown List

Let us see an example of a Combo Box control here. This is drawn using the Combo Box tool and setting the properties for the same (Fig. 4.18).

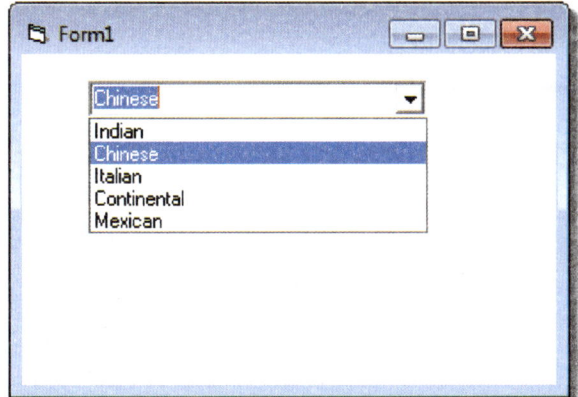

Property	Value
Name	Combo1
List	Indian
	Chinese
	Italian
	Continental
	Mexican
Text	Chinese
Locked	True
Sorted	False

Fig. 4.18 *Drawing Combo Box control using ComboBox tool and setting its properties*

ACTIVITY

A. **In the club membership form create the following:**
   1. One list box for languages known with items – English, German, French, Spanish, Italian, Japanese, Chinese, or other regional language.
      Allow multiple selection from the list box.
   2. One combo box for currently studying in class – 6, 7, 8, 9, 10, 11, and 12.

B. **Set the appropriate properties for the controls designed on the form.**

Timer tool

The timer control on the form is used to fire an event at specific intervals. It is invisible at run time. The code to fire an event is placed in the timer event (Fig. 4.19).

Some of the commonly used properties of the Timer tool are given in Table 4.9.

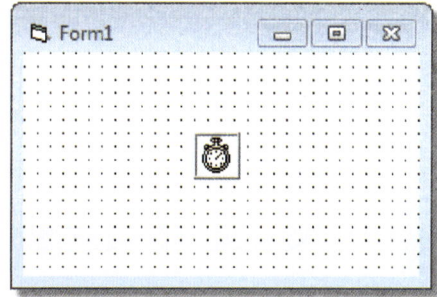

Fig. 4.19 *Using Timer tool*

Table 4.9 *Properties of Timer Tool*

Property Name	Property Function	Property Task Pane
Name	It specifies the name of the timer. The default name is Timer1, Timer2 and so on.	(Name) Timer1
Enabled	It sets the value of True or False that determines whether the timer will be available for the user-generated events or not.	Enabled True
Interval	It sets the number of milliseconds between the calls to a timer.	Interval 0

Shape tool

The shape tool is used to draw different shapes on the form. The Shape property is used to create a specific shape on the form by using different integer values (Table 4.10). Some of the commonly used properties of the Shape tool are given in this table.

Table 4.10 *Properties of Shape Tool*

Property Name	Property Function	Property Task Pane
Name	It specifies the name of the Shape tool with which it will be identified in the code. The default name is Shape1, Shape2 and so on.	(Name) Shape1
Shape	It sets the value returning the appearance of the Shape tool.	Shape 0 - Rectangle 0 - Rectangle 1 - Square 2 - Oval 3 - Circle 4 - Rounded Rectangle 5 - Rounded Square

Let us see an example of a Shape control here. This is drawn using the Shape tool and setting the properties for the same (Fig. 4.20).

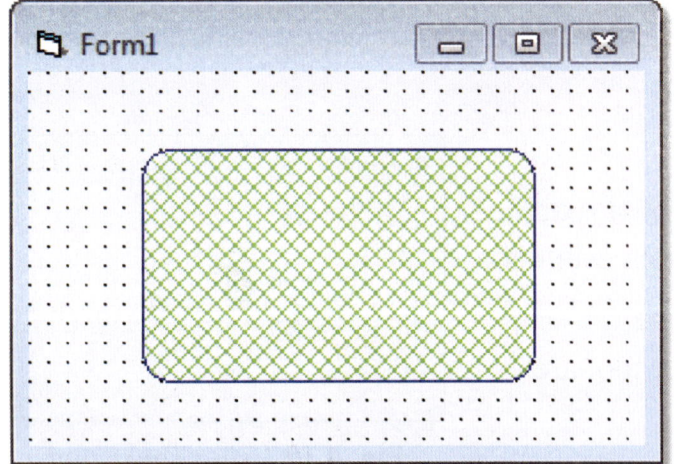

Property	Value
Name	Shape1
Shape	4-Rounded Rectangle
BorderColor	Dark blue
FillColor	Light green
FillStyle	7-Diagonal Cross

Fig. 4.20 *Drawing Shape control using Shape tool and setting its properties*

Picture tool

The picture box is one of the control that is used to handle graphics. You can load a picture at design phase by clicking on the picture item in the Properties window and select the picture from the desired folder. It can load the images in many different formats like BMP, DIB, JPEG, GIF, etc. You can also load the picture at run time using the LoadPicture method. For example, the following statement will load the picture grape.gif into the picture box at run time.

Picture1.Picture=LoadPicture ("C:\VB program\Images\grape.gif")

Some of the commonly used properties of the picture tool are given in Table 4.11.

Table 4.11 *Properties of the Picture Tool*

Property Name	Property Function	Property Task Pane
Name	It specifies the name of the picture tool. The default name is Picture1, Picture2, and so on.	(Name) Picture1
Picture	It sets the image that will be displayed. It can also be used for a company logo, etc.	Picture (None)
AutoSize	It automatically resizes to display the entire content of the picture.	AutoSize False / True / False

Let us see an example of a Picture Box control here. This is drawn using the Picture tool and setting the properties for the same (Fig. 4.21).

Property	Value
Name	Image1
Picture	C:\My Documents\star.jpg
AutoSize	False

Fig. 4.21 *Drawing a Picture control using picture tool and setting its properties*

Image tool

The image box is another control that handles images and pictures. It functions almost identically to the picture box. However, there is one major difference, the image in an image box is stretchable, which means it can be resized. This feature is not available in the picture box. Similar to the picture box, it can also use the LoadPicture method to load the picture.

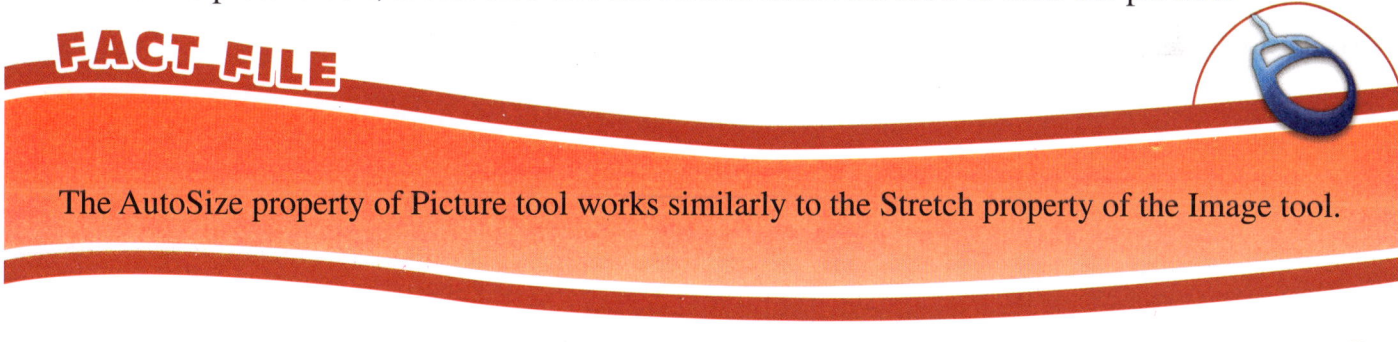

FACT FILE

The AutoSize property of Picture tool works similarly to the Stretch property of the Image tool.

For example, the following statement loads the picture grape.gif into the image box at run time.

Image1.Picture=LoadPicture ("C:\VB program\Images\lion.gif")

Some of the commonly used properties of the Image tool are given in Table 4.12.

Table 4.12 *Properties of Image Tool*

Property Name	Property Function	Property Task Pane
Name	It specifies the name of the image tool. The default name is Image1, Image2, and so on.	(Name) Image1
Picture	It sets the image that will be displayed in the image control.	Picture (Bitmap)
Stretch	It determines whether the graphics can resize to fit the size of the Image control.	Stretch False / True / False

Let us see an example of an Image control here. This is drawn using the Image tool and setting the properties for the same (Fig. 4.22).

Property	Value
Name	Image1
Picture	C:\My documents\My picture\star.jpg
Stretch	True

Fig. 4.22 *Drawing an Image control using Image tool and setting its properties*

ACTIVITY

A. **Place your photograph at the left top corner of the club membership form by using an appropriate tool.**
B. **Design a text box with multiline as True for giving your comments.**
C. **Save the form and execute it.**

GLOSSARY

Command button: It works when the user clicks on it.
CheckBox tool: It is used when the user has got the choice to select one or more options.
ComboBox tool: It allows the user to make a selection of items in the drop-down list.
Frame tools: It is used to group the controls together.
ImageBox tool: It is another control that handles images and pictures.
Label tool: It is used to display text on the form.
ListBox: It allows the user to make a selection from a number of items.
Msgbox command: This command can be used to display a message in a separate window when an event is occurring.
Option buttons: It is used to display options from which the user is allowed to select only one.
PictureBox tool: It is one of the controls that is used to handle graphics.
Pointer tool: It is used to select an object.
Shape tool: It is used to draw different shapes on the form.
TextBox tool: It draws a rectangular box on the form to accept input from the user.
Timer tool: It is used to fire an event at specific intervals.

NOW YOU KNOW

1. ToolBox contains a set of controls that are placed on a form at design time thereby creating the user interface area.
2. Frame tools are generally used when a group of choices are given in the form of a checkbox or an option button.
3. The list box occupies more space in form than the combo box.
4. The image in an image box can be resized but not in a picture box.

EXERCISE

A Fill in the blanks.

1. .... is a tool used to select an object on the form.
2. .... and .... tool can be used for displaying the images on the form.
3. .... control is used to group the other controls.

4. .... gives the number of choices from which the user can select only one.

5. .... control is not displayed at the runtime but its event is fired automatically at the specific time interval.

B **Fill up the given table.**

Tool	Name	Purpose
A		
☑		
🗐		
🗏		
◉		
⏱		
🖼		

C **State whether the following sentences are True or False.**

1. The Label tool is used to select an object.

2. ListBox tool is used to display text on the form.

3. Textbox tool draws a rectangular box.

4. Frame tool is used to group the controls together.

5. Timer control is used to fire an event at specific intervals.

D Answer the following questions.

1. What is the purpose of a Toolbox in Visual Basic? Name any five commonly used tools for designing a form.

2. How can a message be displayed on the form? Name any three properties of the tool used.

3. Name and explain any five common properties of all the tools featured in the Toolbox.

4. How can you draw different shapes on the form? Which property enables these shapes?

5. What is the use of a Timer tool?

LAB WORK

Design the following user interface forms with the help of the tools of Visual Basic. (Any additional tool can be added as per your requirement.)

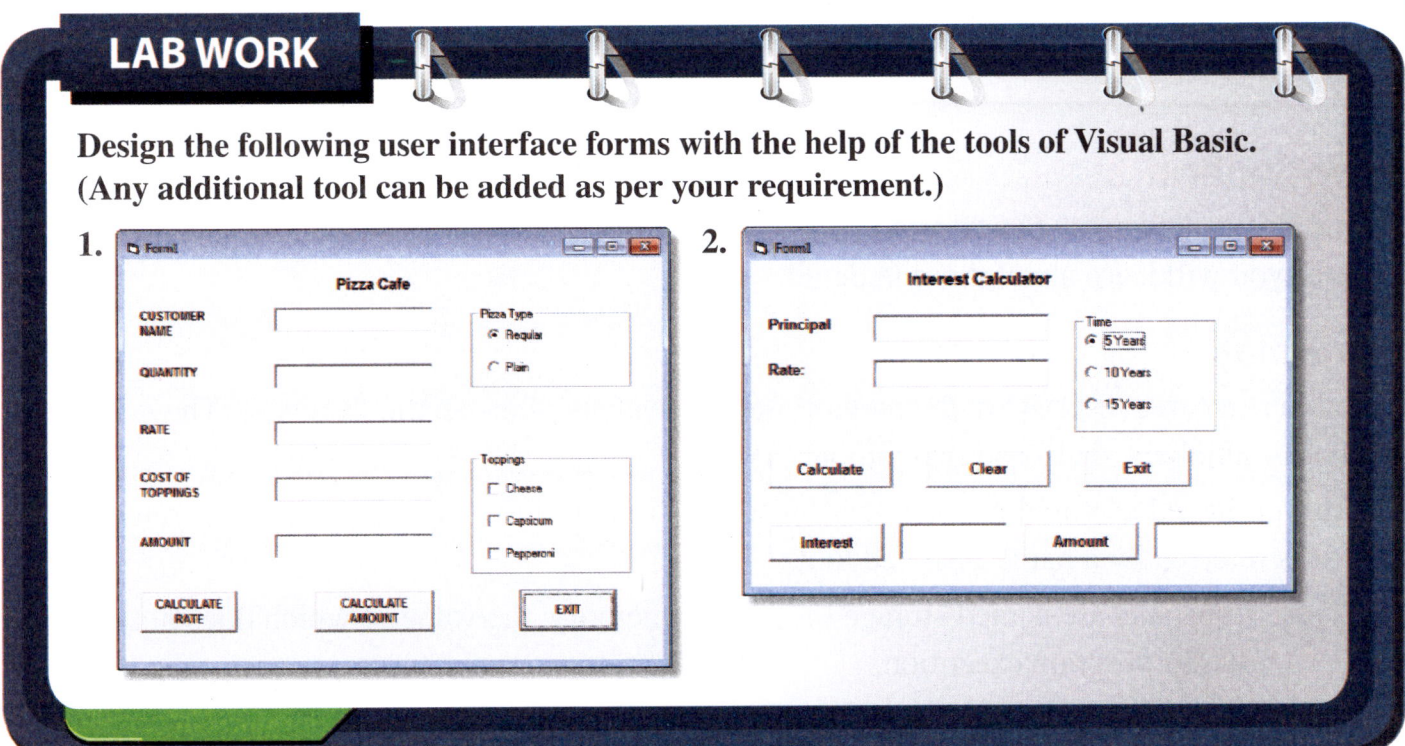

TEACHER'S NOTES

1. Tell the students how they can remove a control from a program.

   (**Hint** : Project Menu ⟹ Components option)

2. A tool has many properties. Explore all the properties along with the students.

5. Operators and Functions

LEARNING OBJECTIVES

You will learn about:
1. Variables – Rules, Data types, Declaration, Assignment of values
2. Operators – Arithmetic, Relational, String, Logical
3. Functions – Integer, String, Date
4. some important functions – MsgBox( ) and InputBox( )

Introduction

Visual Basic allows you to perform various types of operations on numbers and text. In this chapter you will learn about these in detail.

Variables

Variable is an area reserved in the memory to store values of a specific data type. The value can be words, numbers, dates and many more.

Whenever the value stored in a memory location is required to be used, modified or removed, then it is referred by a name assigned to it.

Note: Constants are named storage location in memory, the value of which does not change during program execution.

A Visual Basic variable name must follow the given rules for naming:

- The first character must be a letter, A through Z (uppercase or lowercase letters may be used). Succeeding characters can be letters, digits, or the underscore (_).
- There should not be any space in between any two characters.
- It should not exceed the limit of 255 characters.
- Name cannot be a reserved word (VB keyword).
- It should not contain any special character like %, &, !, #, @ or $.

Note: A variable can store only a specific type of a value depending on the data type used at the time of declaring a variable.

FACT FILE

VB is not case sensitive. For example, Num, NUM and num all refer to the same variable. If you type a variable on a line in a case other than the case you used when you declared the variable, VB will change the case to match that of the declared variable when you leave that line.

ACTIVITY

Of the given variables sort out the valid and invalid names.
Myfriend, 1number, first_name, &lastname, .add, 22phone, item name, dim, print, my%school, my@number, my teacher, fathernm, address

Data types in Visual Basic

The data type refers to the kind of data a variable can hold. Data types apply to all values that can be stored in computer memory or can be used in the evaluation of an expression. Every variable, or a constant, must be declared using a specific data type. Visual Basic supports different data types as listed in Table 5.1.

Table 5.1 *Different Data Types Used in Visual Basic*

Data Type	Function
Byte	It shows integer value within the range 0 to 255
Integer	It can only store whole number integers within the range –32,768 to 32,767. Integers should be used when you are working with values that cannot contain fractional numbers.
Long	It is same as Integer data type. However, it can store a value with a range of –2,147,483,648 to 2,147,483,647. For storing bigger integer values, Long can be used.
Single	It represents a floating point number with a decimal. It has a range of -3.402823×10^{38} to $-1.401298 \times 10^{-45}$ for negative numbers, and 1.401298×10^{-45} to 3.402823×10^{38} for positive numbers. When you need fractional numbers within this range, this is the data type to use.
Double	It is same as Single except that it has a huge range for floating numbers as compared to the Single data type. It is generally used for scientific calculations.
String	It stores only alphanumeric values, that is, text and numbers in the form of characters. String data type is generally used as a variable-length type of variable. A variable-length string can contain up to approximately 2 billion characters.

Date	It stores the date value from 1/1/100 to 12/31/9999.
Boolean	It represents either True or False.
Variant	It stores any type of data. It is the default data type.

Declaring a variable

Declaring a variable tells Visual Basic to reserve space in memory. There are two ways of declaring a variable. These are discussed here.

Implicit declaration: It is not always necessary that a variable should be declared before it is used. Automatically whenever Visual Basic encounters a new variable, it is assigned a default variable type and value. This is called implicit declaration. Thus, in this type of declaration it is easier for the user to have more control over the variables.

Explicit declaration: When the declaration of the variable is required before it can be used in a program then it is known as explicit declaration. It is advisable to declare the variables explicitly.

The variables are declared with a Dim statement to specify the name of the variable and its data type.

The syntax used is:

Dim variableName As variableType

Where,

Dim is the keyword that indicates to Visual Basic that a variable is being declared.

variableName is the name assigned to the variable.

variableType is used for the declaration of the data type.

For example, the syntax used for declaring a variable Rate of type Integer to store only integer values is given below:

Dim Rate As Integer

It is also possible to declare multiple variables on the same line by separating each variable with a comma(,). Let us see below different cases where a variable is declared.

1. When the variables are of the same type, the data type declaration only needs to be made once at the end of the declaration. For example,

   Dim Rate, Time, Principal As Integer

2. When the variables are of different types, the data type of variable must be declared at the end of each group of the same type. For example,

   Dim Student_Name As String, Student_Class As Integer

   Dim a, b, c As String, x, y As Double, i As Integer

String variable declaration: String variables can be either variable-length or fixed-length. The difference in declaring them is shown below:

Variable-length string declaration: Length of the data assigned can vary as it happens for any string data type. For example,

Dim Student Name As String

Fixed-length string declaration: It stores a value of fixed length. In the example given below a string variable is declared that stores a string value of only one character long.
For example,

Dim Section As String * 1

Assigning a value to a variable

Visual Basic variables may be initialized either during the declaration or after the declaration. Initialization is performed using the Visual Basic assignment operator (=).

Look at the following examples:

1. To initialize a single variable when it is declared:

    Dim num As Integer = 12

    Dim str As String = "Hello"

2. To declare multiple variables. Each variable may be initialised in a separate declaration line.

    Dim str1 As String = "Abhay", x = 5 As Integer, y As Integer = 10

3. To initialize the variable after the declaration has been done.

    Dim str1

    Str1 = "Welcome"

4. To change the value of the variable anytime during the program after initialization has already been done.

    Dim x As Integer = 10

    x = 20

FACT FILE

When a new value is assigned, the old value is overwritten by the new value because at one time a variable can hold only one value.

ACTIVITY

A. Complete the following activity.
1. Declare the integer variable x, y and z.
2. Assign value 5 to x, 10 to y and 15 to z.

B. What is the value of the variables C, N1, N2, N3 which are given below?

A = 5
B = 10
C = A + B
N1 = A + 10
N2 = B
N3 = 5 + N2

C. Declare a string variable Friend, a numeric variable Num1 to store a decimal value. Assign the value 'Vedika' to the string variable created above.

Operators in Visual Basic

Operators are used to perform different operations on the variables created. These operations can be the mathematical calculation, comparison of the values stored in the variable or some kind of logical operations on the variables. Operators are categorised depending on the type of the expression created. Some of the operators in VB are discussed here.

Arithmetic operators

Arithmetic operators are those operators which does the mathematical manipulation on the values. These operators are written in the order of precedence, that is, exponential operator has got the highest order of execution and subtraction has the lowest order (Table 5.2).

Table 5.2 *Arithmetic Operators*

Operator	Description	Example	Answer
^	Exponential/(Power of)	3 ^ 2	9
*	Multiply	4 * 5	20
/	Division	9 / 2	4.5
\	Integer division	9 \ 2	4
Mod	Modulus/(Remainder)	9 mod 2	1
+	Addition	2 + 5	7
−	Subtraction	6 − 1	5

Example 1:

   Dim x As Integer
   x = 2 ^ 2 * 2 / 2

Here, the variable x will have a value 4.

Example 2:

   Dim y As Integer
   y = 9\2 + 1 – 2

Here, the variable y will have a value 3.

Relational operators

Relational operators are also known as **comparison operators**. These operators are used to do the comparison of the values and return a Boolean value of either True or False depending on the result of the comparison (Table 5.3).

Table 5.3 *Relational Operators*

Operator	Description	Example	Answer
=	Equals to	2 = 5	False
<>	Not equals to	9 <> 9	False
<	Less than	4 < 5	True
>	Greater than	9 > 20	False
<=	Less than or Equals to	10 <= 20	True
>=	Greater than or Equals to	5 >= 6	False

Logical operators

Logical operators allow a program to make a decision based on multiple conditions. Each operand is considered a condition that can be evaluated to a True or False value (Table 5.4).

Table 5.4 *Logical Operators*

Operator	Description	Example	Answer
NOT	Result will be the logical negation of the statement	NOT 10 = 20	True
AND	Result will be True only if both the statements are True	5 < 10 AND 6 > 2 10 = 10 AND 4 = 5	True False
OR	Result will be True only if either of the statements is True	4 < 5 OR 12 > 22 4 > 5 OR 12 > 22	True False

String concatenation operator

String concatenation operators are used to concatenate two strings together. Concatenation means joining two strings side by side (Table 5.5).

Table 5.5 *String Concatenation Operators*

Operator	Description	Example	Answer
+	Joins two strings	"Hello" + "World"	HelloWorld
&	Joins two strings	"Hi" & " " & "Friends"	Hi Friends

ACTIVITY

Find out the value of the given variables.

1. A = 5 * 2 + 3^3 – 4*3 mod 4
2. B = 25 mod 2 * 5 – 2 + 6
3. C = 10>12 AND 12 > 15
4. D = 3 <= 4 OR 5 > 4
5. E = NOT 10>10
6. F = "WE"+" Rock"
7. G = "I AM"+ " &"the" &" " &" Best"

Built-in Functions in VB

A **built-in function** is a predefined formula that accepts an input from the user in the form of arguments and returns a value. They are classified depending on the type of the argument given to these functions.

Date function

These functions work on date values (Table 5.6).

Table 5.6 *Date Functions*

Function	Description
Date( )	Returns the current system date
Time( )	Returns the current system time
Now( )	Returns the current system date and time

For example, to create a form with a Command control called date functions, write the following code in the code window after double-clicking the command box (Fig. 5.1). The output at run time is shown in Figure 5.2.

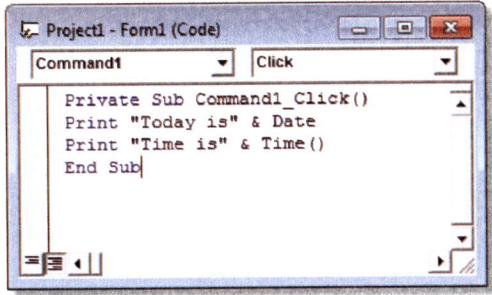

Fig. 5.1 *Using date function*

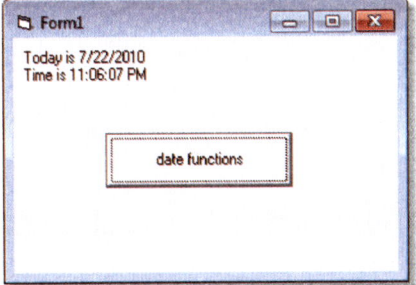

Fig. 5.2 *Output*

String functions

These functions work on string values (Table 5.7).

Table 5.7 *String Functions*

Function	Description	Example
Len( )	Returns the number of characters in string	Print Len("Hello") Displays 5
Left( )	Returns the n number of characters from the left side of string	Print Left("Hello",2) Displays He
Right( )	Returns the n number of characters from the right side of string	Print Right("Hello",3) Displays llo
Mid( )	Returns n number of characters from the middle of the string	Print Mid(Administration",2,3) Displays dm
Ucase( )	Returns the string converted to upper case	Print Ucase("hello") Displays HELLO
Lcase ( )	Returns the string converted to lowercase letters	Print Lcase("Hello") Displays hello
Trim( )	Removes spaces from both the left and right of string	Print trim(" Health ") + " is wealth" Displays Health is wealth
Ltrim( )	Removes space from the left side of the string	Print Ltrim(" Amit ") +"is a good boy" Displays Amit is a good boy
Rtrim( )	Removes space from the right side of string	Print Rtrim(" Amit ") + "is a good boy" Displays Amit is a good boy

Instr( )	Searches for strings within another strings, the first argument is the main string and the second argument is the string to be searched	Print instr("Adminsistration", "is") Displays 7
Val( )	It converts the numbers contained in a string to its numeric equivalent	Val("124566") will produce the number 124566 Val("125.0066") will produce the number 125.0066
Replace( )	It replaces one string with another string a specified number of times.	Print Replace("Hello/world", "/", "–") Displays Hello-world

FACT FILE

The default value accepted in a text box is of the type string. The Val command is used to convert the text into a number format so that calculation can be performed.

FACT FILE

Print statement of Visual BASIC is just like Basic print statement, done in lower classes. The separators, semicolon and comma also works in the same way.

Let us see a few examples of built-in functions:

Example 1: Here the input is given in Figure 5.3 and the corresponding output is given in Figure 5.4.

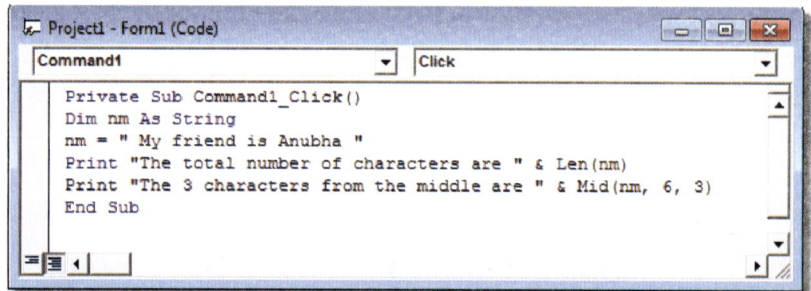

Fig. 5.3 *Using String functions*

Fig. 5.4 *Output*

Example 2: Here the input is given in Figure 5.5 and the corresponding output is given in Figure 5.6.

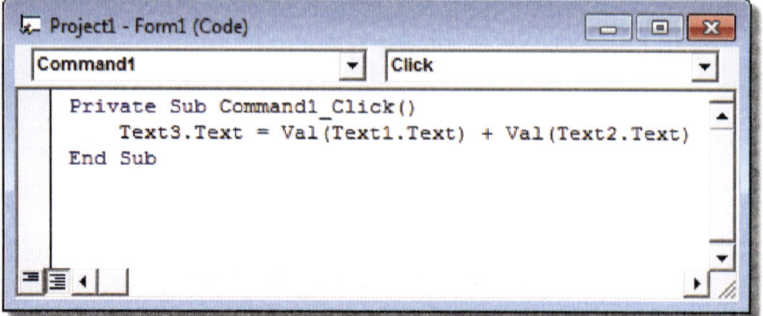

Fig. 5.5 *Adding inputs in a text box*

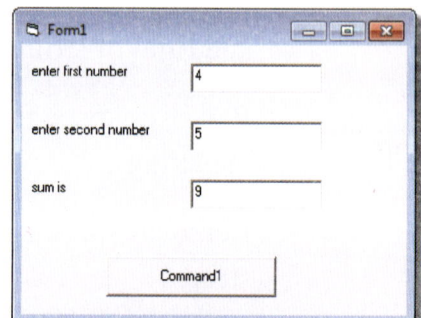

Fig. 5.6 *Output*

**Note:** When you want to get the input entered by the user from the text box, you use the syntax Text1.Text, Text2.Text, Text3.Text and so on, where Text1, Text2, Text3 are the names of the textboxes.

Number functions

These functions work on number values. See Table 5.8

TRY THIS!

Add two numbers in a text box without using Val() and see the difference. Now add two strings in a text box and see the result.

Table 5.8 *Number Functions*

Function	Description	Example
Int( )	Converts a number into an integer by truncating its decimal part and the resulting integer is the largest integer that is smaller than the number.	Int(2.4) = 2, Int(4.8) = 4, Int(–4.6) = –5, Int(0.032) = 0
Sqr( )	Returns the square root of a number	Sqr(4) = 2, Sqr(9) = 2
Abs( )	Returns the absolute value of a number	Abs(–8) = 8 and Abs(8) = 8.
Round( )	Rounds up a number to a certain number of decimal places. The Format is Round (n, m) which means to round off a number n to m decimal places.	Round(7.2567, 2) = 7.26

ACTIVITY

A. Accept a decimal number and create 4 command buttons for calculating the Integer, Square, Absolute and Round of a number.

B. Accept a sentence in a text box and create 5 command buttons for displaying the first 3 letters, 5 letters starting from the fourth position, upper case string, lower case string, total number of characters in string.

C. Create a form to display the current system date at the click of a command button.

**TRY THIS!**

To display the Prompt on multiple lines, you can use either the constant vbCrLf or the combination Chr (10) & Chr (13) between any two strings.

Some Important Functions Used in VB

The MsgBox ( ) function

A message box is a special dialog box used to display a piece of information to the user. The user cannot type anything in the message box.

The syntax used is:

MsgBox (Prompt, Style value, title)

where,

Prompt displays the message in the message box.

Style value determines what type of command buttons appears on the message box (Table 5.9).

Title displays the title of the message board.

Table 5.9 *Style Value for a Message Box*

Style Value	Named Constant	Buttons Displayed
0	vbOKOnly	OK button
1	vbOKCancel	OK and Cancel buttons
2	vbAbortRetryIgnore	Abort, Retry and Ignore buttons
3	vbYesNoCancel	Yes, No and Cancel buttons
4	vbYesNo	Yes and No buttons
5	vbRetryCancel	Retry and Cancel buttons

Let us see a few examples for msgbox function:

Example 1: Here the input is given in Figure 5.7 and the corresponding output is given in Figure 5.8.

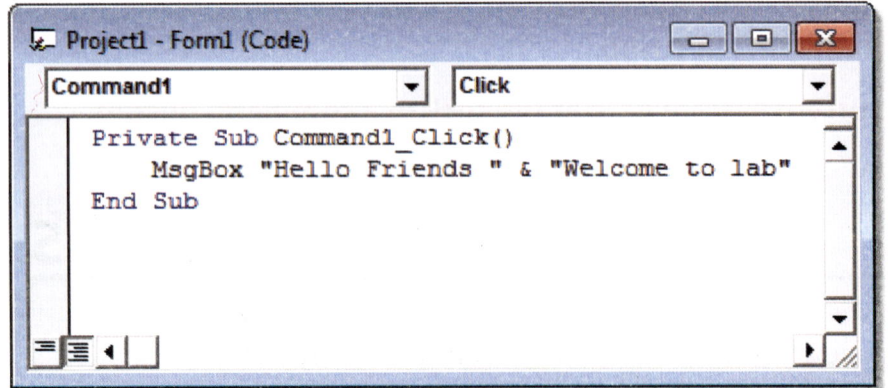

Fig. 5.7 *Displaying only OK button on*   Fig. 5.8 *Output the message box*

Example 2: Here the input is given in Figure 5.9 and the corresponding output is given in Figure 5.10.

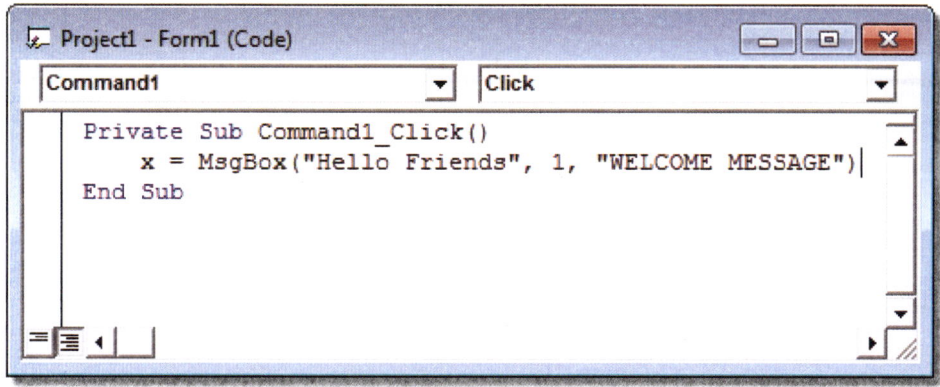

Fig. 5.9 *Displaying OK and Cancel button*

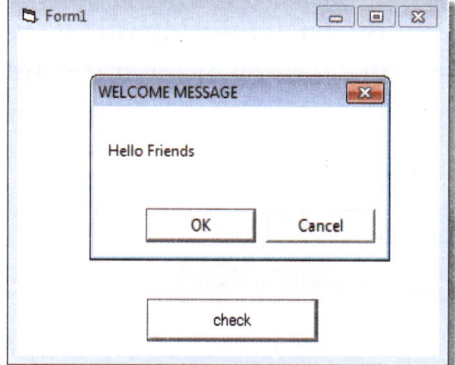

Fig. 5.10 *Output on the message box*

Note: Here the value 1 is returned to the variable x to display both the OK and cancel button on the message box.

The InputBox ( ) function

This function displays a small dialog box where the user can enter a value or a message in form of the text. It has a text box with OK and Cancel buttons (Fig. 5.11).

The InputBox () function returns a string data value that holds the answer that was typed in by the user.

The syntax used for InputBox( ) is:

   InputBox (prompt, title, Default text)

where,

   Prompt is the message to be displayed for the user.
   Title is the title of the InputBox ( ) window
   Default value is the value displayed if the user does not enter anything.

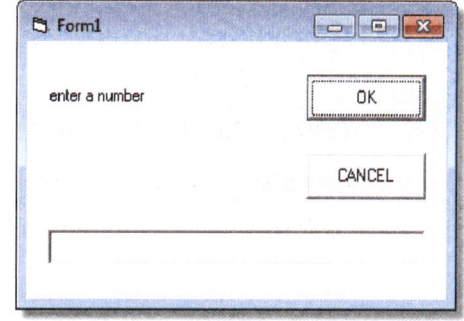

Fig. 5.11 *Input Box*

In the following example the code to display an input box is given in Figure 5.12. The corresponding output is given in Figure 5.13.

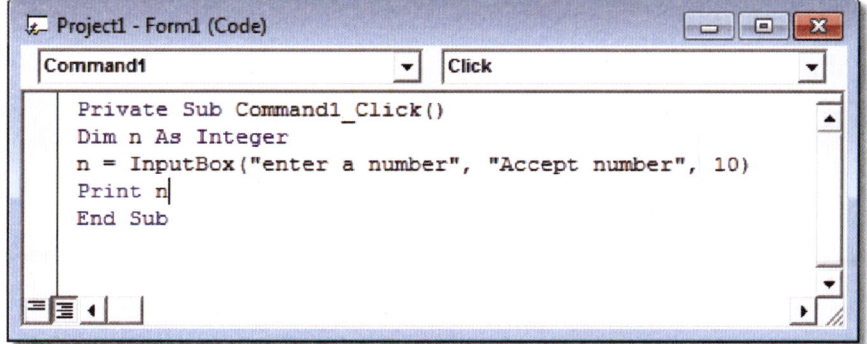

Fig. 5.12 *Using InputBox () function*

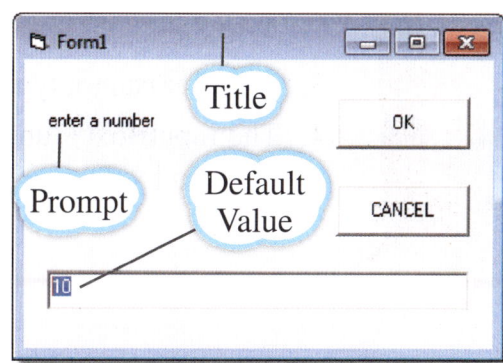

Fig. 5.13 *Output*

TRY THIS!

By default the InputBox() is displayed in the middle of the screen. If you want, you can specify the position of Input Box by giving the x and y coordinates of the screen as the fourth and the fifth argument in the function.

ACTIVITY

A. Accept two numbers using an InputBox in two different variables and print the sum of two in a message box.

B. Accept a name of a person and display a welcome message along with the name in a message box.

GLOSSARY

Built-in function: It is a pre-defined formula that accepts an input from the user in the form of arguments and returns a value.

Data type: It refers to what kind of data it can hold and how it stores that data.

Inputbox(): It displays a small dialog box where the user can enter a value or a message in the form of text.

Message box: It is a special dialog box used to display a piece of information to the user.

Operators: They are used to perform different operations on the variables created.

Variable: It is an area reserved in the memory to store values of a specific data type.

NOW YOU KNOW

1. A variable in Visual Basic can be declared by Dim statement either explicitly or implicitly.
2. Depending on the type of the expression created operators are categorized as Arithmetic, Logical, Comparison and String operators.
3. The user cannot type anything in the message box.
4. The InputBox() function returns a string data value that holds the answer that was typed in by the user.

EXERCISE

A **Fill in the blanks.**

1. ……………………. and ……………………. are two ways to declare a variable in Visual Basic.
2. Giving a value to a variable is known as ……………………. .
3. A variable can be declared by using ……………………. statement.
4. A ……………………. data type stores only two values.
5. A ……………………. data type stores the numbers in decimal where accuracy is more important.
6. ……………………. and ……………………. are two important functions in Visual Basic which interacts with the user in the form of a small window.

B **Give the difference between:**

1. InputBox( ) and Msgbox( )
2. Rtrim( ) and Ltrim( )
3. Date( ) and Now( )
4. Lcase( ) and Ucase( )
5. Mid( ) and Instr( )

C **Match the following.**

1. String concatenation Operator — a. Characters from left side
2. Logical Operator — b. String
3. Len( ) — c. &
4. Left( ) — d. And
5. Variable name — e. total characters in string
6. Data type — f. str

D **Answer the following questions.**

1. What are variables? How do we declare a variable in Visual Basic?
2. What are the rules for creating a variable in Visual Basic?
3. What are data types? Name all the possible data types that can be created in Visual Basic?

4. Which data types are used to store numeric values with and without decimal? Explain all with examples.

5. How is string values handled in Visual Basic? Explain the data type along with declaration and assignment of the value.

6. What are built-in functions? Name the different types.

LAB WORK

A. Write the Visual Basic code for the following command buttons:

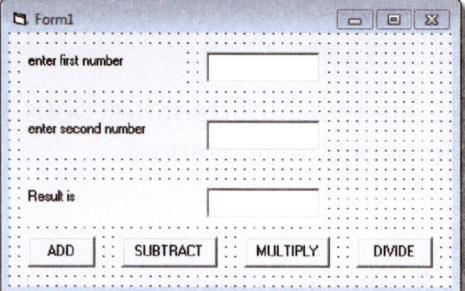 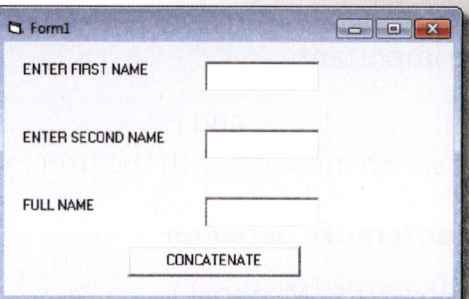

B. Accept the marks of three subjects in an input box and display the percentage in the message box.

C. Accept the name of your favourite food in a text box and display the total characters in it in another text box at the click of a command button.

TEACHER'S NOTES

1. Tell the students that they can add an icon besides the message. There are four types of icons available in VB: Critical ❌, Question ❓, exclamation ⚠️, and information ℹ️. For Example,

6 Sequential Programming in VB

LEARNING OBJECTIVES

You will learn about:
1. sequential programming
2. giving comments in Visual Basic
3. End statement in Visual Basic

Introduction

Programming can be a complex and complicated process or it can be quite straightforward. In either case, the basic programming concepts remain the same. Most programs are built out of a standard set of programming constructs. For example, to write a useful program, one should be able to store values in variables, test these values against a condition, or loop through a set of instructions a certain number of times.

As with any modern programming language, Visual Basic supports three common programming constructs. These are given here.

1. *Sequence:* It refers to the ordered execution of statements.
2. *Selection:* One of a number of statements is executed depending on the state of the program. This is usually expressed with keywords such as IF ... THEN ... ELSE ... ENDIF
3. *Repetition:* A statement is executed until the program reaches a certain state or operations are applied to every element of a collection. This is usually expressed with keywords, such as, FOR ... NEXT, DO ... LOOP.

Let us learn about sequential programming in Visual Basic here.

Sequential Programming in Visual Basic

Any program that executes the instructions written one-by-one in a specific order is known as a sequential programming (Fig. 6.1).

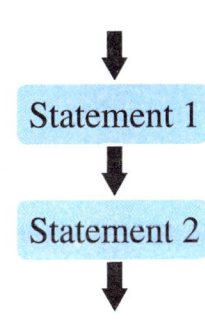

Fig. 6.1 *Sequential flow of statements*

For example, to calculate the area of a circle, you may follow the following sequence of instructions:

1. Create variables for accepting the radius.
2. Input the radius.
3. Calculate the area.
4. Display the area.

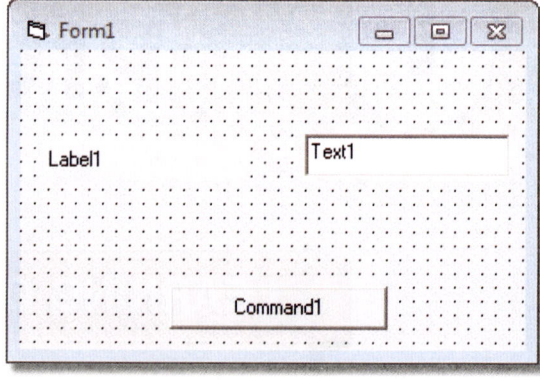

Let us see how the above instructions are executed in Visual Basic. Follow the steps here:

1. Design a form using the controls from the Toolbox (Fig. 6.2).
2. Set the properties of the controls as shown in Table 6.1

Fig. 6.2 *Designing a form*

Table 6.1 *Properties of control used*

Control Name	Property Name	Value
Label1	Caption	ENTER RADIUS
Text1	Text	Blank
Command1	Caption	AREA OF CIRCLE

3. Double-click on the Command box and write the following code (Fig. 6.3).
4. Execute the form by pressing F5 Function key.

OR

Click tool from the Standard Toolbar (Fig. 6.4).

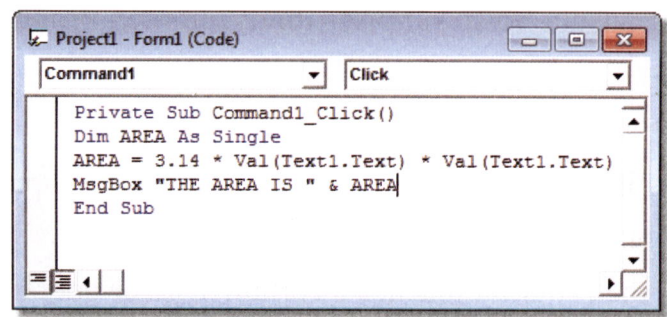

Fig. 6.3 *Writing the code to calculate the area of a circle*

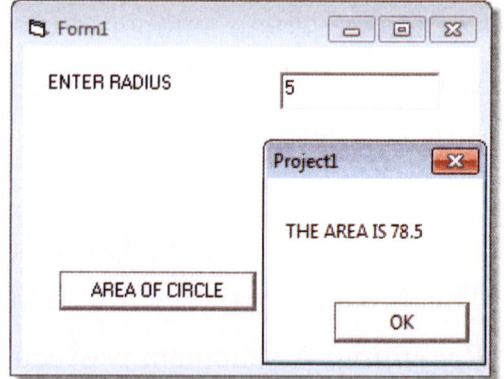

Fig. 6.4 *Calculating the area of a circle*

ACTIVITY

A. Accept the length and breadth from the user in a text box. Calculate and display the area and perimeter in a message box.

B. Accept the marks of English, Computer Science and Maths in three different text boxes and calculate the average percentage. Display the average percentage in the fourth text box.

Giving Comments in Visual Basic

Comments serve as inline documentation that helps to read, reuse and maintain existing code. They make the source code more understandable. While creating large programs, it is considered a good programming practice to include comments for explaining the work of any specific block of codes. The Visual Basic interpreter ignores comment lines when the program is run.

To give a comment in Visual Basic, you can use an **apostrophe** (') or a **Rem Statement**. Look at the example given below:

' This is a comment line.

Rem this is a comment line.

FACT FILE

Rem as a comment is inherited from old DOS version BASIC, and is not frequently used in Visual Basic.

 You can make an entire line a comment, or you can append a comment to the end of another statement.

End Statement

End statement in Visual Basic is used to stop the execution of a form. It is equivalent to pressing the Stop tool ■ present on the Standard Toolbar.

 The End Statement stops code execution abruptly, without invoking proper exit code or any other Visual Basic code.

Let us see some solved examples.

Example 1

To add and delete entries from the list box follow these steps:

1. Design the form as shown in Figure 6.5.
2. Set the property of the controls as given in Table 6.2

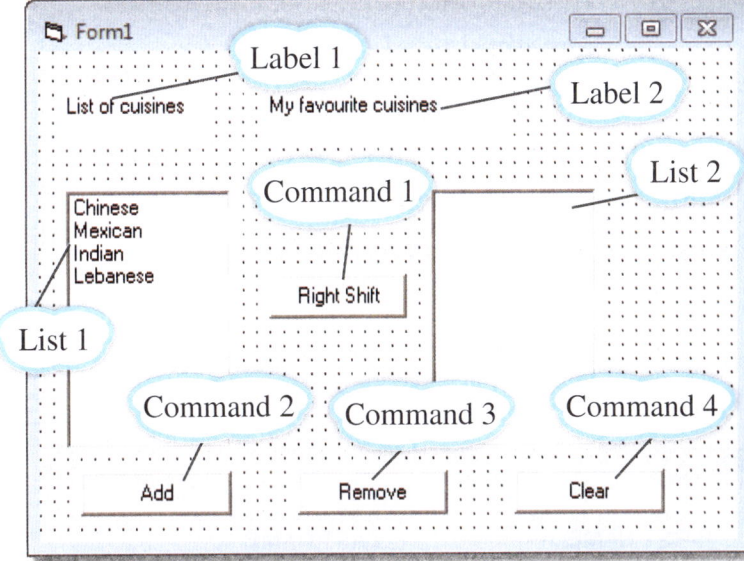

Fig. 6.5 *Designing a VB Form*

Table 6.2 *Property Names and Values*

Control Name	Property Name	Value
Label1	Caption	List of Cuisines
	ForeColor	Highlight
	Font	Size = 10 Bold

Label 2	Caption	My Favourite Cuisine
	ForeColor	Highlight
	Font	Size = 10 Bold
Command1	Caption	Right Shift
	Name	Shift
Command2	Caption	Add
	Name	Add
Command3	Caption	Remove
	Name	Remove
Command4	Caption	Clear
	Name	Clear
List1	List	Chinese
		Mexican
		Indian
		Lebanese

 **Note:** In this code (Fig. 6.6), AddItem is a method used.

Once you have completed designing the form and writing the code, run the project. You will be able to add and delete items in the lists using various Command controls.

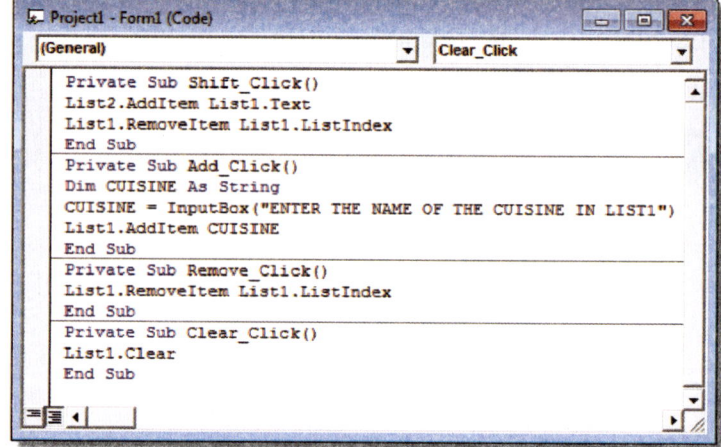

Fig. 6.6 *Code window*

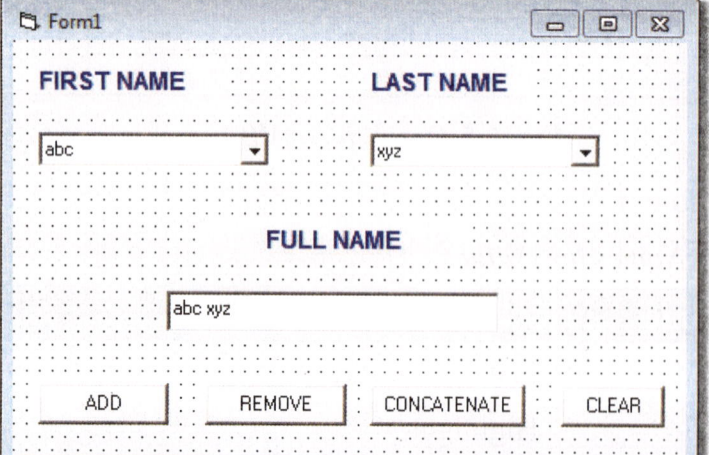

Fig. 6.7 *To add the two strings*

Example 2

To add the two strings follow the steps given below:

1. Design the form as shown (Fig. 6.7).
2. Set the desired properties for the controls created on the form.

3. Write the code in the code window (Fig. 6.8).
4. You will be able to add the two strings in the form using various controls (Fig. 6.9).

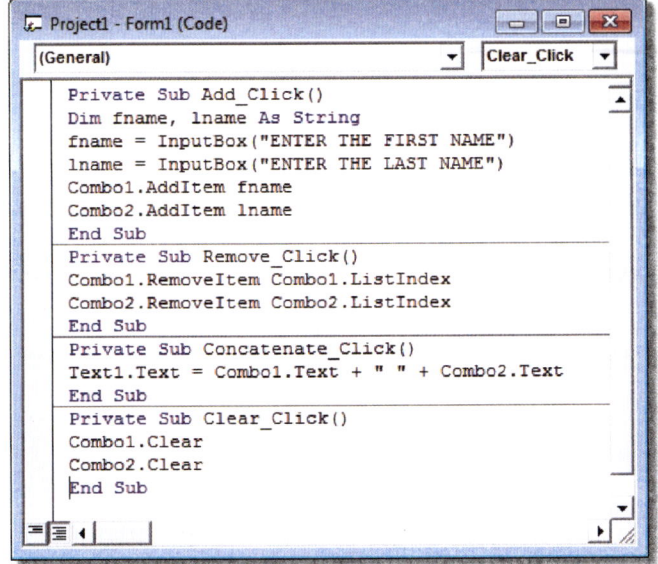

Fig. 6.8 *Code to add two strings*

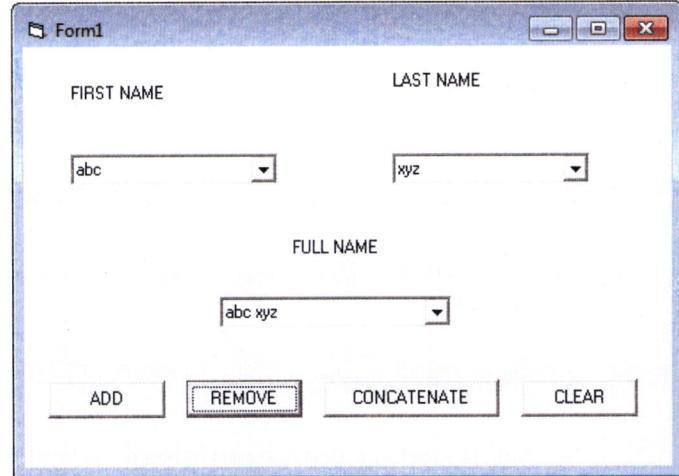

Fig. 6.9 *Concatenating strings*

GLOSSARY

Comments: It is inline documentation that helps to read, reuse and maintain existing code.

End statement: It is used to stop the execution of a form.

Selection programming: It is the execution of a number of statements depending on the state of the program.

Sequence programming: It is the execution of the instructions written one-by-one in a specific order.

Repetition programming: It is the execution of a statement until the program reaches a certain state or operations are applied to every element of a collection.

NOW YOU KNOW

1. Visual Basic supports three common programming constructs – Sequence, Selection, Repetition.
2. Comments make the source code more understandable. To give a comment in Visual Basic, you can use an apostrophe (') or a Rem Statement.
3. End statement is equivalent to pressing a Stop button present on the Standard Toolbar.

EXERCISE

A Fill in the blanks.

1. ...., ... and .... are three types of programming constructs that are supported in VB.

2. .... statement is used to stop the execution of a form.

3. Comments help to ...., ... and .... existing code.

4. Rem is given to write ....

5. FOR ... NEXT is an example of .... type of programming construct.

B Write sequential codes for the following algorithm: HOTS

1. Get the value of principal, time and rate of interest.

2. Calculate the interest.

3. Display the result in a message box

C Read the code given here. Design a form where this code can be used to get the output. Also write the appropriate Rem statement along with each line of the code.

Dim Area As Single

Area = val(TB_Length.Text) * val(TB_Length)

Msgbox("Area of a square is " & Area)

D Answer the following questions.

1. Explain the three types of programming constructs that are supported by Visual Basic.

2. What is the use of comments in VB? Give examples.

3. Why is the End statement used? Which tool is similar to the End statement?

4. Can we use both apostrophe (') and Rem for adding comments in the same program? Justify the answer with an example.

LAB WORK

Design the forms for the following and write the appropriate codes.

1. Accept the marks of three subjects and calculate the total and average percentage.
2. Accept the name and age and display the welcome message.
3. Accept the radius of the circle and display its area and circumference in 2 different text box. The events to be added to 2 different command buttons AREA and CIRCUMFERENCE.
4. Accept two numbers from the user and swap their contents. The output should be displayed in the message box.
5. Accept the size of a square from the user and display its area and perimeter in two different text boxes. The action to be performed on the click of CALCULATE button.

JERRY YANG

Jerry Yang was born on 6 November, 1968 in Taipei, Taiwan.

Jerry Yang co-created Yahoo! Internet navigational guide in April 1994 with David Filo, a native of Moss Bluff, Louisiana. In April 1995, Yang and Filo co-founded Yahoo! Inc.

TEACHER'S NOTES

1. Talk to the students about drawbacks of using the End statement. Tell them how it can cause the VB IDE to crash.

7 Conditional Programming in VB

LEARNING OBJECTIVES

You will learn about:
1. Conditional statement – Definition
2. IF…THEN…ELSE statement
3. SELECT CASE statement

Introduction

In this chapter, you will learn how to write a VB code that can make decisions when it processes input from the user, and controls the program flow in the process. Decision making process is an important part of programming because it can help to solve practical problems intelligently and provide useful output to the user. This kind of decision making program uses conditional statements. For example, you can write a program that can ask the computer to perform a certain task until a certain condition is met.

Conditional Statements

Conditional statements control the flow of execution of a program or one of its sections. Conditional statements perform comparisons and take appropriate actions depending on the outcome of such comparisons. VB provides two conditional statements:

- IF … THEN … ELSE statement
- SELECT CASE statement

IF … THEN … ELSE statement

The IF … THEN … ELSE statement is used to evaluate whether a condition is True or False. Depending on the result of the condition, the specific statements are executed. This condition can be a simple expression or a combination of expressions that uses a comparison operator to compare a value or variable with another.

The IF … THEN … ELSE statement can be used in many ways. These are discussed here.

Type 1

This is the simplest form of the IF statement. In this case, the program will examine the condition. If the condition is True, then the program will execute the statement or statements following it. However, if the condition is False then nothing will happen, as there is no alternative statement in the code.

You can also make use of the flowchart shown (Fig. 7.1) to understand the IF ... THEN statement.

Syntax

   IF Condition THEN
   Statement
   END IF

   IF Condition THEN
   Statement1
   Statement2
   Statement3
   END IF

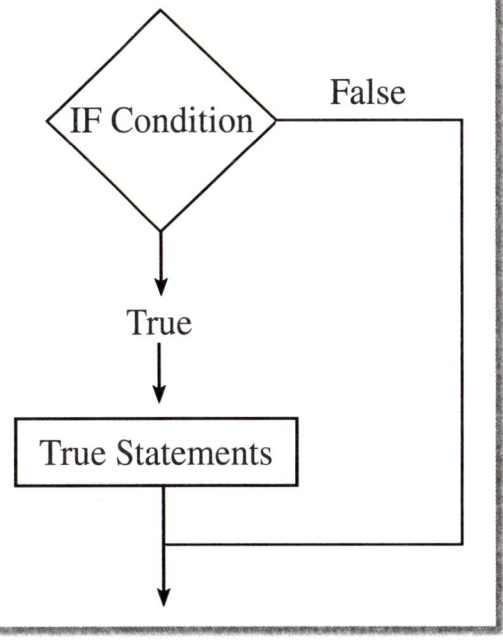

Fig. 7.1 *Flowchart of IF...THEN statement*

Let us see an example for calculating discount of a given amount using VB controls to understand this type of coding.

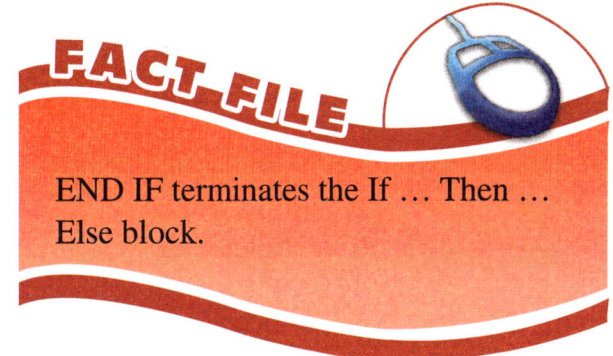

END IF terminates the If … Then … Else block.

1. Design the form as in Figure 7.2.

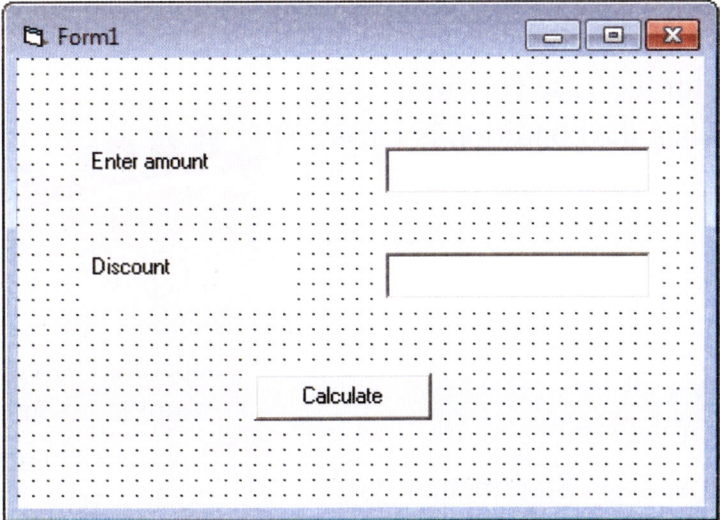

Fig. 7.2 *Designing the form*

2. You may write the code using IF ... THEN statement without END IF as well as with END IF.

a. The code using IF ... THEN statement without END IF is shown in Figure 7.3. The corresponding output is shown in Figure 7.4.

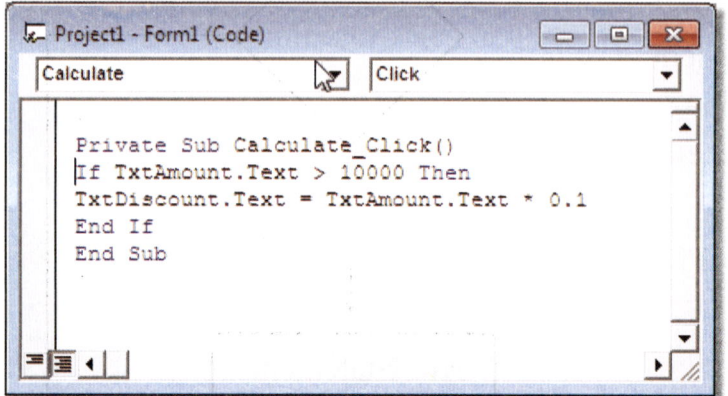
Fig. 7.3 *Code without END IF Statement*

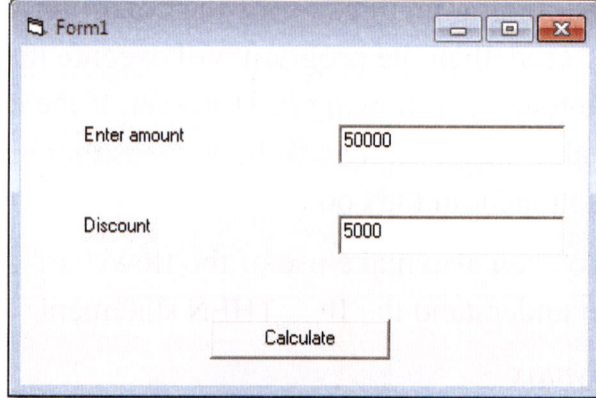
Fig. 7.4 *Output*

b. IF ... THEN Statement with END IF is shown in Fig. 7.5. The corresponding output is shown in Fig. 7.6.

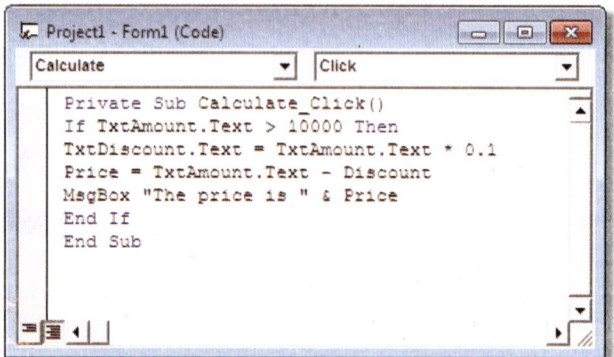
Fig. 7.5 *Using END IF Statement*

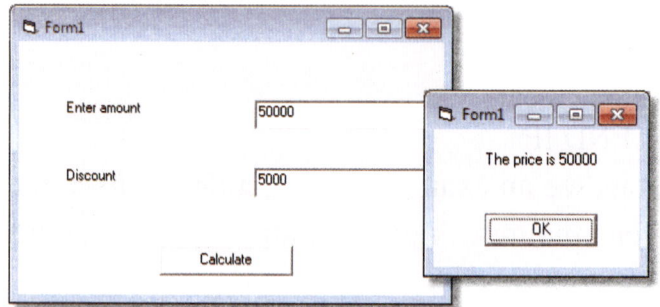
Fig. 7.6 *Output*

Type 2

The IF ... THEN statement offers only one alternative if the condition is True. Here, the one set of statement is executed for the True condition and another set is executed when the condition is False.

Syntax

    IF Condition THEN
    Statement 1
    ELSE
    Statement 2
    END IF

In this case the condition is True, Statement 1 will be executed but if the condition is False, Statement 2 will be executed.

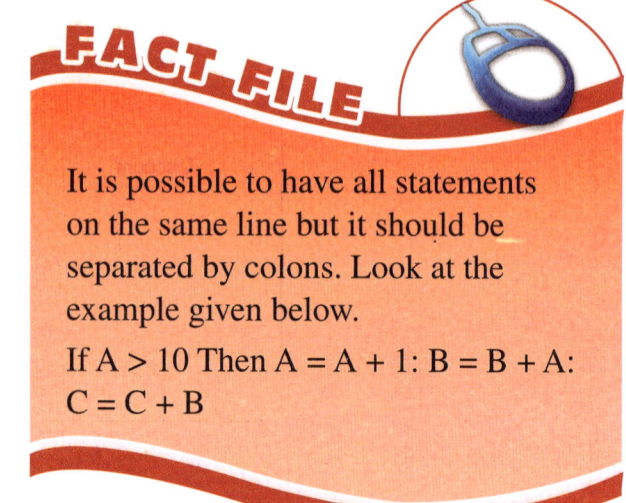

It is possible to have all statements on the same line but it should be separated by colons. Look at the example given below.

If A > 10 Then A = A + 1: B = B + A: C = C + B

The IF ... THEN ... ELSE statement of such type can be understood by the flowchart given here (Fig. 7.7).

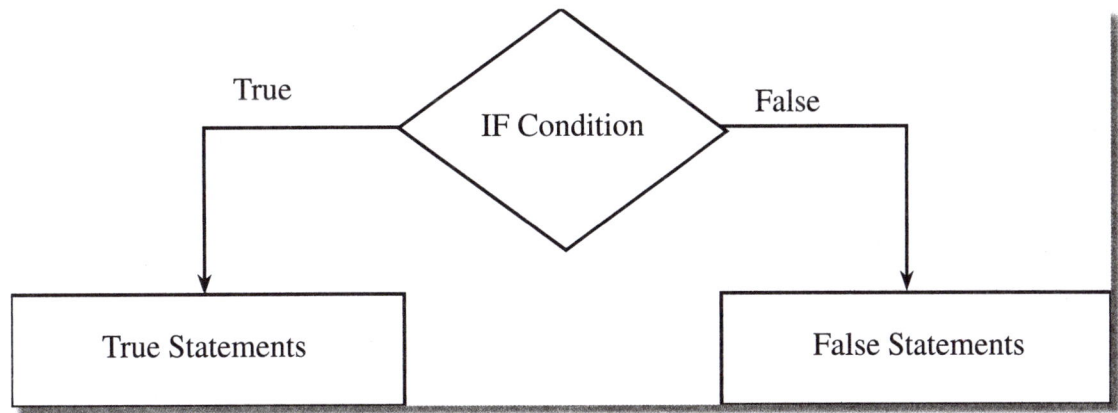

Fig. 7.7 *Flowchart for IF ... THEN ... ELSE statement*

Let us see an example of such type of coding using VB controls for calculating discount when an amount is given (Fig. 7.8).

The output will be as shown in Figure 7.9.

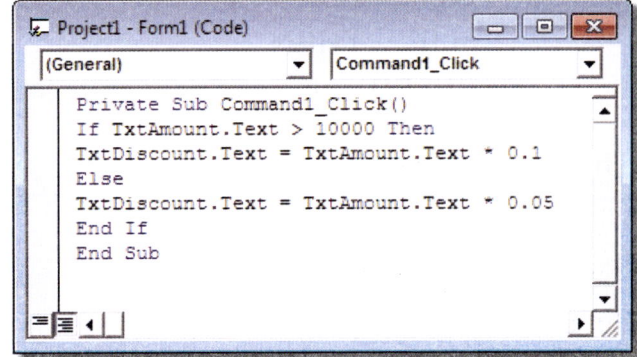

Fig. 7.8 *Using IF...THEN...ELSE*

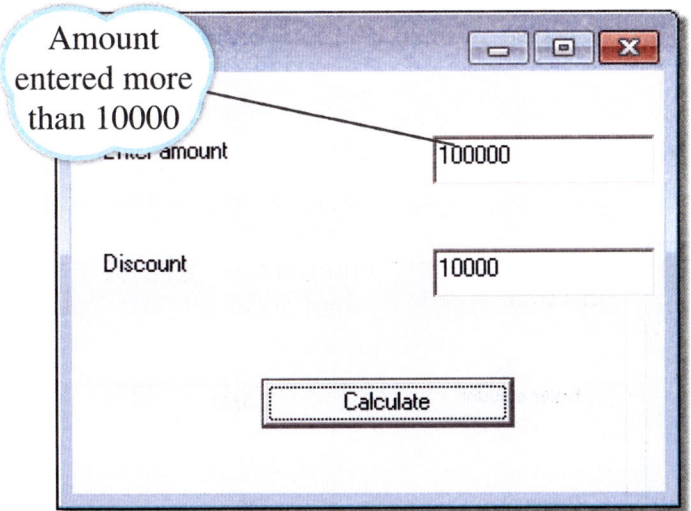

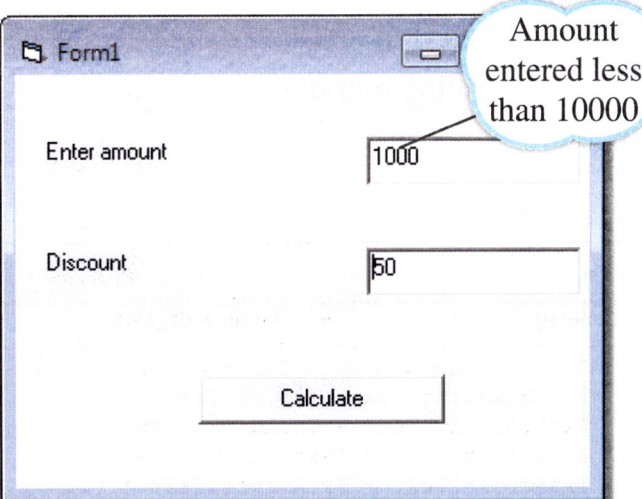

Fig. 7.9 *Output*

Type 3

The IF ... THEN ... ELSEIF statement is similar to IF ... THEN ... ELSE statement, except that it offers as many choices as necessary. Here, the IF statement checks each of the conditions until it finds one that is True, and if none of the conditions are True then it executes the ELSE statement.

Syntax

```
IF Condition 1 THEN
Statement 1
ELSEIF Condition 2 THEN
Statement 2
:
:
ELSEIF Condition k THEN
Statement n
ELSE
Statement
END IF
```

**Note:** Using ELSE is optional in IF ... THEN ... ELSEIF statement.

The flowchart helps (Fig. 7.10) to understand such types of IF... THEN... ELSEIF statement.

Let us see an example of such type of coding using VB controls for calculating discount when an amount is given (Fig. 7.11).

The corresponding output is shown in Figure 7.12.

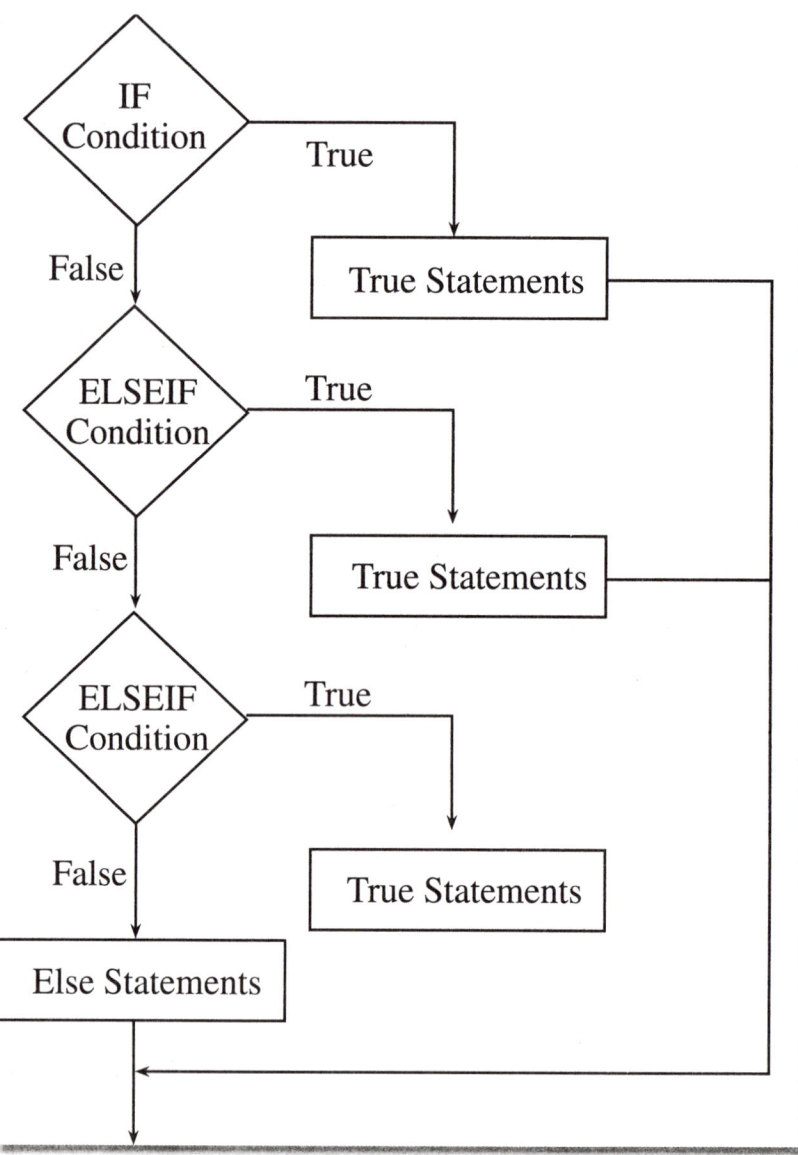

Fig. 7.10 *Flowchart of IF ... THEN ... ELSEIF statement*

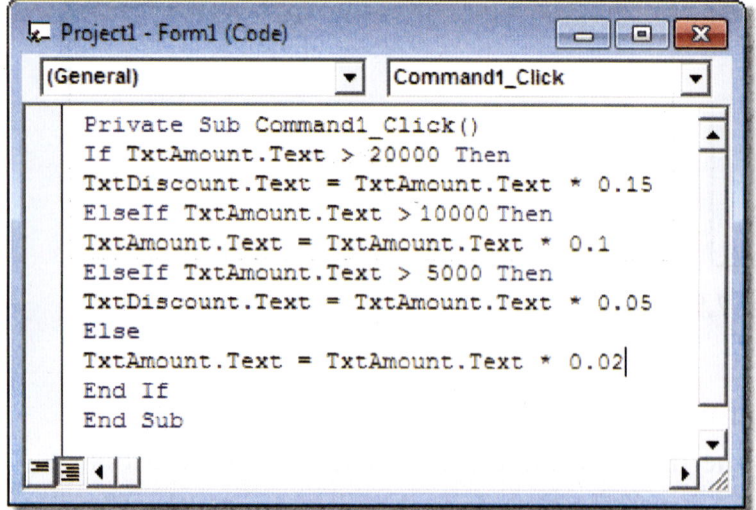

Fig. 7.11 *Using IF ... THEN ... ELSEIF*

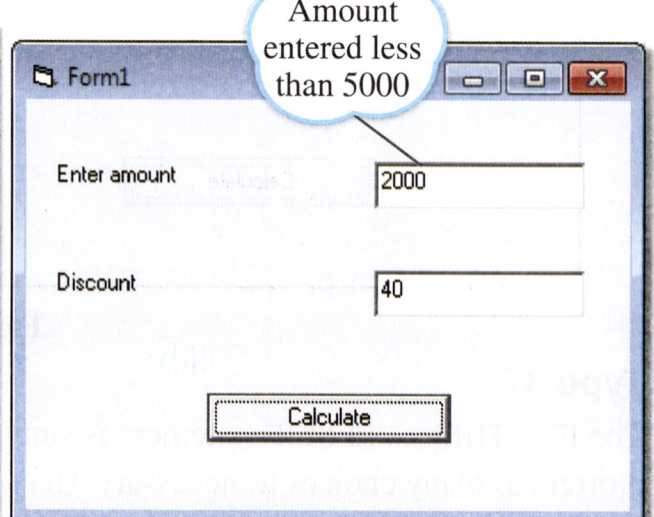

Fig. 7.12 *Output*

ACTIVITY

A. Accept the percentage of a student in a text box and calculate whether he/she has failed or passed.

B. Accept the age of a person in a text box and display an appropriate message whether he/she is eligible for a driving licence or not.

A few solved examples

Let us now see some more solved examples.

Example 1: To compare two given numbers, write the code as shown here (Fig. 7.13). The output is given in Figure 7.14.

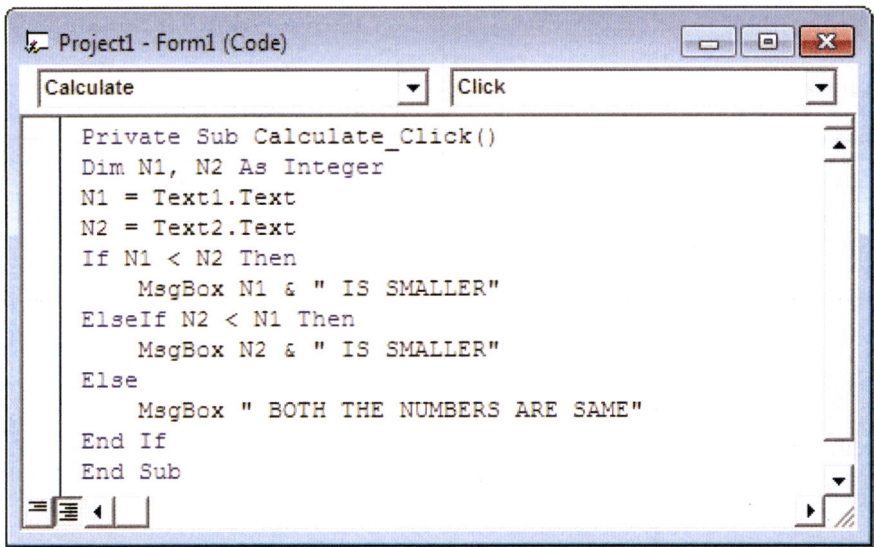

Fig. 7.13 *The code for comparing the two given numbers*

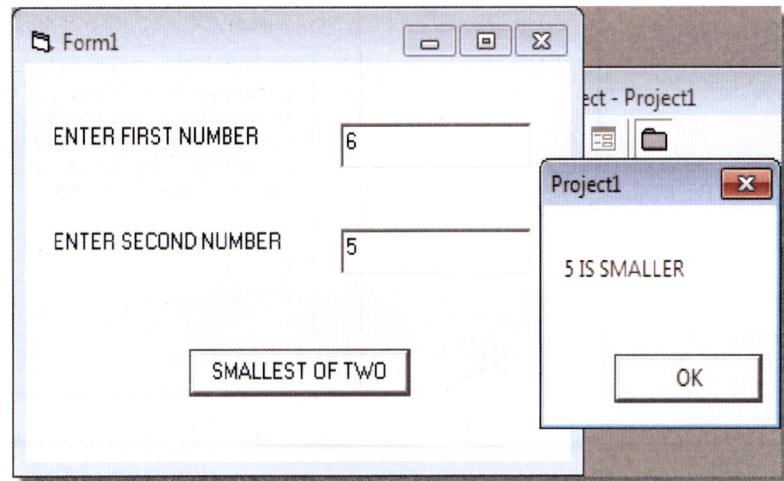

Fig. 7.14 *Output*

Example 2: To format a given text write the code as shown here (Fig. 7.15).

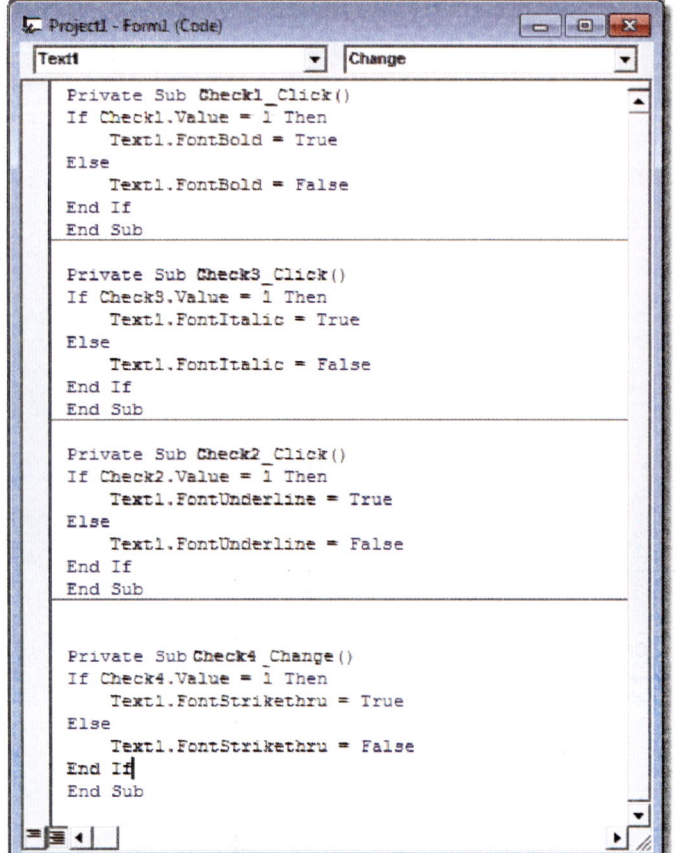
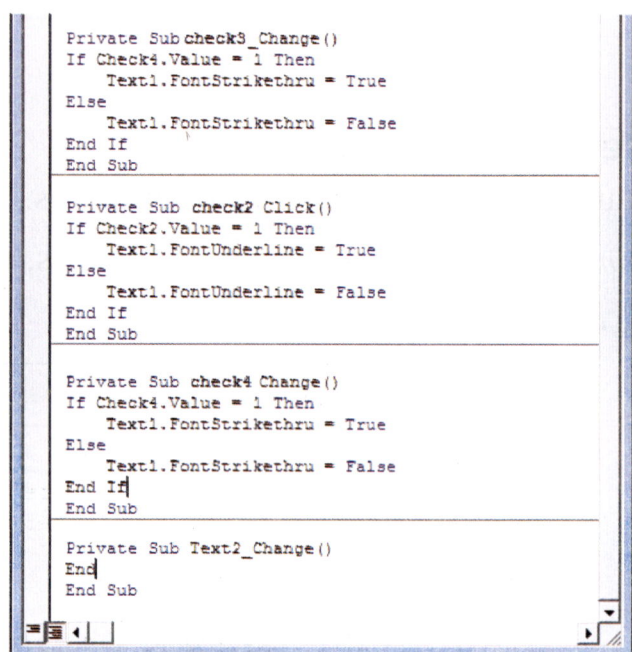

Fig. 7.15 *The code for formatting the given text*

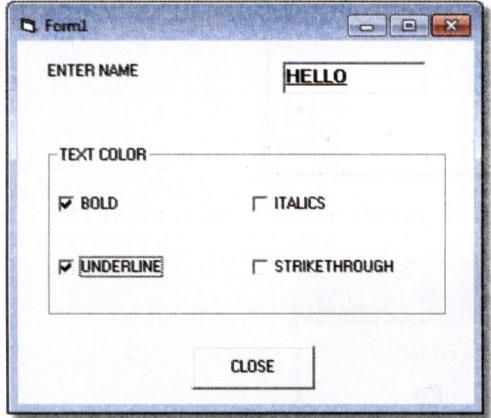

Fig. 7.16 *Output*

The output is given here (Fig. 7.16).

Example 3: To calculate and display a message for addition of two numbers, write the code as shown here (Fig. 7.17).

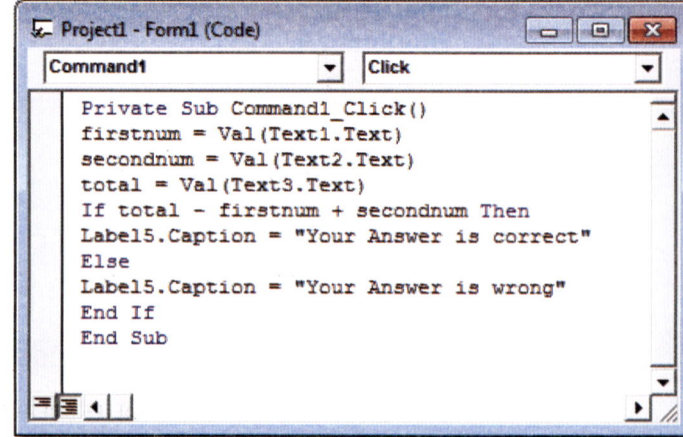

Fig. 7.17 *The code for calculating and displaying a message for addition of two numbers*

The output is given in Figure 7.18.

Fig. 7.18 *Output*

Example 4: To calculate the area of a rectangle and a circle, write the code as shown here (Fig. 7.19). The output is given in Figure 7.20.

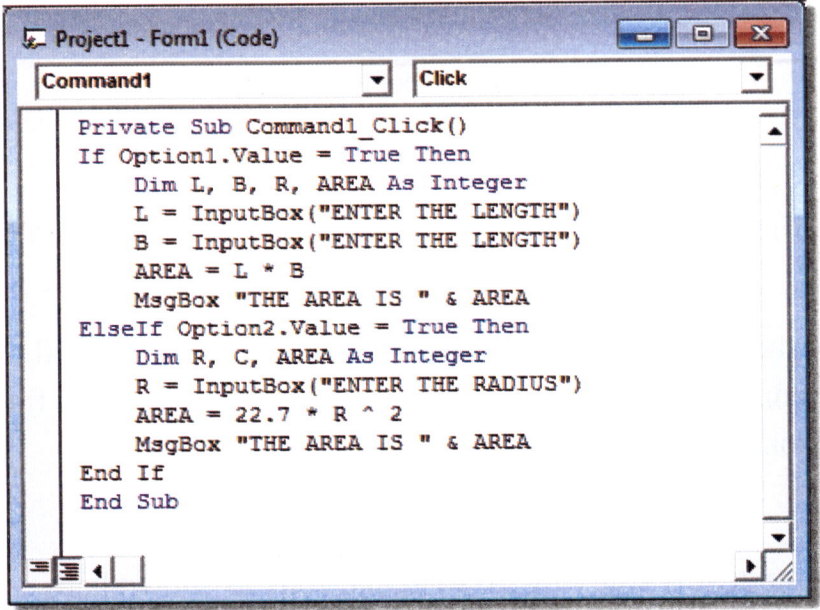

Fig. 7.19 *The code for calculating the area of a rectangle and a circle*

Fig. 7.20 *Output*

FACT FILE

If there are many statements, it is necessary to terminate the Conditional Statement with END IF but if there is only one statement then END IF is optional.

SELECT CASE statement

The SELECT CASE statement provides an alternative to the IF ... THEN ... ELSE statement, providing additional control and readability. However, the SELECT CASE control structure is slightly different from the IF .... ELSEIF control structure. The difference is that the SELECT CASE control structure makes decision on one expression while each IF .... ELSEIF statement can compute entirely different expressions.

SELECT CASE is preferred for situations where there are a large number of possible conditions for the value being checked. Similar to the IF ... THEN ... ELSE, statement, the SELECT CASE structure checks a condition, and if that condition is True, it executes a series of statements.

Syntax

SELECT CASE TestExpression
CASE Expression 1
Statement 1
CASE Expression 2

Statement 2
CASE Expression ... k
Statement ... k
CASE ELSE
Statement ... k + 1
End SELECT

where,

End Select terminates the SELECT... CASE construction.

TestExpression is any statement or variable that is evaluated by a string or a number.

 The interpreter will examine the TestExpression and evaluate it once. Then it will compare the result of this examination with the expression of each case. Once it finds one that matches, the corresponding statement will be executed.

Let us study a few solved examples.

Example 1: To display which grade the student is studying in, write the code as shown here (Fig. 7.21).

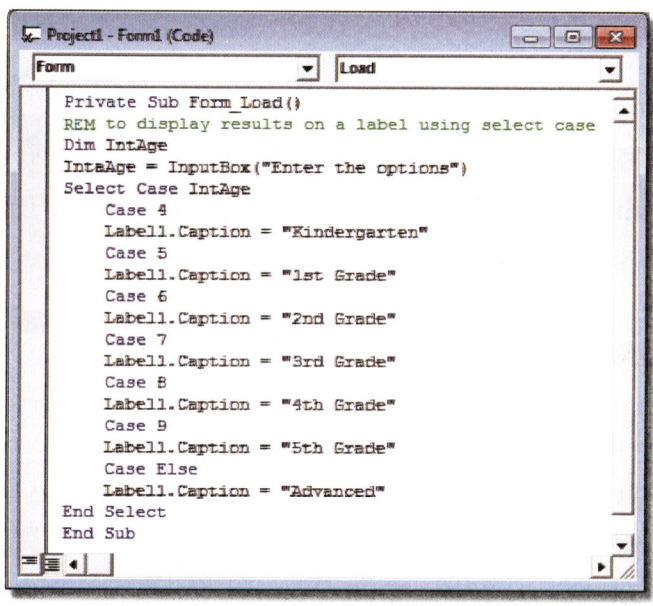

Fig. 7.21 *The Code*

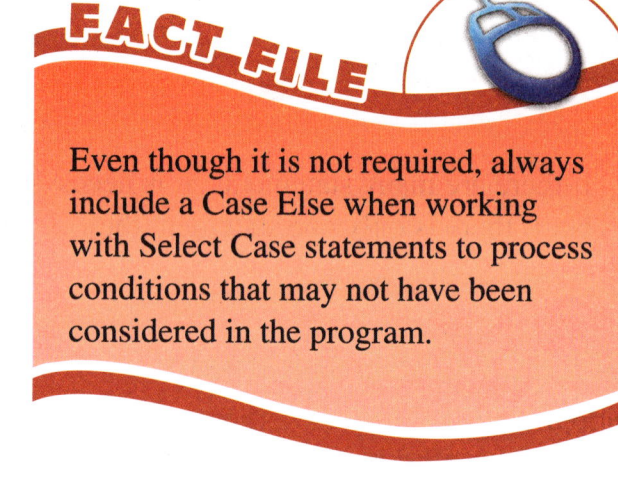

Even though it is not required, always include a Case Else when working with Select Case statements to process conditions that may not have been considered in the program.

The output is shown here (Fig. 7.22).

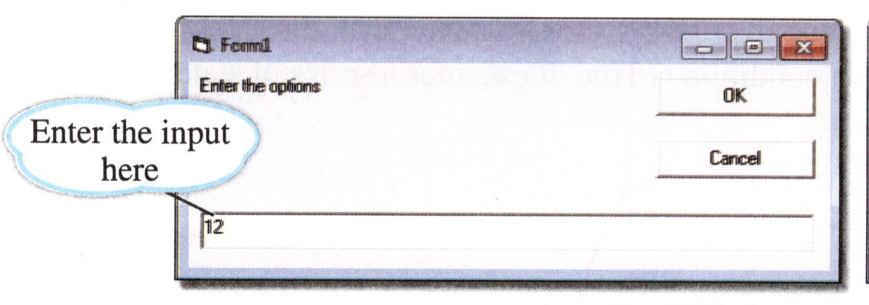
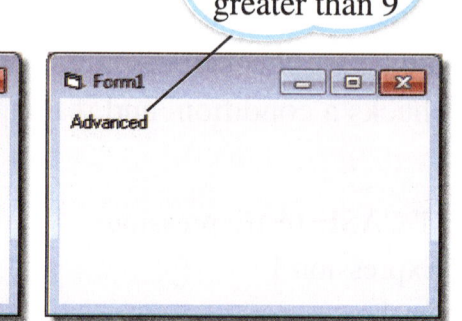

Fig. 7.22 *Output*

Example 2: To display which school the student is in, write the code as shown here (Fig. 7.23).

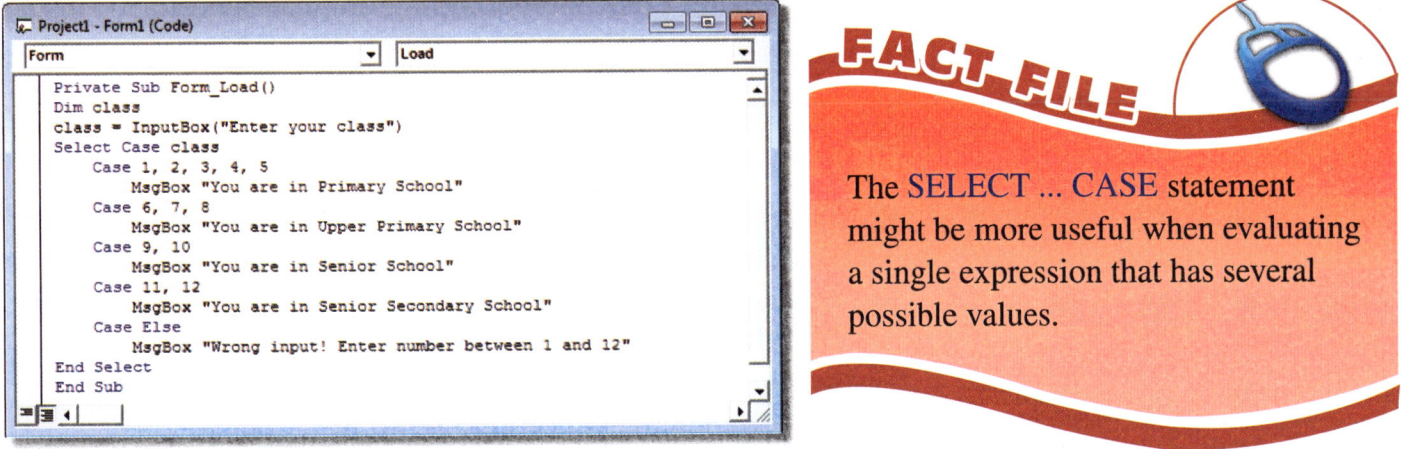

Fig. 7.23 *The Code*

FACT FILE

The SELECT ... CASE statement might be more useful when evaluating a single expression that has several possible values.

The output is given here (Fig. 7.24).

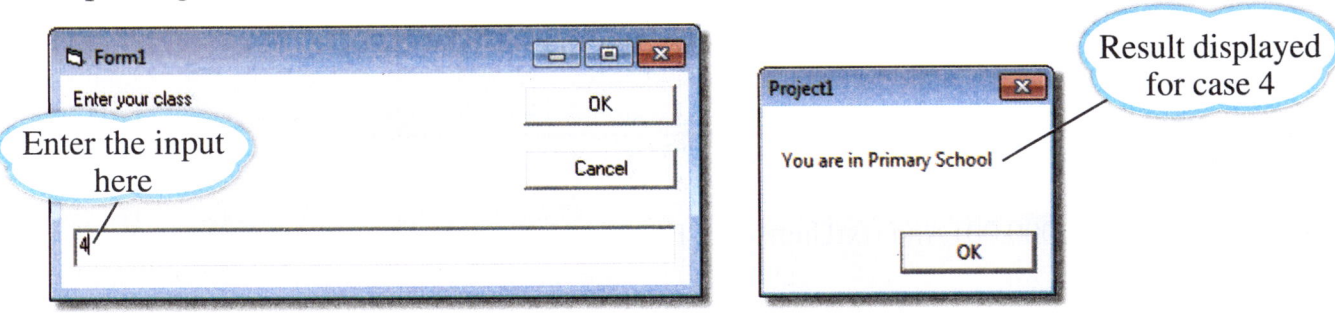

Fig. 7.24 *Output*

Note: Each case branch in a SELECT CASE statement can have more than one possible value. Each value will be separated by a comma.

FACT FILE

SELECT CASE construction can be nested but each SELECT CASE must select statement.

ACTIVITY

A. Accept class of a child in which he/she is studying in the form of a number and display an appropriate message as Pre-school, Junior, Middle, Senior.

B. Accept the month in the form of a number and display the appropriate message as Summer, Autumn, Winter and Spring.

Compound Comparisons with the Logical Operators

You have learnt in the previous lesson that Visual Basic supports three logical operators. These are And, Or, and Not. Logical operators lets you combine two or more comparison tests into a single compound comparison (Table 7.1).

Table 7.1 *Compound Comparisons*

Operator	Usage	Description
And	If (A > B) And (C < D)	Produces True if both sides of the And operator are True. Therefore, A must be greater than B and C must be less than D. Otherwise, the expression produces a False result.
Or	If (A > B) Or (C < D)	Produces True if either side of the Or operator is True. Therefore, A must be greater than B or C must be less than D. If both sides of the Or are False, the entire expression produces a False result.
Not	If Not(Ans = "Yes")	Produces the opposite True or False result. Therefore, if answer holds "Yes", the Not operator turns the True result to False.

A few examples

Example 1: To calculate bonus

If (txtSales.Text > 5000.00) And (txtUnitsSold.Text > 10000) Then
Bonus = 50.00
End If

Example 2: To find whether a given figure is a square, write the code as shown here (Fig. 7.25).

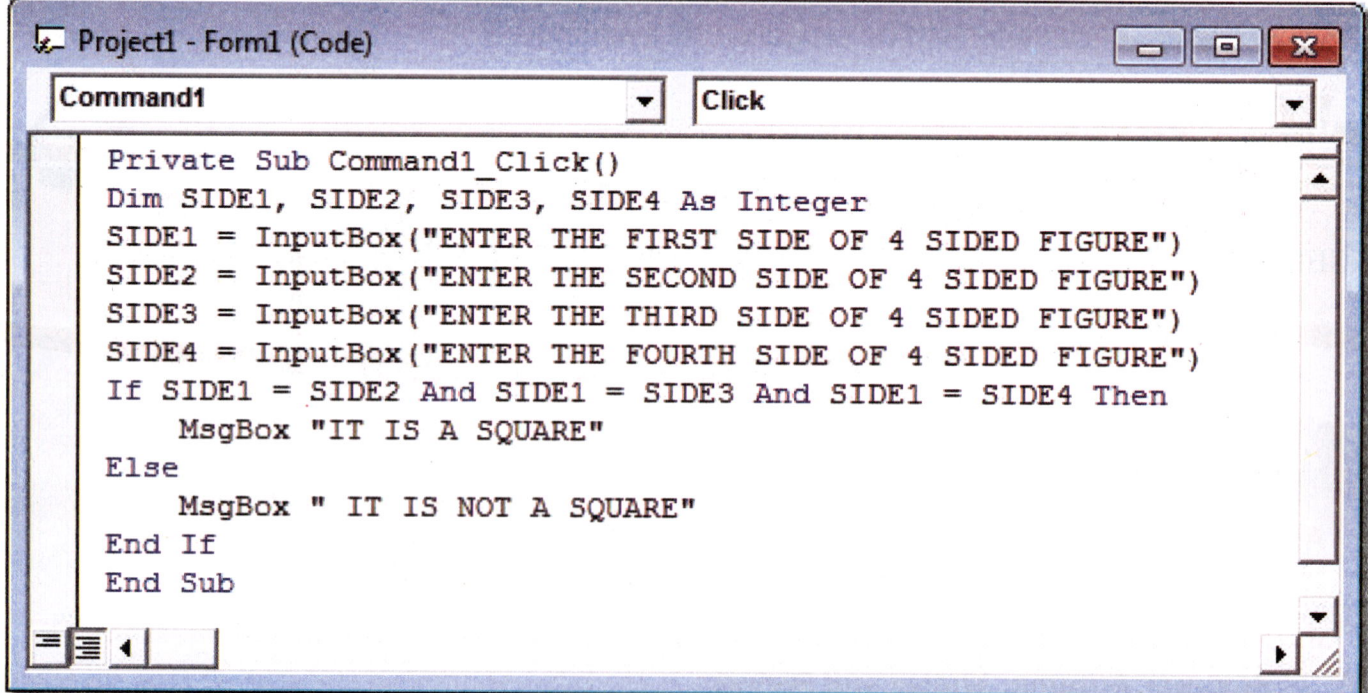

Fig. 7.25 *The Code*

The output is shown here (Fig. 7.26).

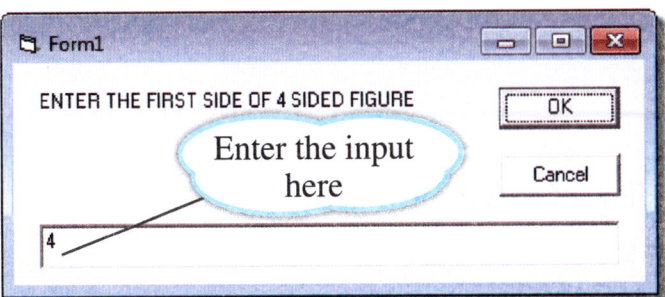
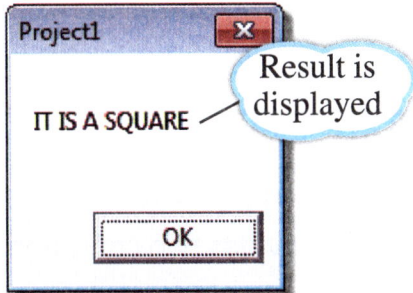

Fig. 7.26 *Output*

ACTIVITY

A. Accept a number and check whether it is in the range of 100 to 200. Display an appropriate message.

B. Accept an employee, department and salary. If the dept = accounts and salary >= 5000 then the incentive = 500. If dept = Research and salary >= 10000 then incentive = 1000 otherwise incentive = 200. Calculate the salary as salary + incentive with an appropriate message.

C. Accept the login name. Display a welcome message if the login = ABC or login = XYZ or login = AAA.

GLOSSARY

Conditional statements: They control the flow of execution of a program or one of its sections.

IF ... THEN ... ELSE statement: It is used to evaluate whether a condition is True or False.

Select Case statement: It helps to make decision on one expression.

NOW YOU KNOW

1. VB provides two conditional statements:
   a. If ... THEN ... ELSE statement
   b. SELECT CASE statement.
2. Logical operators lets you combine two or more comparison tests into a single compound comparison.
3. The SELECT CASE statement provides an alternative to the If ... THEN ... ELSE statement, providing additional control and readability.

EXERCISE

A Fill in the blanks.

1. ……………… statements control the flow of execution of a program.
2. VB provides two conditional statements: ……………………… and ……………………….
3. In …………………… nothing will happen if the condition is false.
4. To deal with multiple conditions, …………………… is used.
5. The …………………… statement provides an alternative to the IF… THEN … ELSE statement.

B Find out the output of the following code for the given input.

1. Dim favourite_food as string
   favourite_food = Inputbox("My Favourite Food")
   SELECT CASE favourite_food
      CASE "Indian"
      Print "My all-time favourite"
      CASE "Chinese"
      Print "My weekend favourite"
      CASE "Continental"
      Print "My special occasion favourite"
      CASE ELSE
      Print "Sorry! Not my choice"
   END SELECT
   Input: Chinese

2. Dim a as integer
   If a > 5 THEN
   a = a * 2
   else
   a = a + 2
   END IF
   print a
   print "program ends"
   Input: 3

C Find the errors in the given code.

1. Dim num1,num2 with integer
   2 = num1
   3 = num2
   IF num1 < num2
      Print num1 is smaller
   ELSE
   IF num2 < num1
      Print num2 is smaller
   ELSE
      Print both are equal
   ENDIF

2. Dim login as integer
   login = "abc"
   IF login is "abc or login is "ABC"
      Msgbox Allowed to work
   ELSIF
      Msgobx Not allowed to work
   END

116

D   Answer the following questions.

1. What is the use of a conditional statement?
2. How many types of conditional statements are available?
3. What is the purpose of IF … THEN statement? Give a small code to support your answer.
4. When do you use Select case statement? Give a small code to support your answer.

LAB WORK

A. Accept a number from the user in a text box and find out whether it is an even or odd number. Display an appropriate message in a message box.

B. Design the given form and do the appropriate coding.

C. Accept the percentage in a text box and display the appropriate grade according to the given criteria:

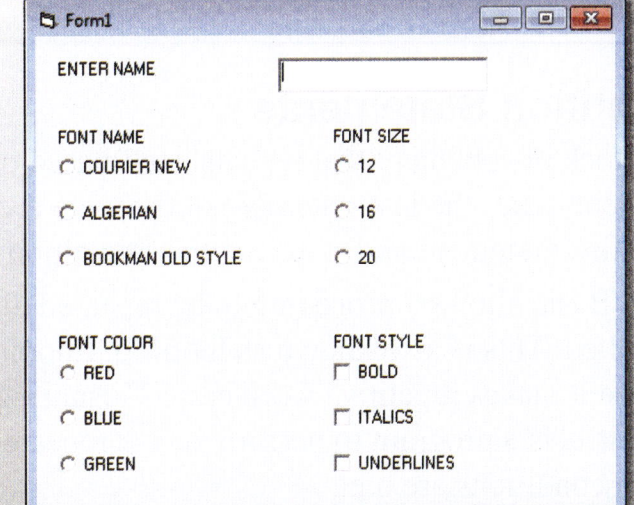

Percentage	Grade
<=40	D
41 to 60	C
61 to 80	B
81o 100	A

D. Calculate the electricity bill according to the given criteria:

Meter Reading	Charges per unit
100 units	INR 2.50/-
101 to 300	INR 4.00/-
301 and above	INR 6.00/-

E. Accept the three angles in three text boxes and find out whether it will form a triangle or not. (Sum of three angles for a triangle should be 180 degrees).

F. Accept a year from the user and find out whether it a leap year or not.

TEACHER'S NOTES

1. Explain the concept of short-circuiting in Case statement to the students.
2. Emphasise on the importance of creating flowchart before writing any code. Help the students create flowchart for every code.

8 Repetition Programming in VB

LEARNING OBJECTIVES

You will learn about:
1. Repetition statements
2. FOR ... NEXT loop
3. DO ... LOOP – Pre-Tested, Post-Tested
4. Nested Loops

Repetition Statements

Any block of statement that repeats itself based on a condition is known as a repetition statement. After the last statement of the code is executed, the program branches, or loops back to the first statement and starts another repetition through the code.

Visual Basic allows a procedure to be repeated many times as long as a set of conditions is fulfilled. This is also known as **looping**. Looping is a very useful feature of Visual Basic because it makes repetitive work easier. Visual Basic provides a number of language structures that instructs a program to perform a task repeatedly, either a specific number of times, or until certain conditions are met.

Every loop consists of the following three parts.

1. *The loop termination condition:* This determines when the loop will be terminated. A loop that does not stop is called an **endless loop** or **infinite loop**.

2. *The body of the loop:* This is a set of statements that are required to be repeated a specific number of times.

3. *Transfer back to the beginning of the loop:* It returns control to the beginning of the loop so that a new repetition can begin.

Some of the commonly used repetition constructs in Visual Basic are:
- FOR ... NEXT
- DO LOOP – this is further divided into:
  - DO WHILE ... LOOP
  - DO ... LOOP WHILE

FOR ... NEXT Loop

In Visual Basic, FOR ... NEXT loop is ideal for situations where a task needs to be performed a specific number of times.

FOR ... NEXT loop consists of the following parts.

- *Header* that contains information about the number of times the loop is to be performed.
- *Code block* that contains the VB statements to be executed on each iteration.
- *Next statement* that sends the loop back to the header to repeat.

Syntax

FOR counterVariable = fromValue To toValue Step Value
...VB Statements...
NEXT counterVariable

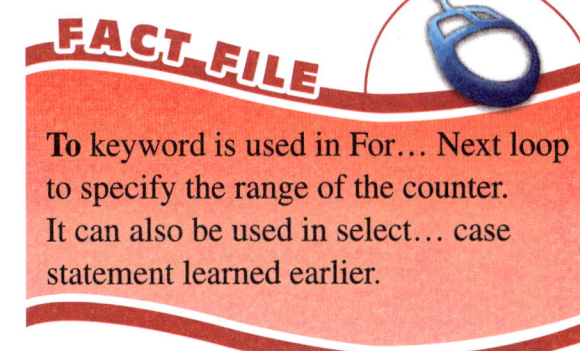

FACT FILE

If you do not provide a Step value, VB takes a default step value = 1

where,

counterVariable is the variable that changes a specific number of times in the loop.

start value is the beginning value of the counter variable.

end value is the end value of the counter variable.

Step value is the amount the counter variable changes each time through the loop.

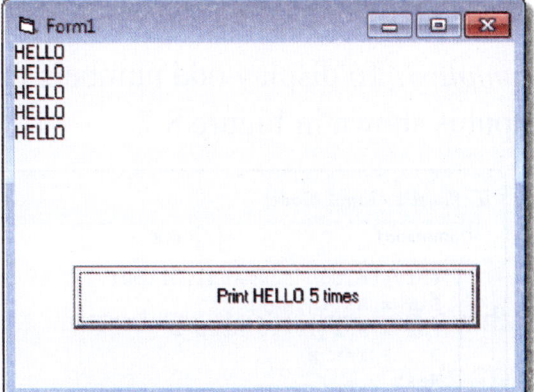

FACT FILE

To keyword is used in For... Next loop to specify the range of the counter. It can also be used in select... case statement learned earlier.

A few solved examples

Example 1: To display HELLO 5 times, write the code as shown here (Fig. 8.1). The output is shown in Figure 8.2.

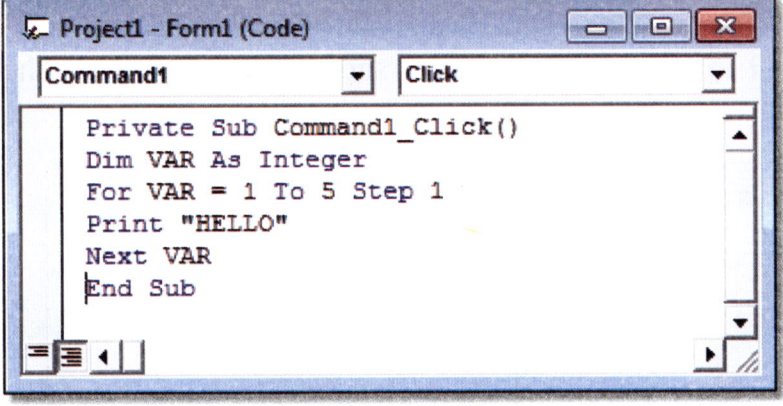

Fig. 8.1 *The code*

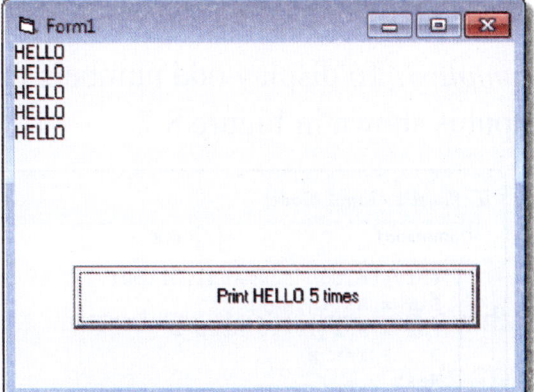

Fig. 8.2 *Output*

Let us understand the FOR ... NEXT loop used in the above code using a flowchart (Fig. 8.3).

In the above code for displaying HELLO 5 times:

- When the loop begins the counter variable var will be initialized with the initial value 1.
- Subsequently, a test will be made to see that the value of var should not exceed the end value 5.
- If the value of var exceeds the end value, the loop will end, and control will pass to whatever statement follows the NEXT statement.
- If the value of var is less than or equal to the stop value, the body of the loop will be executed.
- At the end, the NEXT statement will check the step value to automatically increment the value of var by 1. The NEXT statement also causes a transfer of control back to the FOR statement to begin another repetition of the loop.

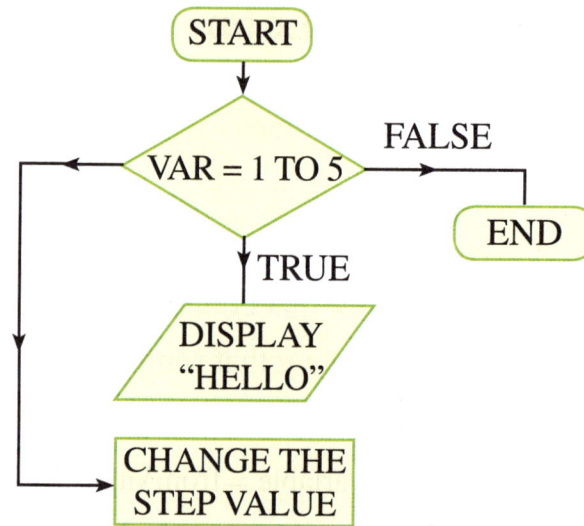

Fig. 8.3 *Flowchart of FOR ...NEXT*

Example 2: To display the numbers from 1 to 10, write the code as shown here (Fig. 8.4). The output is shown in Figure 8.5.

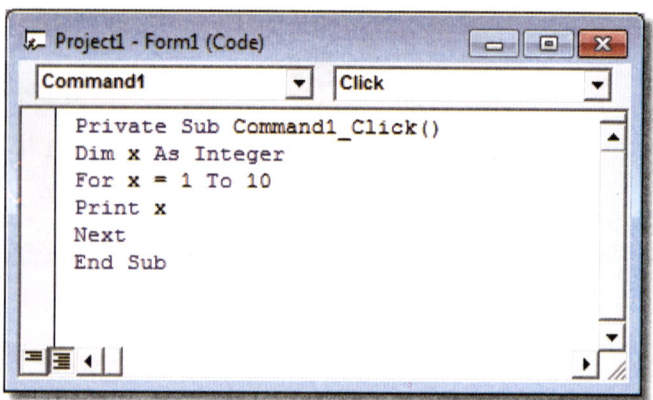

Fig. 8.4 *The Code*

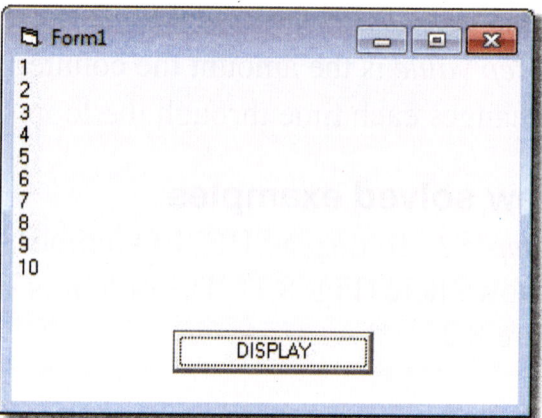

Fig. 8.5 *Output*

Example 3: To display odd numbers from 1 to 10, write the code as shown here (Fig. 8.6). The output is shown in Figure 8.7.

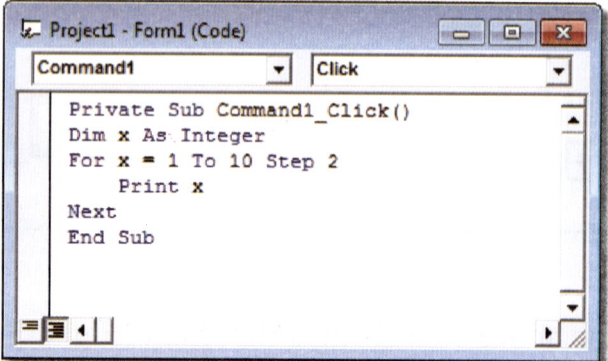

Fig. 8.6 *The Code*

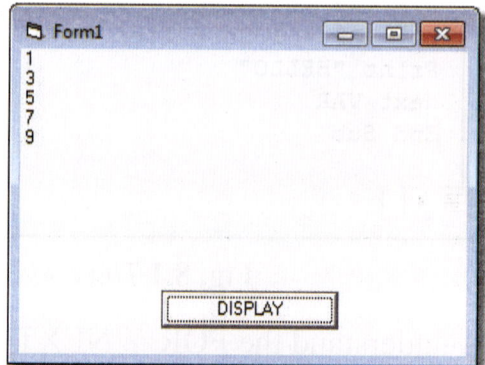

Fig. 8.7 *Output*

Example 4: To display the series of 5 in the same line, write the code as shown here (Fig. 8.8). The output is shown in Figure 8.8.

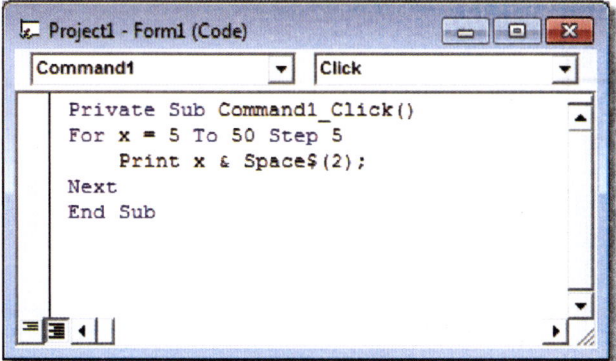

Fig. 8.8 *The Code*

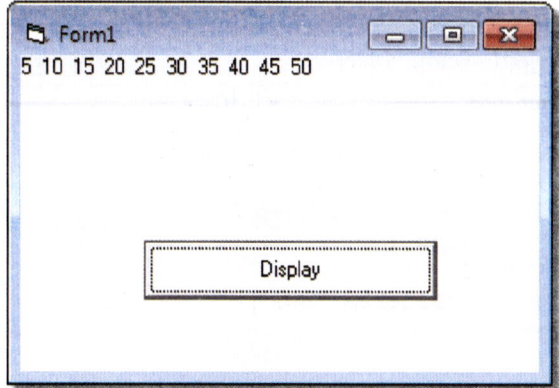

Fig. 8.9 *Output*

Note: In the above code, Space$() is given to print the numbers on the same line. The number within the argument denotes the space between the numbers.

Example 5: To display the sum of 5 numbers entered by the user, write the code as shown here (Fig. 8.10). The output is shown in Figure 8.11.

Note: In the above code the value of sum has been initialized with 0. This is to avoid printing of any unwanted value on the output screen. This unwanted value is called the **garbage value**.

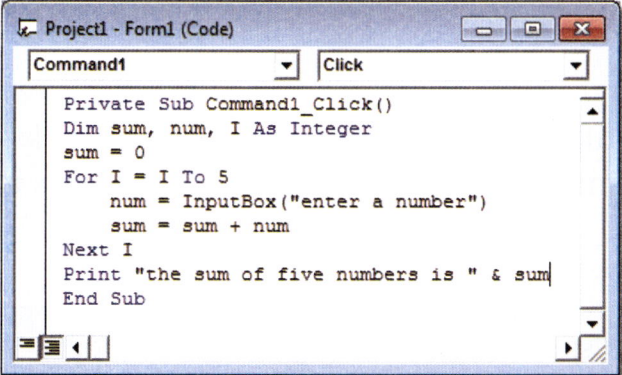

Fig. 8.10 *The Code*

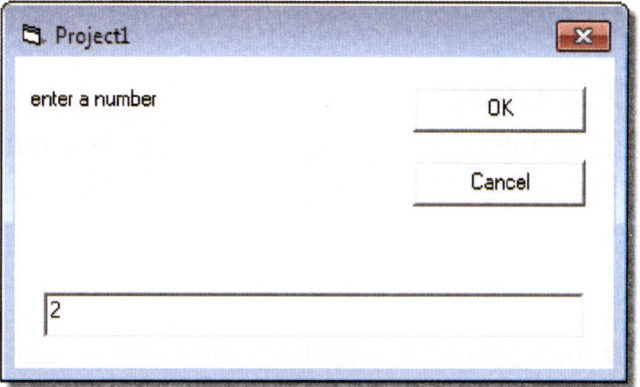

a. *Output 1*

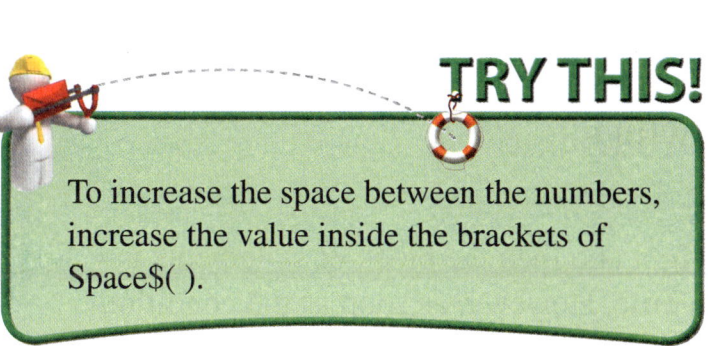

TRY THIS!

To increase the space between the numbers, increase the value inside the brackets of Space$( ).

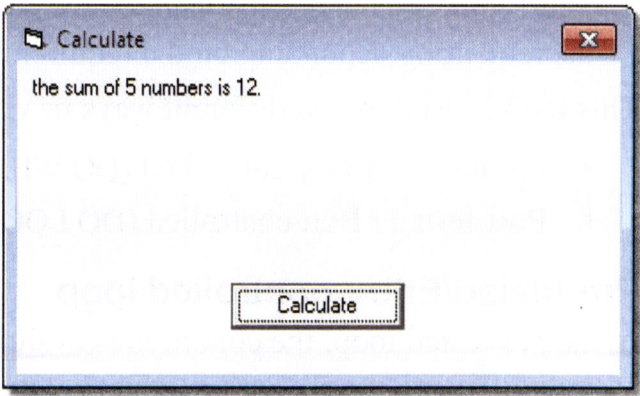

b. *Output 2*

Fig. 8.11

Example 6: To print the series from 1 to 10 in reverse order, write the code as shown here (Fig. 8.12). The output is shown in Figure 8.13.

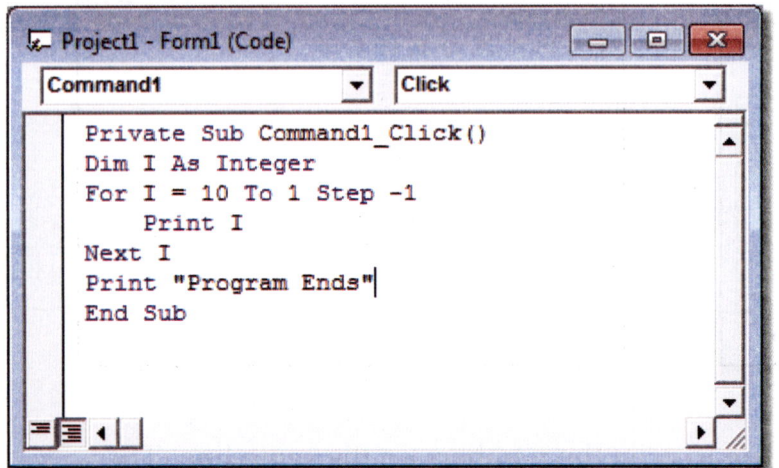

Fig. 8.12 *The Code*

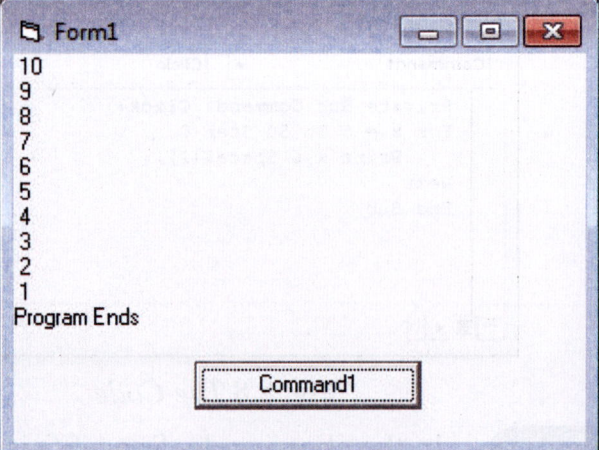

Fig. 8.13 *Output*

ACTIVITY

A. Accept a name of your friend and display it 5 times.

B. Display the even numbers from 1 to 10.

C. Display the multiple of 3 till 30.

DO ... Loop

DO ... LOOP is used to repeat a block of statements till the condition is True. This loop works well when you do not know in advance how many times you need to execute the statements in the loop.

It has the following three parts.

1. *Initialization*: It initializes the counter variable to specify the starting point of the loop.
2. *Condition:* It makes the loop work till the condition is True.
3. *Step value:* It changes the value of the counter variable either by incrementing or decrementing depending on the requirement of the code.

This loop is used in two different ways in Visual Basic:

- Pre-tested / Entry controlled (DO WHILE ... LOOP)
- Post-tested / Exit controlled (DO LOOP ... WHILE)

Pre-tested/Entry controlled loop

In the pre-tested loop, the condition is evaluated first and then the block of statements is executed. The loop will work till the condition is True. However, as soon as the condition becomes False the control exits from the loop. If condition is False on the first pass, the statements are never executed.

Syntax

<Initialization>
Do While <condition>
..Block of statements..
<Step value>
loop

Let us write the code for displaying HELLO 5 times again, however, using DO ... LOOP this time.

To understand the code using DO WHILE ... LOOP (Fig. 8.14), look at Table 8.1 and the flowchart (Fig. 8.15)

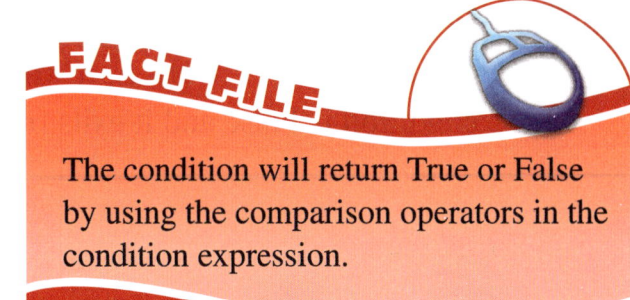

The condition will return True or False by using the comparison operators in the condition expression.

Table 8.1 *Explanation of the Code Using DO WHILE ... Loop*

VAR	Condition	Output
1 (INITIALISATION)	1 <= 5 TRUE	HELLO
VAR = VAR + 1 VAR = 1 + 1 = 2	2 <= 5 TRUE	HELLO
VAR = VAR + 1 VAR = 2 + 1 = 3	3 <= 5 TRUE	HELLO
VAR = VAR + 1 VAR = 3 + 1 = 4	4 <= 5 TRUE	HELLO
VAR = VAR + 1 VAR = 4 + 1 = 5	5 <= 5 TRUE	HELLO
VAR = VAR + 1 VAR = 5 + 1 = 6	6 <= 5 FALSE	EXITS FROM LOOP

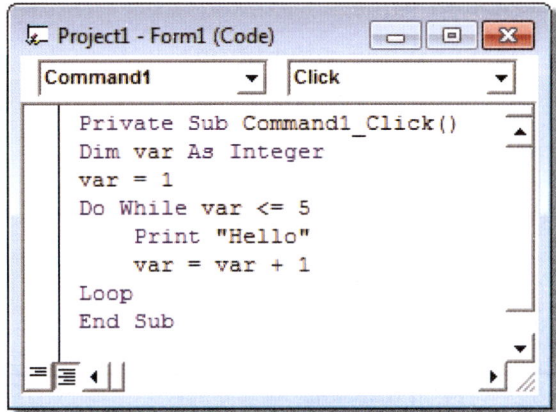

Fig. 8.14 *The code*

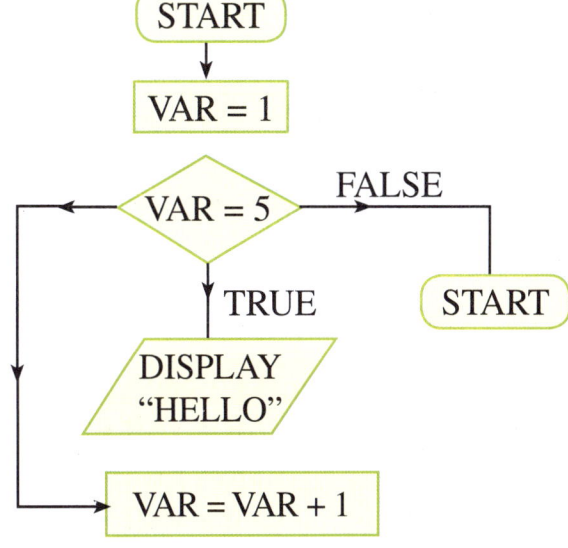

Fig. 8.15 *Flowchart of DO WHILE... Loop*

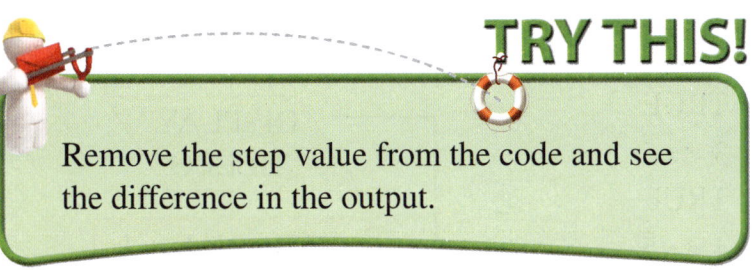

TRY THIS!

Remove the step value from the code and see the difference in the output.

Post-tested/Exit controlled loop

In post-tested loop, the block of statement is executed first and then the condition is evaluated. The loop will work till the condition is True. As soon as the condition becomes False, the control exits from the loop. In this structure, the loop condition is checked after the loop body is performed. Thus, it executes the loop body at least once irrespective of the condition.

Note: DO UNTIL ... LOOP and DO ... LOOP UNTIL works just like DO WHILE ... LOOP and DO LOOP ... WHILE. It works with one difference that the loop executes till the condition is False and it exits from the loop when the condition is True.

Syntax

<Initialization>
DO
..Block of statements..
<Step value>
Loop While <condition>

Let us write the code for displaying HELLO 5 times again, however, using DO LOOP ... WHILE this time.

Write the code as shown here (Fig. 8.16). The output is shown in (Fig. 8.17).

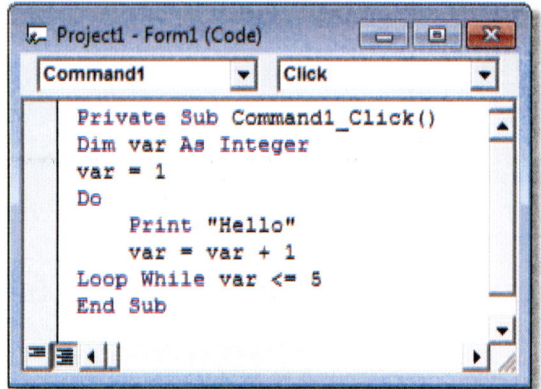

Fig. 8.16 *The code*

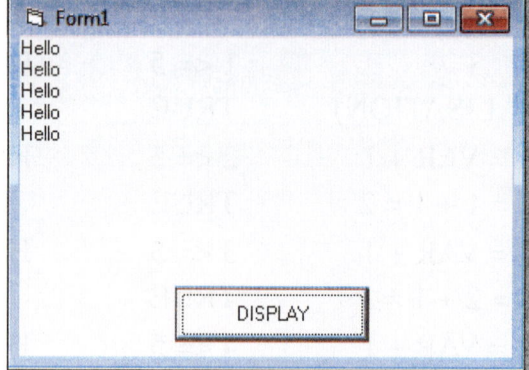

Fig. 8.17 *Output*

The explanation of the above code using DO WHILE is given in Table 8.2 and the flowchart (Fig. 8.18).

Table 8.1 *Explanation of the code for printing*

Output	New Value of vaR	Condition
HELLO	VAR = VAR + 1	2 <= 5
	VAR = 1 + 1 = 2	TRUE
HELLO	VAR = VAR + 1	3 <= 5
	VAR = 2 + 1 = 3	TRUE
HELLO	VAR = VAR + 1	4 <= 5
	VAR = 3 + 1 = 4	TRUE
HELLO	VAR = VAR + 1	5 <= 5
	VAR = 4 + 1 = 5	TRUE
HELLO	VAR = VAR + 1	6 <= 5
	VAR = 5 + 1 = 6	FALSE
EXITS FROM LOOP		

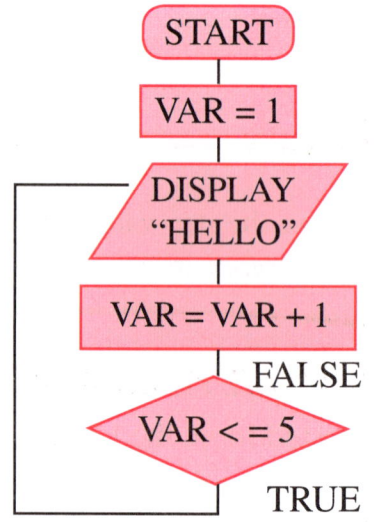

Fig. 8.18 *Flow chart of DO WHILE ... Loop*

ACTIVITY

A. Accept a number from the user and print the table of a number using DO WHILE ... LOOP.

B. Print the square of numbers from 1 to 10 using DO ... LOOP WHILE.

C. Try to do the questions given in the above activity by using both the ways of DO ... LOOP.

A few examples

Example 1: To accept a name in a text box and print the following pattern write the code as shown here (Fig. 8.19). The output is shown in Figure 8.20.

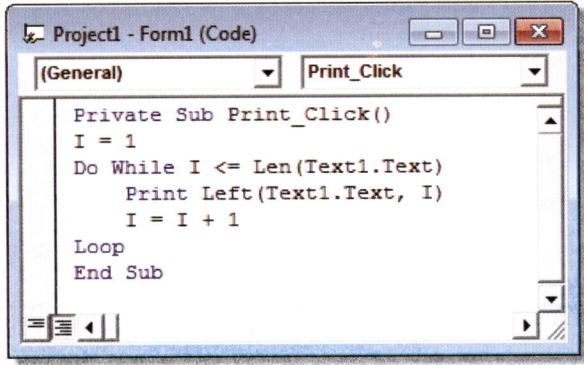
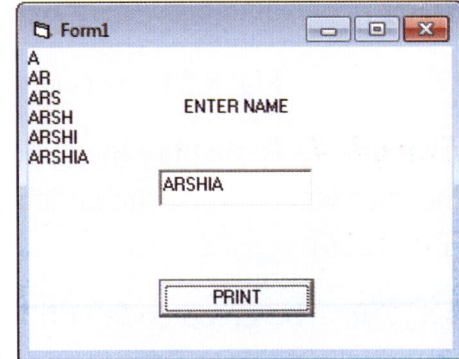

Fig. 8.19 *The Code* **Fig. 8.20** *Output*

Example 2: To print the last three characters of the 5 names entered by the user in an input box, write the code as shown here (Fig. 8.21).

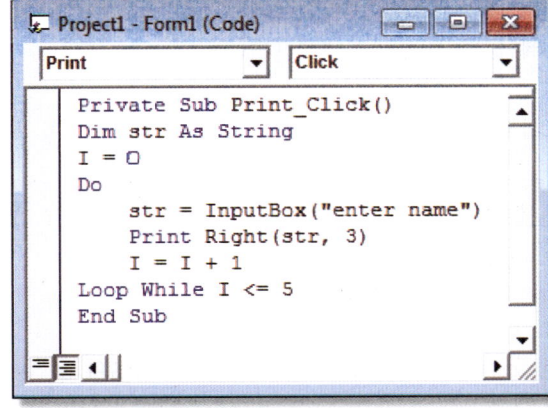

The output is given here (Fig. 8.22).

Fig. 8.21 *The Code*

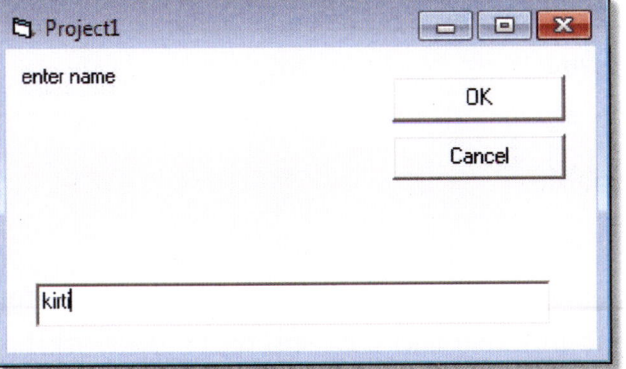

Fig. 8.22 *Output*

Example 3: To accept a number and display the sum of the digits of the number, write the code as shown here (Fig. 8.23). The output is shown in Figure 8.24.

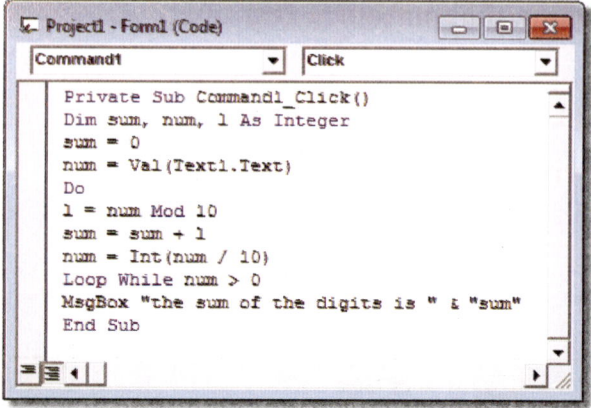

Fig. 8.23 *The Code*

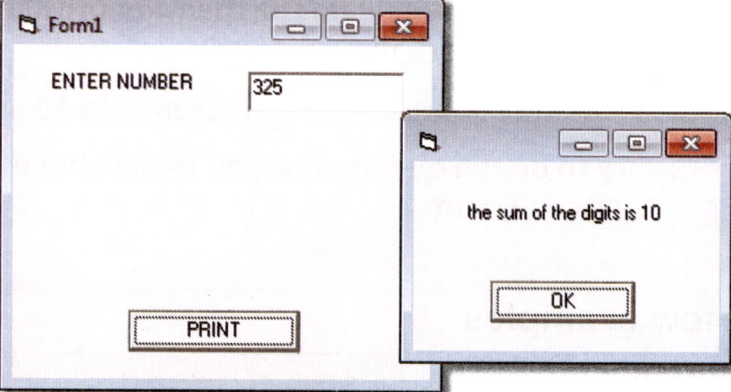

Fig. 8.24 *Output*

Example 4: To display the cube of a number till the user wants, write the code as shown here (Fig. 8.25).

Note: The given code will work for indefinite number of times until the condition is True as compared to FOR ... NEXT which works only a fixed number of times.

The output is given here (Fig 8.26).

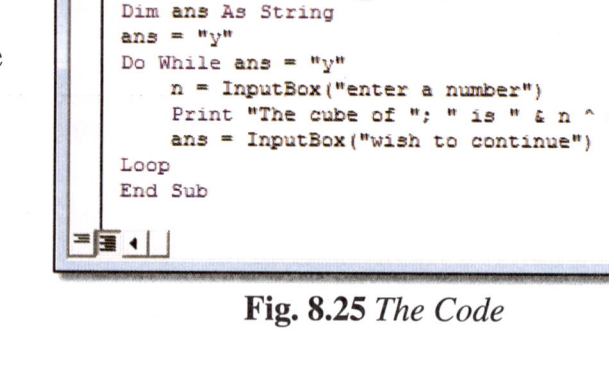

Fig. 8.25 *The Code*

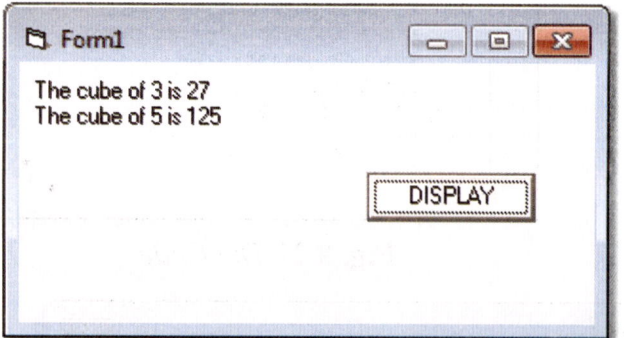

Fig. 8.26 *Output*

In the above code:

- ans = "y" is the initialization of the string variable.
- DO WHILE ans = "y" is the condition.
- ans = InputBox("wish to continue") will work as the step value. If the user enters a letter other than "y" then the condition will evaluate to False and the loop will stop working.

Nested Loops

Using one loop within another loop is known as nested loop. In many situations, it is convenient to use a loop contained within another loop. Any looping construct can be nested inside another loop.

The following important points should be remembered at the time of using nested loop:

- The execution starts from the outer loop.
- For each value of the outer loop counter variable the inner loop executes completely.
- The outer loop generates the rows and the inner loop generates the columns to print the pattern in a matrix format.

Note: A matrix is a grid of values arranged in rows and columns.

- Always use different counter variables for the outer and the inner loop.
- Always have the NEXT statement for the inner FOR ... NEXT loop before the NEXT statement of the outer FOR ... NEXT loop.

A few solved examples

Example 1: To print the given pattern:

```
***
***
***
```

Write the code as shown here (Fig. 8.27).

In the above code:

- For each value of row (outer loop counter variable) the inner loop runs 3 times.
- Print "*", prints the output on the same line thus creating multiple columns.
- Print in the outer loop will shift the cursor to the new line thus creating multiple rows.

The output is shown here (Fig. 8.28).

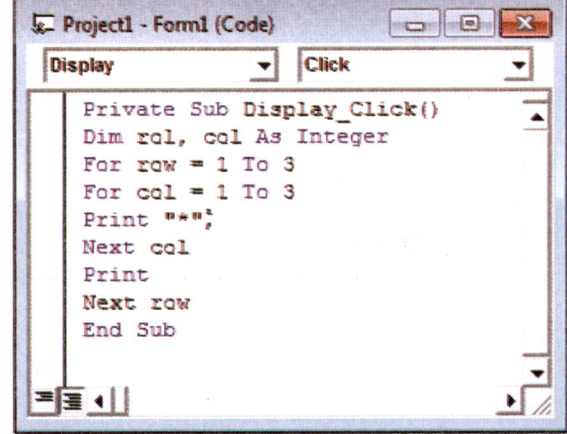

Fig. 8.27 *Writing the code*

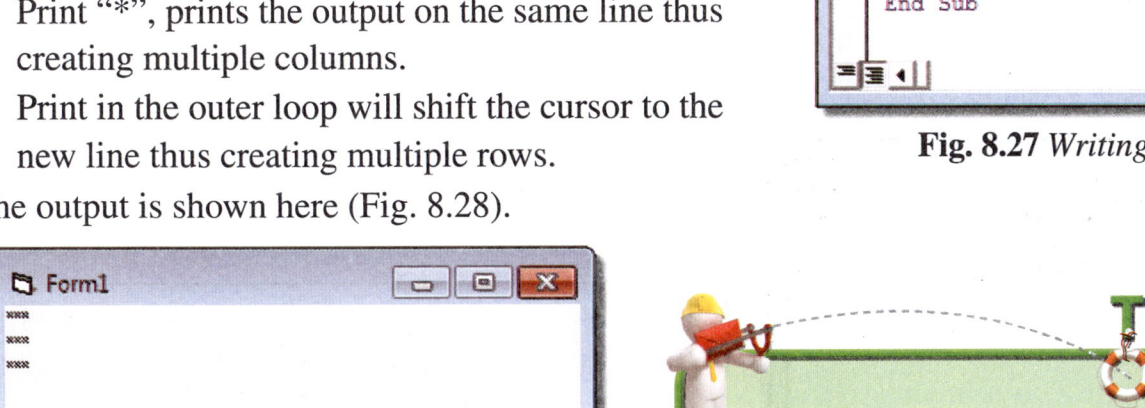

Fig. 8.28 *Output*

TRY THIS!

Do the same code again using nested DO ... Loop and find out which looping construct is easier in nested looping.

Example 2: To print the numbers in the form of a right angled triangle, write the code as shown here (Fig. 8.29). The output is shown in Figure 8.30.

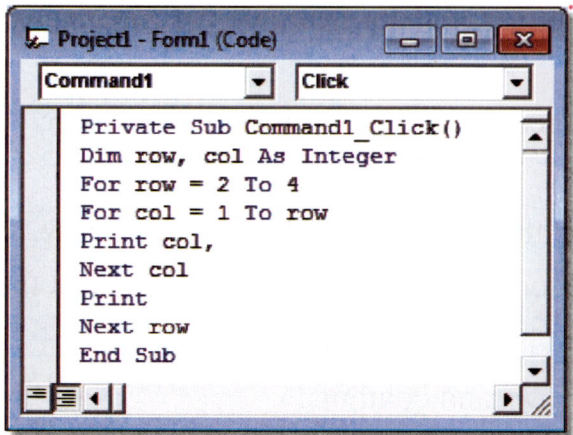

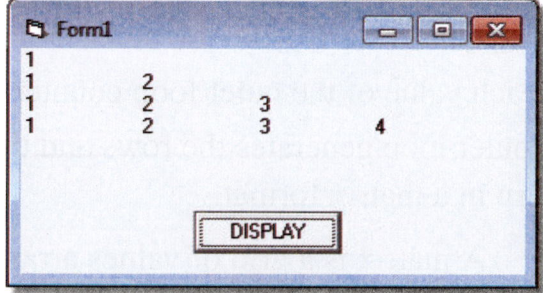

Fig. 8.29 *The Code*   Fig. 8.30 *Output*

Example 3: To print the numbers in the decreasing order as shown in the pattern here, write the code as shown here (Fig. 8.31). The output is shown in Figure 8.32.

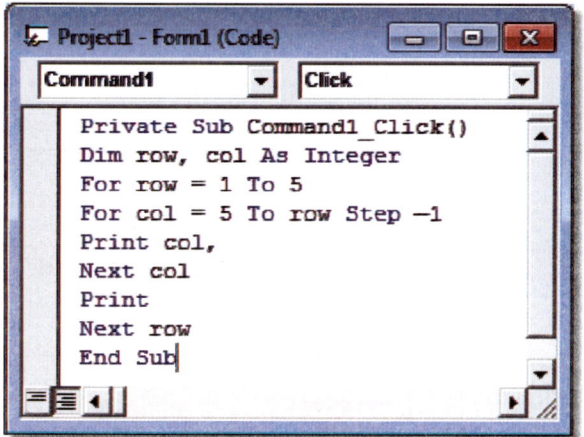

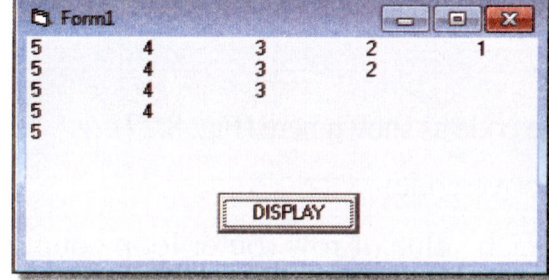

Fig. 8.31 *Writing the code*   Fig. 8.32 *Output*

Example 4: To print the numbers in the pattern shown here, write the code as shown here (Fig. 8.33). The output is given in Figure 8.34.

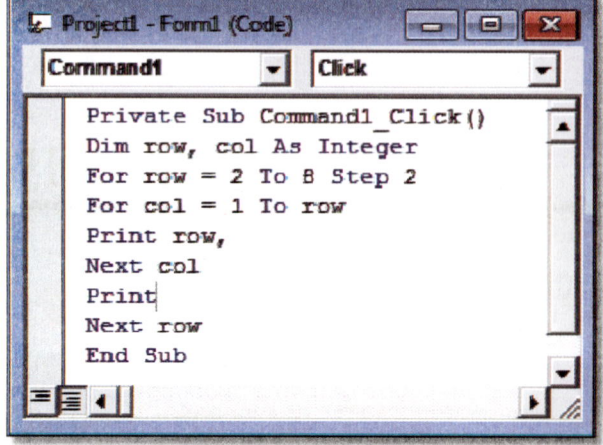

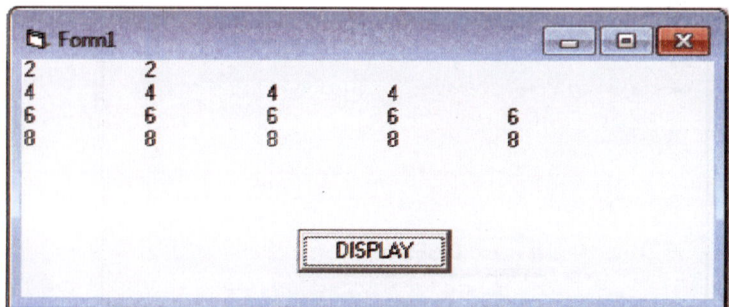

Fig. 8.33 *The Code*   Fig. 8.34 *Output*

Example 5: To accept a number and generate the next 5 consecutive numbers and to repeat the whole process till desired, write the code as shown here (Fig. 8.35).

The output is shown here (Fig. 8.36).

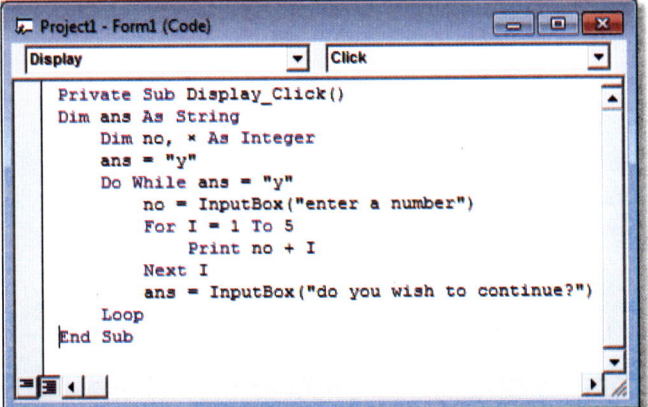

Fig. 8.35 *The Code*

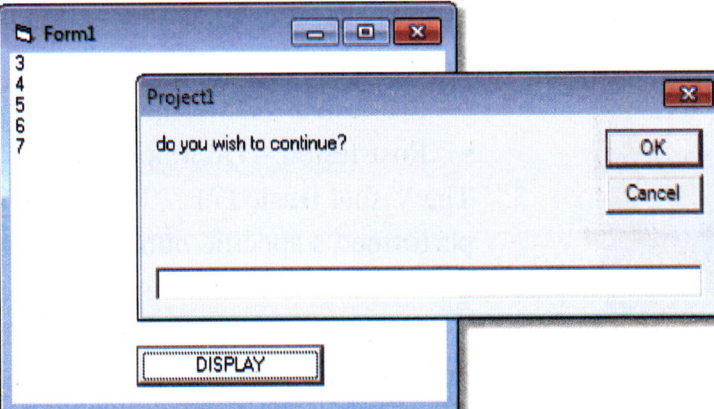

Fig. 8.36 *Output*

ACTIVITY

A. Accept a number from the user and generate the table of each number. Repeat the whole process till desired.

B. Generate the following pattern:

111	1234	321
222	1234	321
333	1234	321

C. Accept the 5 favourite numbers of the user and display the sum of them. Repeat the whole process three times.

GLOSSARY

Looping: It is repeating a program structure until the condition specified is met.

Nested loop: It is using one loop within another loop.

Pre-tested: It is the entry controlled loop where the condition is evaluated first and then the block of statements is executed.

Post-tested: It is the exit controlled loop where the block of statement is executed first and then the condition is evaluated.

Repetition statement: It refers to any block of statement that repeats itself based on a condition.

NOW YOU KNOW

1. Visual Basic allows a procedure to be repeated many times as long as a set of conditions is fulfilled.
2. Some of the commonly used repetition constructs in Visual Basic:
   - For ... Next
   - Do Loop
   - Pre-tested – Do While
   - Post-tested – Do loop While
3. The Visual Basic For ... Next loop is ideal for situations where a task needs to be performed a specific number of times.
4. DO ... Loop is used to repeat a block of statements till the condition is true. This loop works well when you do not know in advance how many times you need to execute the statements in the loop.
5. Any looping construct can be nested inside another loop.

EXERCISE

A Fill in the blanks.

1. When a procedure repeats many times as long as a set of conditions is fulfilled is known as ……………………. .
2. Visual Basic allows …………………… and …………………… construct for repeating the code.
3. DO … loop can be …………………… and …………………… controlled loop.
4. Writing a loop within another loop is called …………………… .
5. The …………………… loop executes completely for each value of …………………… loop in the nested looping.

B Find out the errors in the given code:

1.
```
Dim counter, no as string
Counter=1
Do while counter is <= 5
No=inputbox(enter a number)
If no mod 2 is 0
Print "number is even"
Otherwise
Print "number is odd"
End
Counter is counter+1
End loop
```

2.
```
Dim no as number
For no from 1 to 10
Messagebox the cube of number is
 no*no*no
End for
Print Program Ends
```

C. Answer the following questions

1. What is looping? How many types of looping constructs are available in Visual Basic?
2. When do you use FOR ... NEXT loop? Give a small code.
3. When do you use DO ... Loop?
4. How many types of DO ... Loop are available? Explain with the help of a small code?
5. What is nested looping? Give a small code.

LAB WORK

A. Write a VB code for the following instructions using For ... Next:

1. Accept the number from the user and display the factorial of the number.
2. Accept 6 numbers and print the count of even and odd numbers separately.
3. Accept 5 numbers and print the square of the number if the number is an odd number otherwise print the message "sorry! Number is even".

B. Write a VB code for the following instructions using any form of DO ... Loop:

1. Accept a number from the user and check if it is a prime number or not.
2. Accept 10 numbers from the user and display the sum of all multiples of 10 entered by the user.
3. Accept the number from the user till user wants and calculate the sum of the even numbers entered.
4. Accept an odd number from the user and print the count. The program should terminate if the number entered is even.

TEACHER'S NOTES

1. Help the students create mathematical patterns like Fibonacci series using Visual Basic.
2. Create as many nested loops with the students as possible because they are a difficult construct.

9 Creating Menu in MDI Application

LEARNING OBJECTIVES

You will learn about:
1. SDI and MDI forms
2. creating MDI application with SDI and MDI forms
3. creating Menu Bar in the MDI application

Introduction

Like any other Windows application, VB consists of multiple windows which appear at startup. The windows that are displayed when you start VB are collectively known as the Visual Basic Integrated Development Environment (IDE). This IDE can be used to create different types of document interfaces. In this lesson, you will learn about them in detail.

SDI and MDI Forms

You can view the forms in Visual Basic IDE in two ways:
- Single document interface forms
- Multiple document interface forms

Single Document Interface (SDI) forms

In SDI forms, single document is supported in a window, that is, if the user tries to open another document then the previously opened document closes first and then a new document is opened. The best example is a document that you create in WordPad, Notepad or Paint.

In Visual Basic, the forms that you usually create are SDI forms that work independently of the other forms created. You can work on one form at a time.

Multiple Document Interface (MDI) forms

In MDI forms, multiple documents are supported by window, that is, the user is allowed to open another document irrespective of the previously opened documents. For example, in MS Word multiple documents can be opened at one time.

In Visual Basic, you can implement this by converting a usual single form to a MDI form. After this, the MDI form will become the parent form and any other form (child form) can be accessed within the parent form, that is, it cannot be moved outside the boundaries of the parent form. There can be many child forms created within the parent form.

FACT FILE

The MDI form cannot contain any tools from the ToolBox as the tools are used to design the form and MDI form only acts a container for the SDI forms.

ACTIVITY

A. Open Paint and create one file. Now create another file before closing the previous one. What message you will get? Why?

B. Open Excel 2007 and find out whether it supports SDI or MDI.

Creating MDI Application

An MDI form or the parent form can work as a complete independent application with many features like Menu Bar, Toolbars, Status Bar, etc.

Follow these steps for creating a parent form:

1. Create a blank project.
2. Click on **Project** menu ⇒ **Add MDI Form** option (Fig. 9.1).
3. **Add MDI Form** dialog box appears (Fig. 9.2).
4. Select the **MDI Form** under the **New Tab**.
5. Click on the **Open** command button.

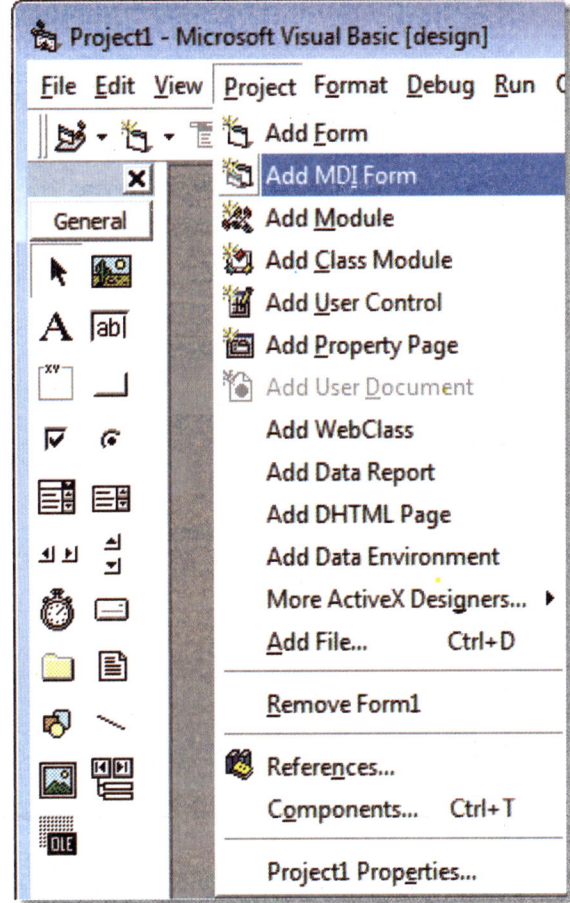

Fig. 9.1 *Creating an MDI form*

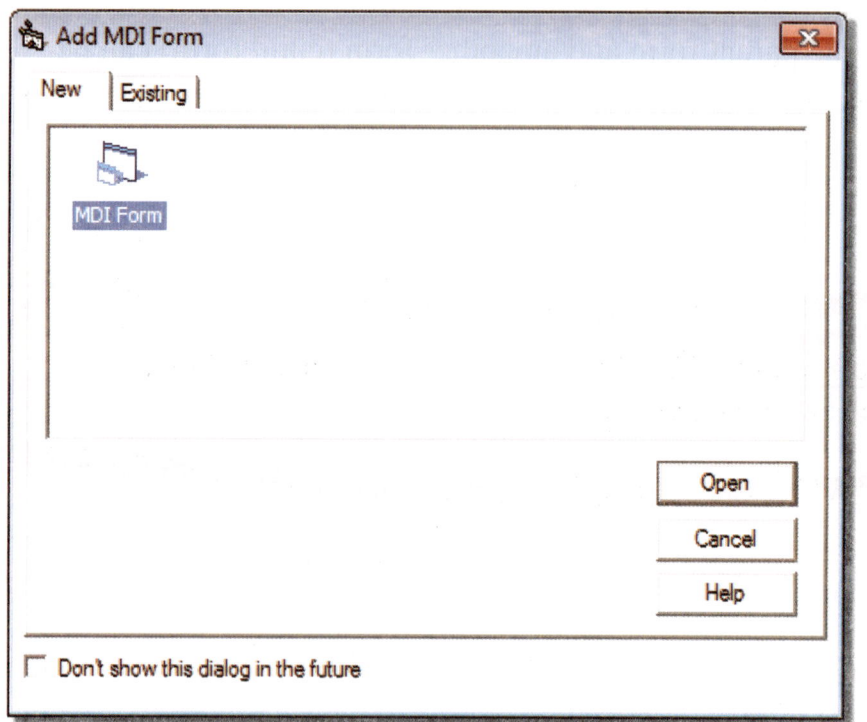

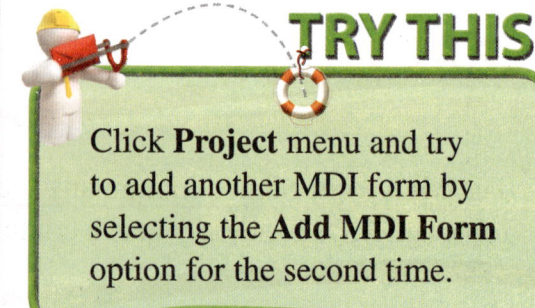

TRY THIS!

Click **Project** menu and try to add another MDI form by selecting the **Add MDI Form** option for the second time.

Fig. 9.2 *Add MDI Form dialog box*

6. The new MDI Form will be displayed (Fig. 9.3). This is named as MDIForm1 by default.

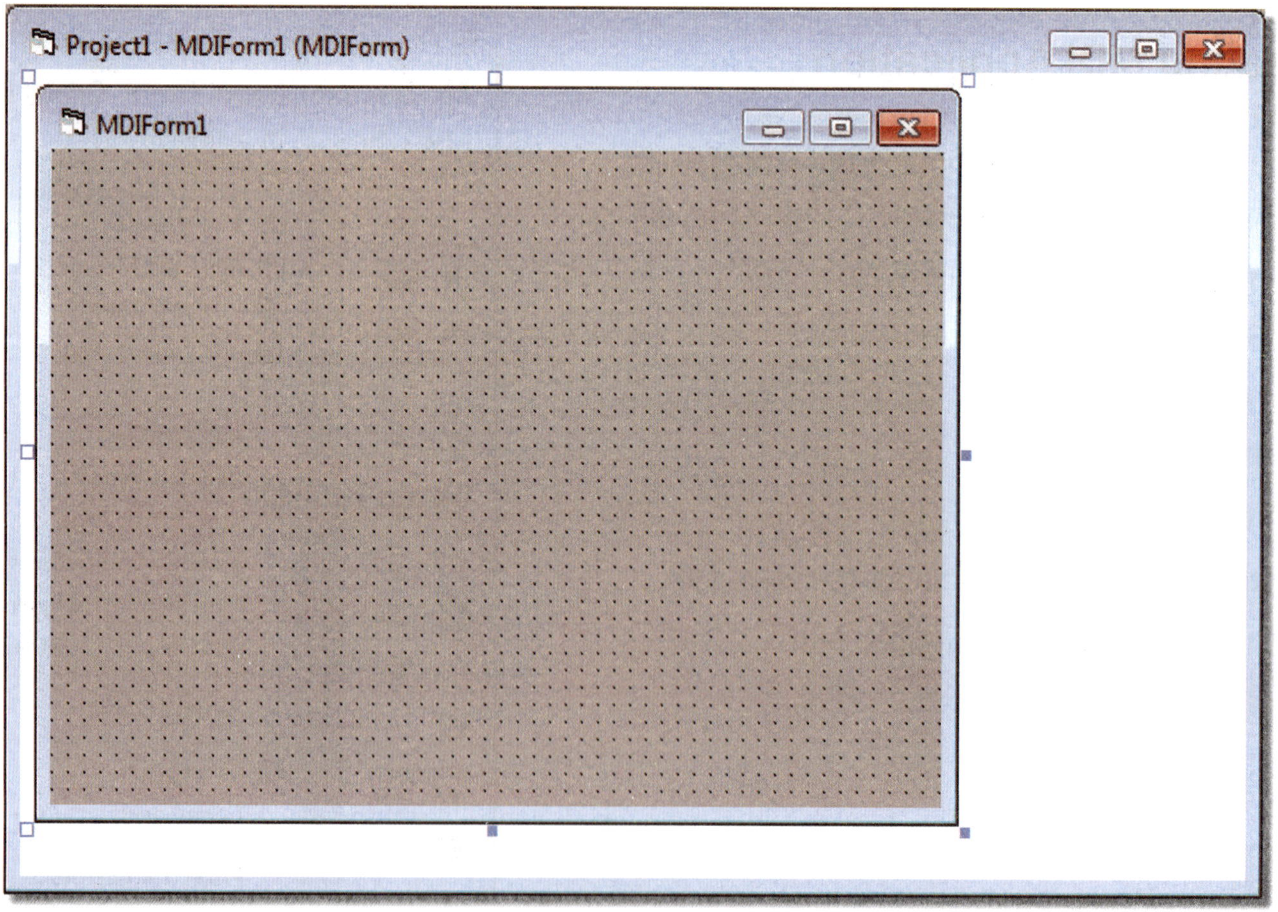

Fig. 9.3 *A new MDI Form*

Now, follow these steps for creating a child form:

1. The default Form1 created earlier in Project1 can behave as a child form by setting the **MDIChild property** (Autoshow children) to **True**. So, do the changes in the properties of the form.

2. Add a label to the form and change the caption name property to THIS IS CHILD FORM 1 (Fig. 9.4).

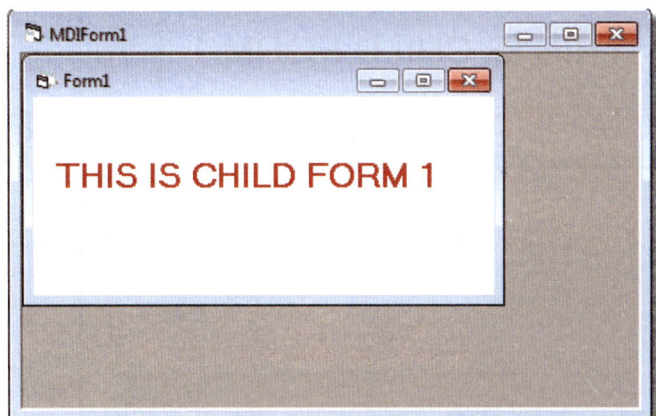

Fig. 9.4 *Child Form 1*

3. Execute your application. You will see that the child form is always a part of the parent form irrespective of the fact whether you maximize, restore or minimize the child form.

4. Now click on **Minimize** option of Form1. You will see it in the form of a small window at the bottom of the parent form as shown (Fig. 9.5).

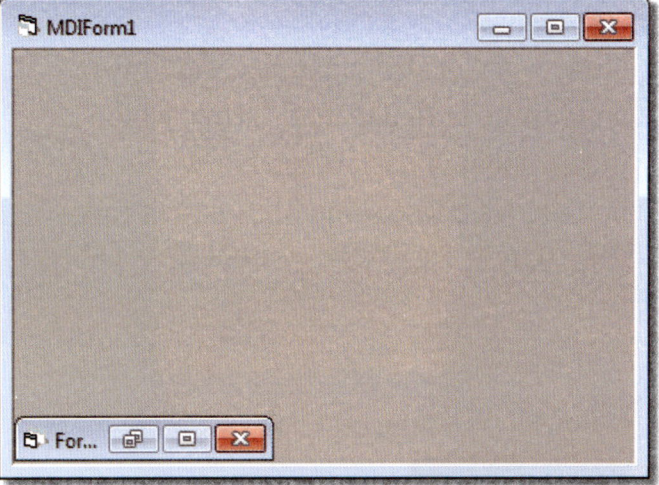

Fig. 9.5 *Child form minimized*

5. Add another child form to the same application by clicking on the **Project** menu ⟹ **Add Form** option.

6. Add a Label to Form2 and change the caption name property to THIS IS CHILD FORM 2 (Fig. 9.6).

7. Change the **MDI Child property** to **True** for Form2 in the same way you did for Form1.

Fig. 9.6 *Child Form 2*

8. Click anywhere on Form1. The code window appears. In the load event of Form1 do the following changes in the code (Fig. 9.7):

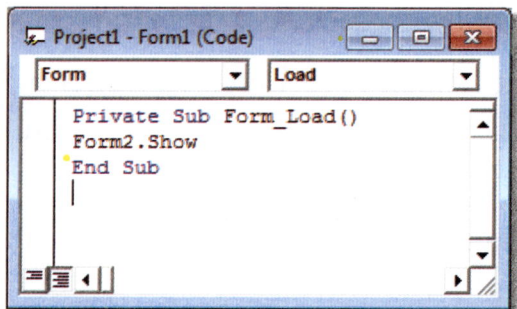

Fig. 9.7 *Writing the code to show Form2*

9. This code will display the second form as soon as the first form is loaded in the memory. Thus, both the forms will be displayed at the same time when you execute your MDI application (Fig. 9.8).

Fig. 9.8 *Displaying the two child forms in the parent form window*

Fig. 9.9 *Sizes of both the forms can be altered together*

10. Now, you can also maximize, minimize and restore both the child forms, which are independent of each other, but within the boundaries of the same MDI parent form (Fig. 9.9).

ACTIVITY

Complete the following activity.

1. Add a third child form in the above project created and display some message in a label.
2. Change the MDIChild property to False
3. Write Form3.show in the load event of Form2.
4. Execute your application and see how these three forms behave with respect to the parent form.
5. Maximize, minimize and restore to the normal size Form1, Form2 and Form3 and see the difference.

Creating Menu Bar in MDI Application

You already know that Menu Bar is the standard feature of most of the window's applications. It is mainly used for easy navigation and control of an application. Some of the most common menu items of Menu Bar are File, Edit, View, Tools, Help, etc. Each item on the main Menu Bar also provide a list of options in the form of a drop-down list showing the submenus. You may also insert these menus in your Visual Basic forms. To insert Menu Bar in VB, you need to follow the steps given below here:

1. Click on **Tools** menu ⇒ **Menu Editor**… option (Fig. 9.10).

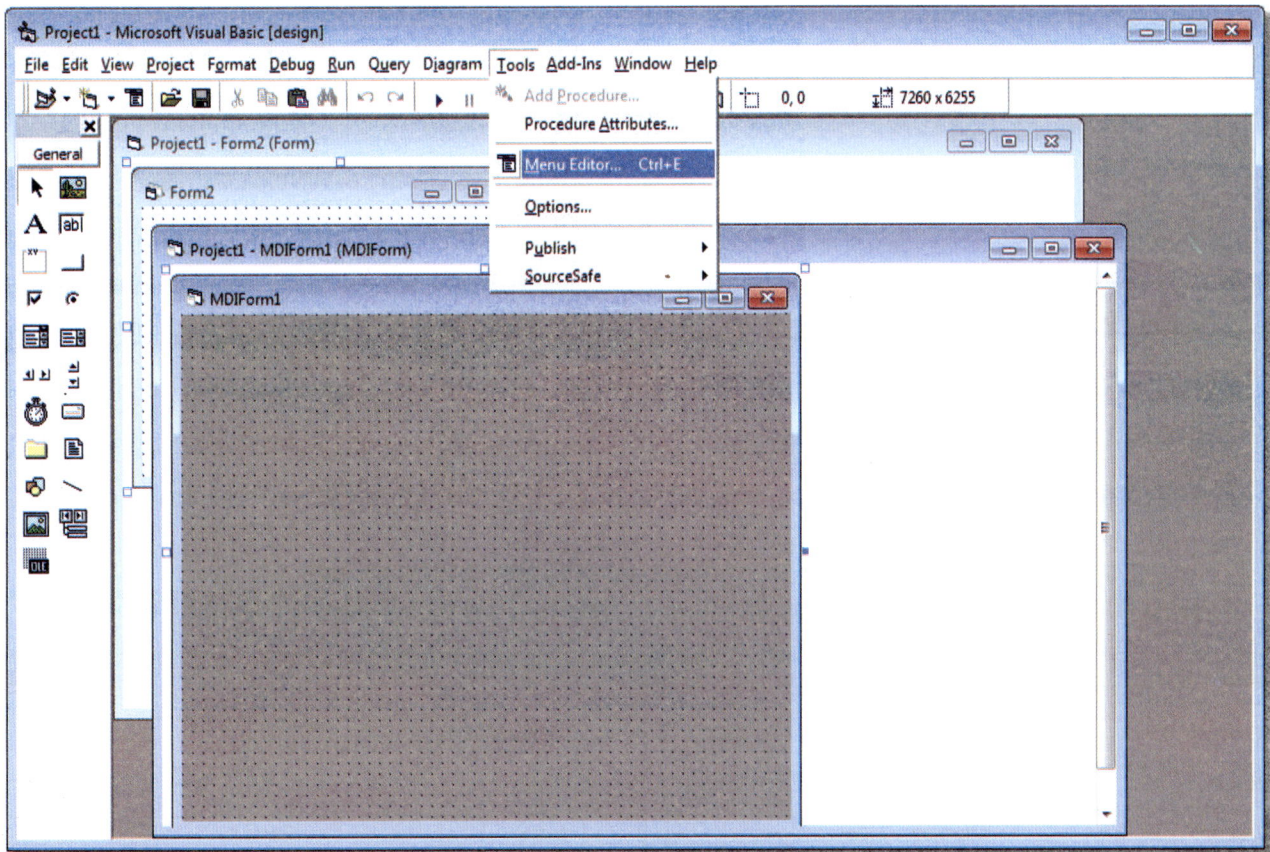

Fig. 9.10 *Opening the Menu Editor*

2. The Menu Editor dialog box appears (Fig. 9.11).

3. In the Menu Editor dialog box fill the options as follows:

   a. Type File in the **Caption:** text box.

   b. Type F in the **Name:** text box.

Note: You can use the ampersand (&) sign in front of File in the Caption name box as done in Figure 9.11. This would make F the **hotkey**, which is used to initiate any action. This action can now also be done by pressing the **Alt** key and the letter F (the hotkey). You can recognise a hotkey as this will be underlined when it appears in the menu.

c. Click on **Next** command button. The blue bar shifts to the next line (Fig. 9.12).

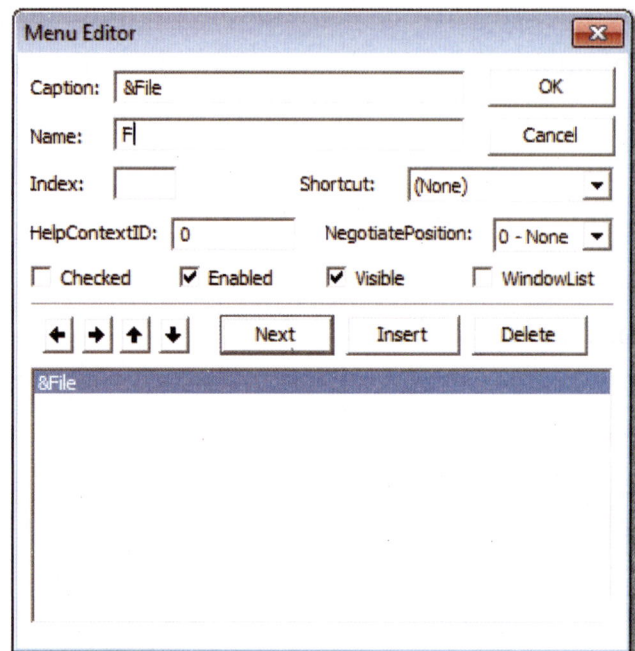

Fig. 9.11 *Menu Editor dialog box*

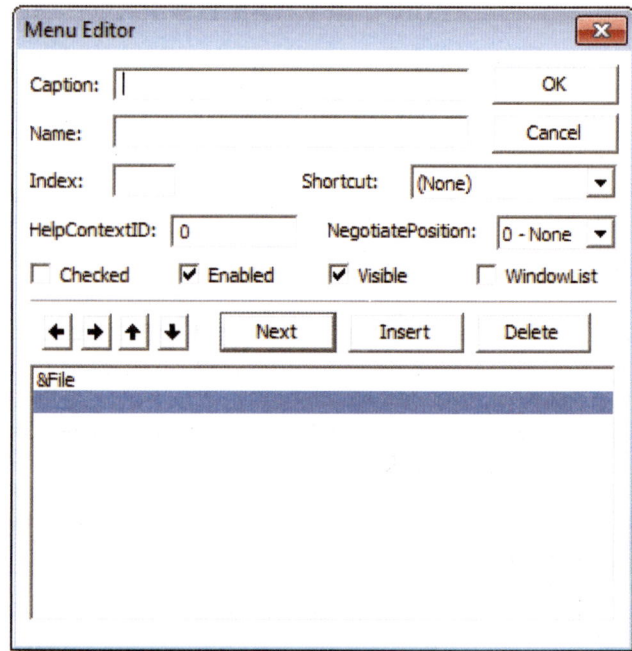

Fig. 9.12 *Creating a new option or menu*

d. Click on the ➔ to create the options within the **File** menu. This is to create a submenu under the main File menu created.

e. The caption and name textboxes will be blank so that the option caption and name can be added to the File menu as shown (Fig. 9.13).

f. Repeat the above step to add more options and menus to the application (Fig. 9.14).

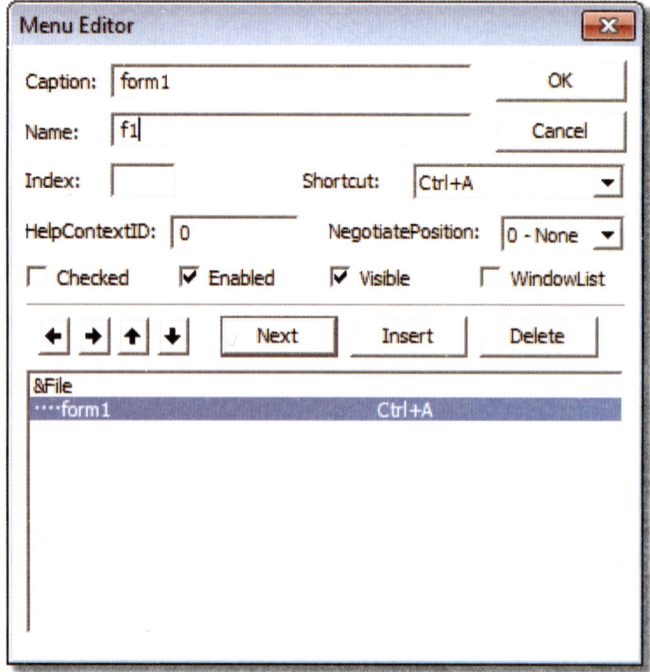

Fig. 9.13 *Adding submenu options*

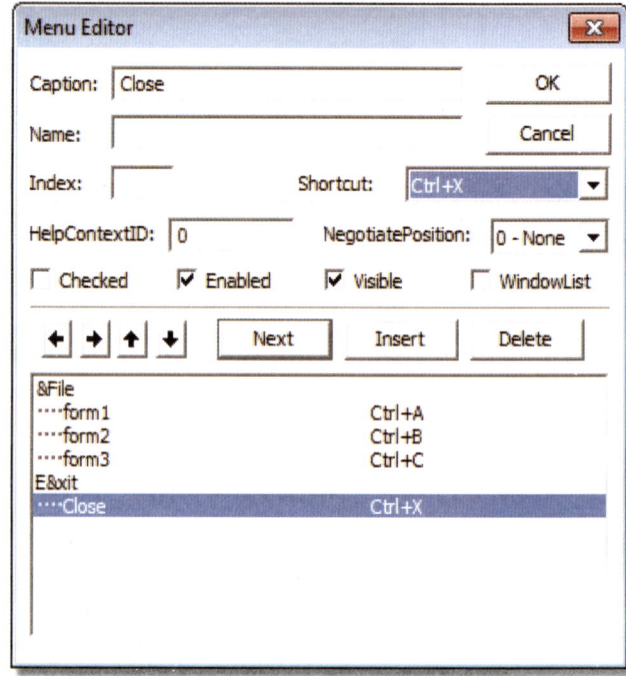

Fig. 9.14 *Adding menus and submenus in the MDI Form*

g. Execute your MDI application to see the Menu Bar with options (Fig. 9.15).

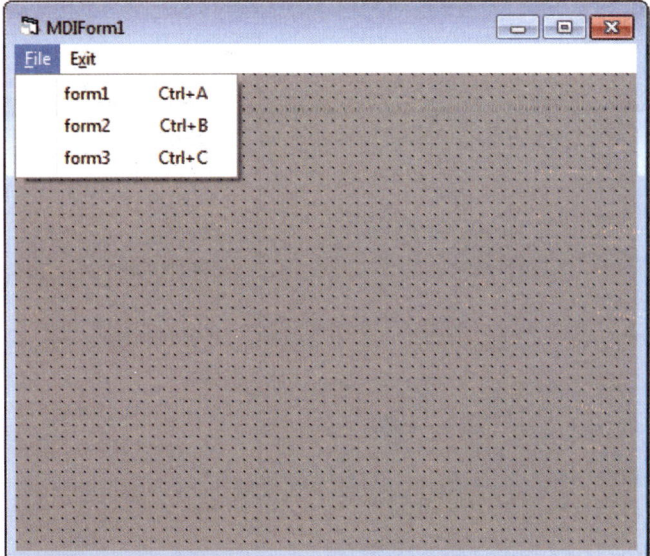

Fig. 9.15 *Displaying the Menu Bar in MDI Form*

h. Do the coding in the Code window of the MDI application as shown in Figure 9.16.

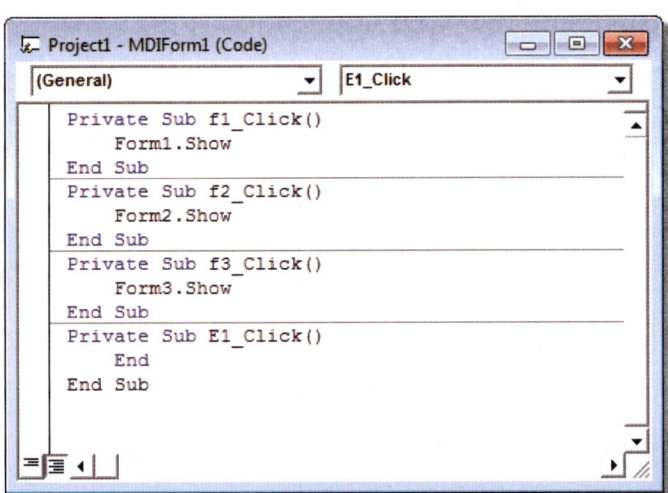

Fig. 9.16 *The code*

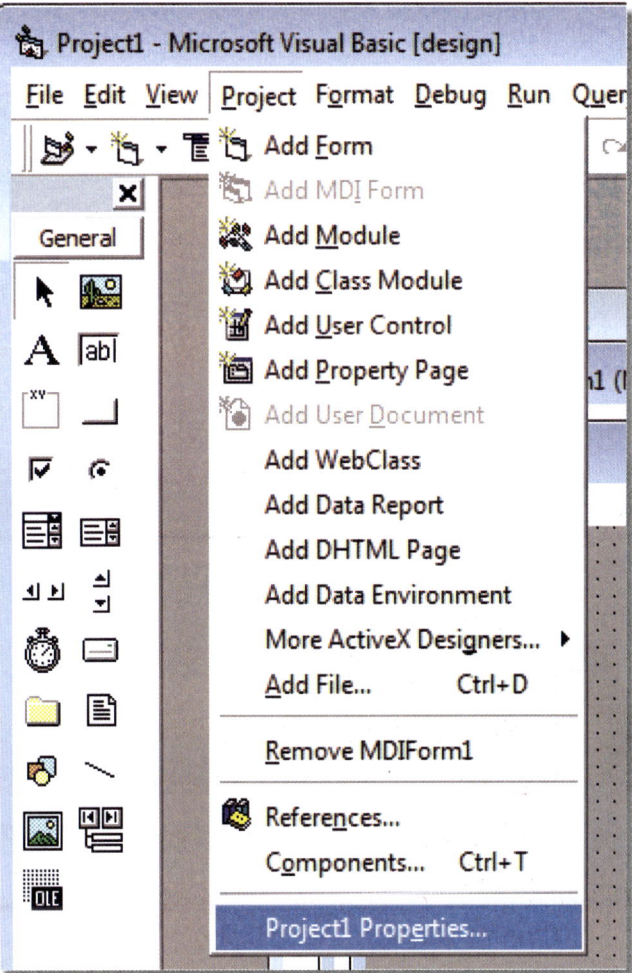

To open the above created MDI application, follow the steps given.

1. Click on **Project** menu ⟹ **Project1 Properties...** option (Fig. 9.17).

Fig. 9.17 *Opening Project Properties*

2. **Project1 - Project Properties** dialog box appears. Under the heading **Startup Object**: select **MDIForm1** option (Fig. 9.18).

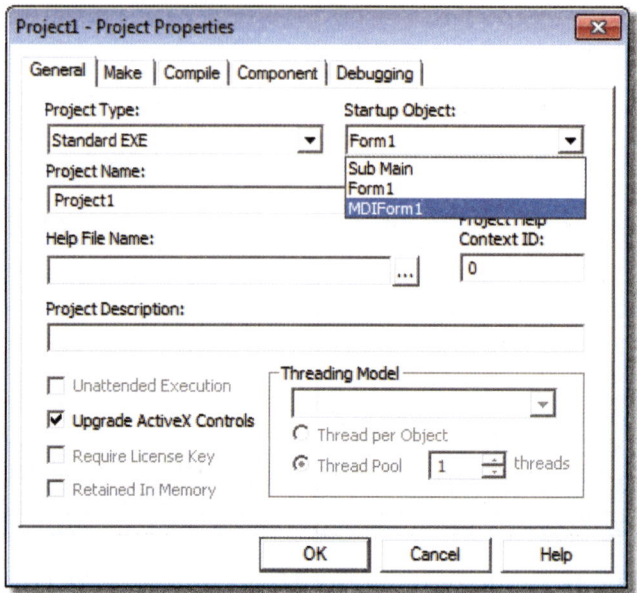

Fig. 9.18 *Setting the properties to the parent form*

3. Click on the **OK** command button.
4. Now, execute your MDI Form and enjoy your own created MDI application (Fig. 9.19).

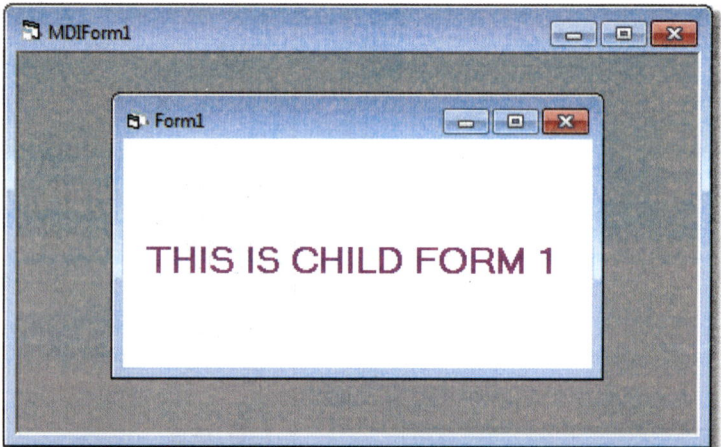

Fig. 9.19 *MDI FORM1 with the Menu Bar and options*

GLOSSARY

Child form: It refers to any other form that can be accessed within the parent form.

Hotkey: It is used to initiate any action.

Multiple Document Interface: It allows more than one form to be opened in the same window at the same time.

Parent form: It is the main MDI form that has the control of the project.

Single Document Interface: It allows only a single form to be opened in a window.

NOW YOU KNOW

1. VB consists of multiple windows which appear at startup.
2. The windows that are displayed when you start Visual Basic are collectively known as the Visual Basic Integrated Development Environment (IDE). This IDE can be used to create different types of document interfaces.
3. An MDI application is made up of parent form and child form. The parent form acts as a container for the child form, and has full control of it. It can work as a complete independent application with many featurs like Menu bar, Toolbars, Status Bar, etc.
4. Menu Bar is the standard feature of most window's applications. The main purpose of the menu is for easy navigation and control of an application. Some of the most common menu items are File, Edit, View, Tools, Help, etc.

EXERCISE

A Fill in the blanks.

1. The windows that are displayed when you start Visual Basic are collectively known as the …………………… .
2. SDI stands for …………………… .
3. An example of MDI application is …………………… .
4. The default form created can be made to work like SDI form by changing the …………………… property to …………………… .
5. Menu Bar can be created in MDI form by using …………………… menu in …………………… option.

B Give the code/steps with statements for: HOTS

1. Adding a code to display a form using an option in a menu.
2. Adding a code for exiting an MDI Form by using an option in a menu.
3. Adding Form1 and Form2 options in the File menu.
4. Adding a horizontal bar in the File menu under Form1 and Form 2 options.

C. Match the following.

1. Ampersand in the Menu Editor — a. Menu Editor... option
2. Notepad — b. MDI application
3. WordPad — c. To make a hot key
4. To change startup use Project menu — d. SDI application
5. To add menu using Tools menu — e. Properties option

D. Answer the following questions.

1. Give two difference between MDI and SDI form.
2. Give the steps for creating MDI form in Visual Basic.
3. What is parent and child form in MDI application? Give two properties of the MDI application. How many MDI forms can be created in a project?
4. What is a Menu Bar? How can you create a menu in Visual Basic?

LAB WORK

A. Create an MDI form with the menu:

1. File
   a. Open Form 1   b. Open Form 2   c. Close Form   d. Save   e. Print
2. Exit
   a. Help
   b. Close
   c. In Save and Help options only an appropriate message in a message box should be displayed.
   d. Give the coding for opening Form1, Form2 and also for closing them.

B. Create the following Menu in a MDI form.

BOOK	MEMBER	ISSUE
Add	Add	Date wise
Modify	Modify	Subject wise
Delete	Delete	Language wise

TEACHER'S NOTES

1. Tell the students about Tabbed Document Interface (TDI).
2. Give students as many examples of SDI and MDI applications as possible.

10 Connecting VB with MS Access 2007

SNAP RECAP

1. The various objects that MS Access identifies are tables, queries, forms, reports, etc.
2. Microsoft Access is a powerful database program that you can use to store all kinds of information in the form of tables, queries, forms, reports, etc.
3. The Toolbox contains a set of controls that are placed on a form at design time, thereby, creating the user interface area.
4. The Properties window displays the various properties of the object selected on the form.

LEARNING OBJECTIVES

You will learn about:
1. ADO Data Control
2. inserting ADO Data Control
3. connecting Visual Basic to MS Access 2007
4. connecting the text box to the fields of the table
5. executing the form
6. modifying MS Access 2007 table using ADO Data Control

Introduction

Visual Basic can be easily used for accessing and modifying databases. There are many ways to work with databases in Visual Basic, but the simplest way to connect with databases is by using the ADO Data Control.

ADO Data Control

ADO is an **ActiveX Data Object** designed as a programming interface to access a database. It is present in form of ADO data control in Visual Basic, and is used as a fast and an easy way to connect the Visual Basic form with an MS Access database. It provides built-in functions that help you to create new records and also navigate, update and delete the records. The resultant form makes it easy for a user to maintain records.

Inserting ADO Data Control

You need to insert ADO Data Control into the Toolbox in order to use the ADO Data Control. To do so, follow the steps given below:

1. Click on **Project** menu ⟹ **Components...** option (Fig. 10.1).

2. **Components** dialog box appears (Fig. 10.2). Select **Microsoft ADO Data Control 6.0 (OLEDB)** check box.

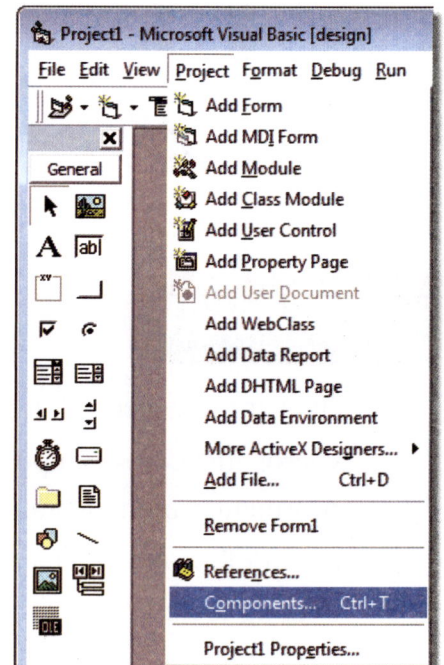

Fig. 10.1 *To insert the ADO Control in the Toolbox*

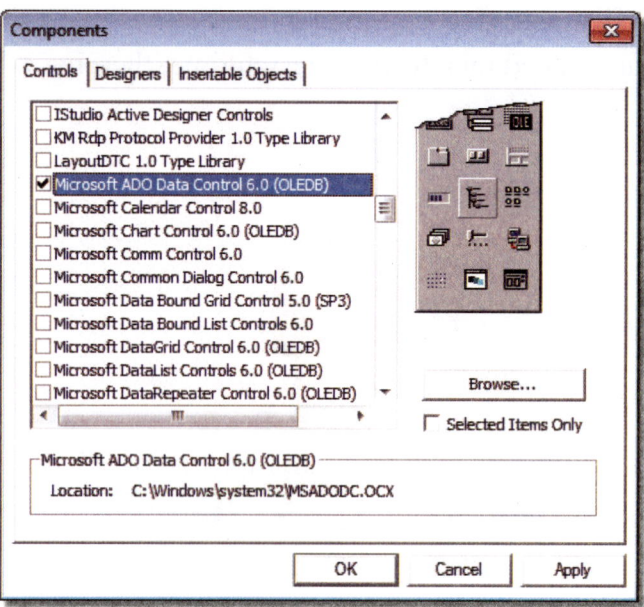

Fig. 10.2 *Components dialog box*

3. Click on the **Apply** button.

4. The **OK** button changes to **Close** button. Click on the **Close** button to close this window.

5. You will see ADO component added to the Toolbox in the Visual Basic IDE (Fig. 10.3).

6. Now you can proceed to build your ADO-based VB database applications.

| Components dialog box opens | Ctrl + T |

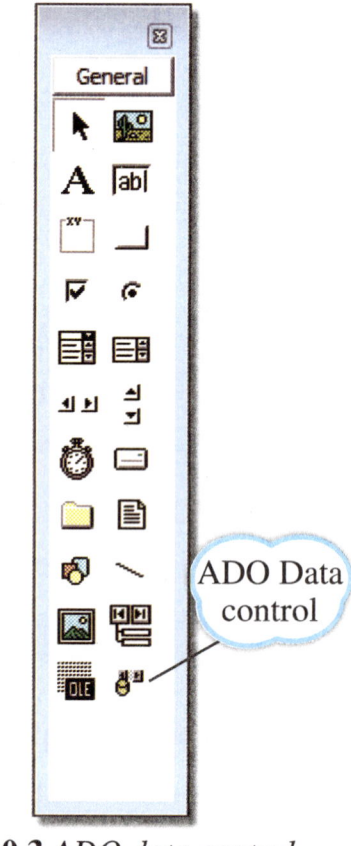

Fig. 10.3 *ADO data control added to Toolbox*

144

Connecting Visual Basic to MS Access 2007

You can establish a connection between the Visual Basic IDE and MS Access 2007 using the ADO controls. To do so, follow the steps given here:

1. Create a table in MS Access 2007 with the given names as shown (Fig. 10.4).

   Here, Database: school.mdb

   Table: Teacher

   Fields: Tcode, Tname, Subject, Date of joining, Phone Number

T code	T name	Subject	Date of Joini
T101	Ms Anita	Science	12/8/2001
T121	Ms Anjali	Computers	5/5/2002
T144	Ms Charvi	Mathematics	1/4/2003
T171	Mr David	Social Science	5/6/2004

   Fig. 10.4 *Creating the table using MS Access*

2. Design your Visual Basic form with labels and textboxes equivalent to the fields in the table created in MS Access 2007 (Fig. 11.5).

3. Select the **ADO data control** icon present on the Toolbox and place it on the Visual Basic form (Fig. 10.6).

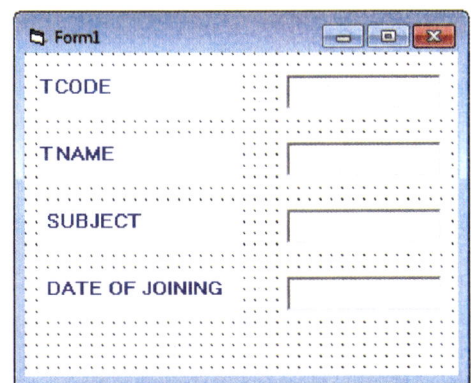

Fig. 10.5 *Creating form in VB as the table in MS Access 2007*

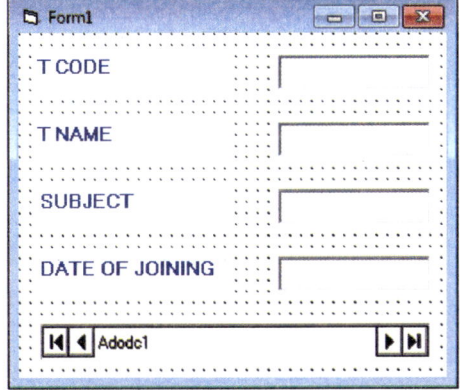

Fig. 10.6 *Creating ADO data control on the form*

FACT FILE

You can save the time spent on creating several controls of the same type by creating one control. Then, use the Copy and Paste option. When VB asks if you're creating a control array, answer No.

4. Now do the following changes in the properties of ADO Data Control, to connect it to MS Access 2007, as shown in the Property window.

   a. Change the **CommandType** property to **2 – adCmdTable** (Fig. 10.7).

   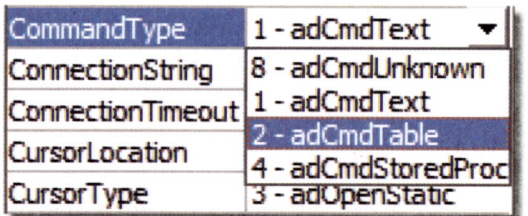

   Fig. 10.7 *Changing properties*

   b. Click on the ⋯ present in the **ConnectionString** property text box (Fig. 10.8).

   Fig. 10.8 *ConnectionString property*

   c. The **Property Pages** dialog box appears (Fig. 10.9). Select the **Use Connection String** button. Click on the **Build…** command button present on its right side.

   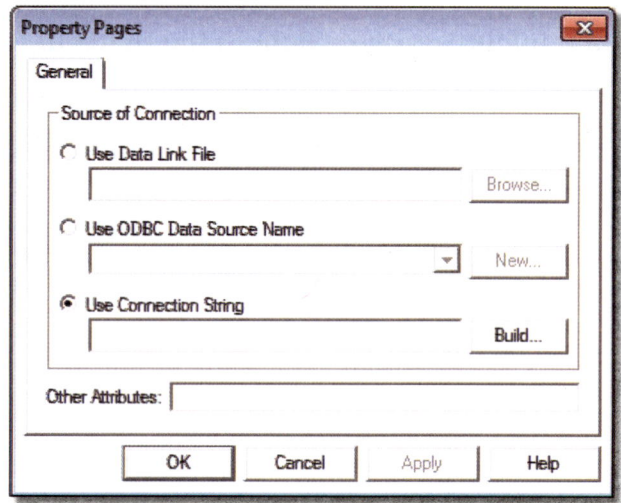

   Fig. 10.9 *Property Pages dialog box*

   d. The **Data Link Properties** dialog box appears (Fig. 10.10). Select the desired **Provider** tab. Here, under OLE DB Provider(s) **Microsoft Jet 4.0 OLE DB Provider** is selected.

   e. Click on the **Next** button.

   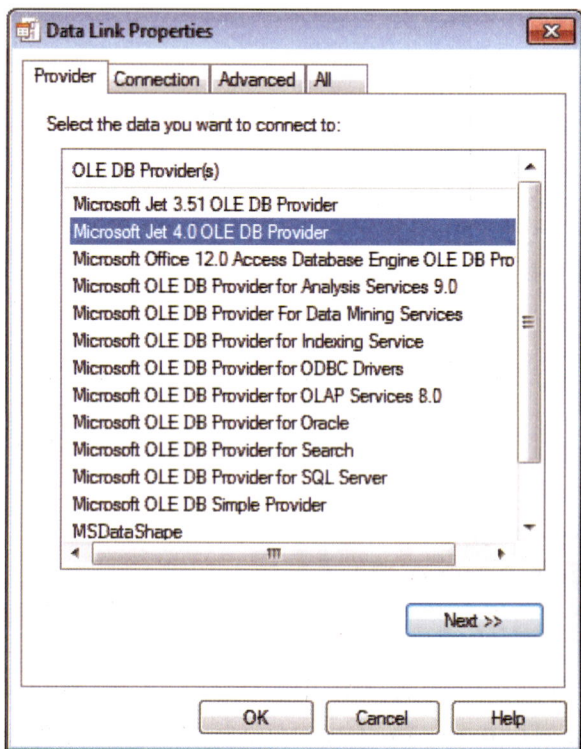

   Fig. 10.10 *Data Link Properties dialog box*

f. The **Connection** tab will be opened in the same dialog box. Here, select 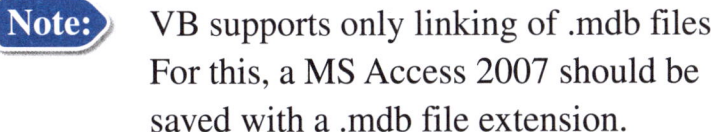 button present on the right side of the **Select or enter the database name:** option (Fig. 10.11).

g. The **Select Access Database** dialog appears (Fig. 10.12). Select the database name. In this case, it is SCHOOL.mdb.

Note: VB supports only linking of .mdb files. For this, a MS Access 2007 should be saved with a .mdb file extension.

h. Click on **Open** command button.

i. You will now come back to **Connection** tab in **Data Link Properties** dialog box, where now you will see that the database name is displayed on its own (Fig. 10.13).

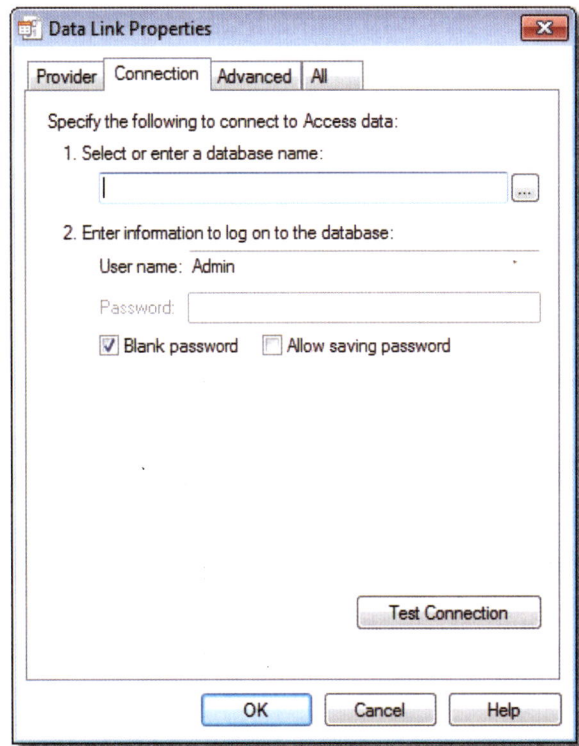

Fig. 10.11 *Connection tab in the dialog box*

Click on **Test Connection** button. If the provider is given correctly and Visual Basic connects successfully to MS Access then you will get a message window with the message 'Test connection succeeded'.

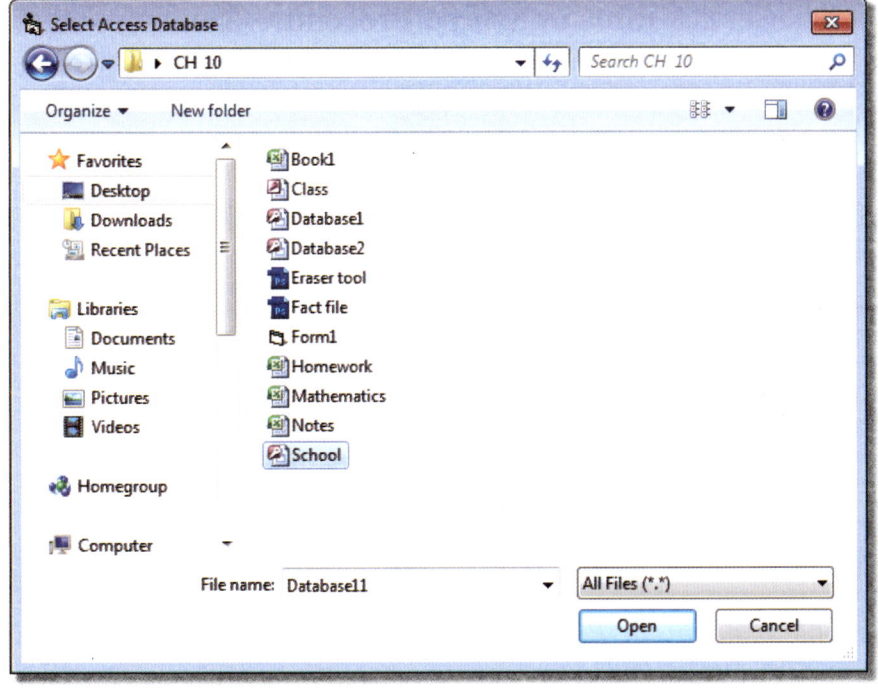

Fig. 10.12 *Select Access Database dialog box*

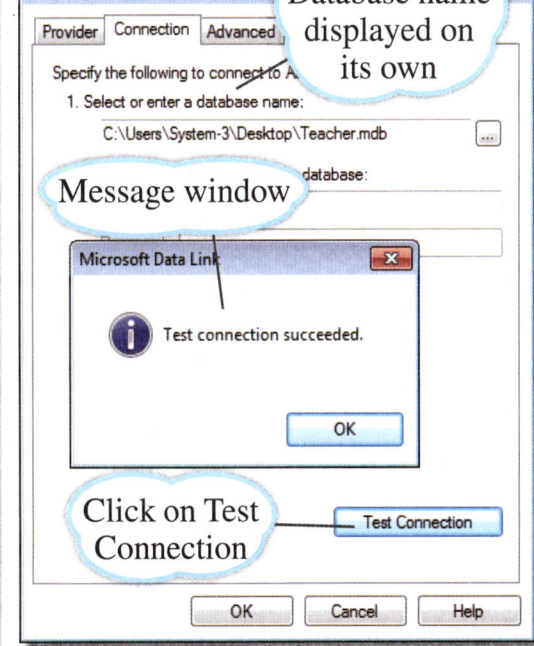

Fig. 10.13 *Testing the connection*

j. Click on **OK** button on the **Microsoft Data Link** message box.

k. You will come back to **Property Pages** dialog box where the **Use Connection String** option has the details of the connection established (Fig. 10.14).

l. Click on the **Apply** button and then on **OK** button. This will bring your control back to the Property window.

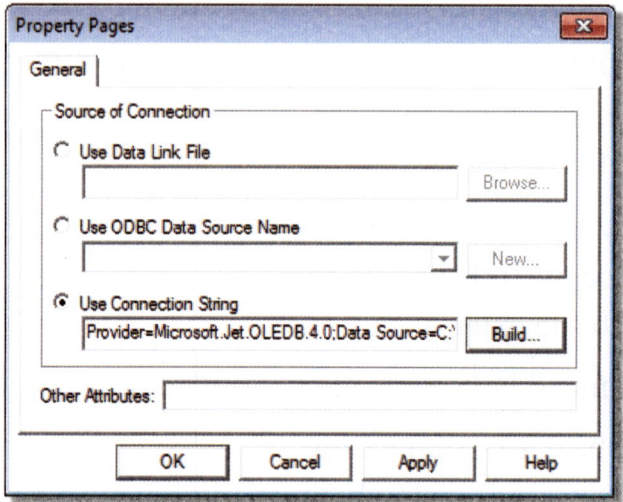

Fig. 10.14 *Connection String in the Properties Pages box*

m. Select ⋯ present on the right side of the **RecordSource** property (Fig. 10.15).

Fig. 10.15 *RecordSource property in the main property window*

n. The **Property Pages** window appears with a different tab opened. Select the Table name of the database selected earlier in the **Table or Stored Procedure Name** option (Fig. 10.16).

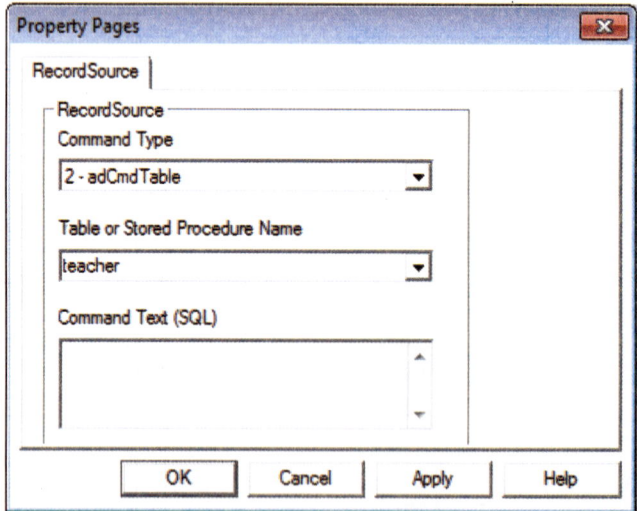

Fig. 10.16 *Selecting the table name in the Property Pages dialog box*

o. Click on the **Apply** button and then on **OK** button.

p. This will bring your control back to the Property window. This will be the end of the steps for connecting Visual Basic with MS Access.

By following the above steps changes can be made in the Property window of the ADO data control as shown in Table 10.1.

Table 10.1 *Properties of the ADO Data Control*

Property Name	Value
CommandType	2 - adCmdTable
ConnectionString	Provider = Micorsoft.Jet.OLEDB.4.0; Data source = D:\My Documents\school.mdb;
RecordSource	Teacher

ACTIVITY

Complete the activity by following the instructions given below.

1. Create a table on My friends in MS Access 2007.
2. Design the VB Form.
3. Connect your form with MS Access 2007.

Connecting the Textbox to the Fields of the Table

After connecting the ADO Data Control to a specific table in MS Access, you need to associate each text box to a specific field of the table so that the values of each record can be displayed in a specific textbox of the form. This is done by following the steps given here:

1. Select **TextBox1** in the **Form Design** window and do the following changes in the **Property** window (Table 10.2):

Table 10.2 *Changes in the TextBox1 Properties*

Property Name	Value
DataSource	Adodc1
DataField	T code

2. Do the similar changes for **TextBox 2** (Table 10.3), **TextBox 3** (Table 10.4), **TextBox 4** (Table 10.5) and **TextBox 5** (Table 10.6).

Table 10.3 *Changes in the TextBox2 Properties*

Property Name	Value
DataSource	Adodc1
DataField	T name

Table 10.4 *Changes in the TextBox3 Properties*

Property Name	Value
DataSource	Adodc1
DataField	subject

Table 10.5 *Changes in the TextBox4 Properties*

Property Name	Value
DataSource	Adodc1
DataField	Date of joining

Table 10.6 *Changes in the TextBox5 Properties*

Property Name	Value
DataSource	Adodc1
DataField	Phone No

Executing the Form

Follow these steps to execute the form:

1. Click on the **F5** Function key.

   Select the **Run** menu ⟹ **Start** Option.

   Select ▶ tool present on the **Standard Toolbar** of Visual Basic to execute your form.

2. You can see the record of the teacher table displayed in the text box (Fig. 10.17).

3. Use the navigation buttons of the ADO Data Control to move to First, Previous, Next and Last record of the table.

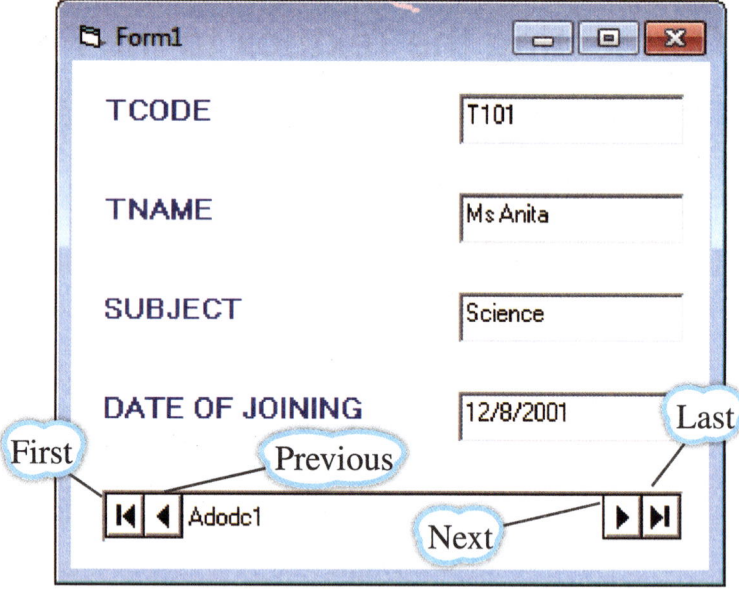

Fig. 10.17 *After the project is run*

ACTIVITY

Complete the following activity based on the instructions given below.

1. Associate each text box with the form and the table created earlier.
2. Same the project and the form.
3. Execute it and do the navigation using ADO data control.

Modifying MS Access 2007 Table Using ADO Data Control

You can do the changes in Access table through little coding using ADO Data Control object. Before doing so, you must add three command buttons, namely, ADD, UPDATE and DELETE in the form (Fig. 10.18).

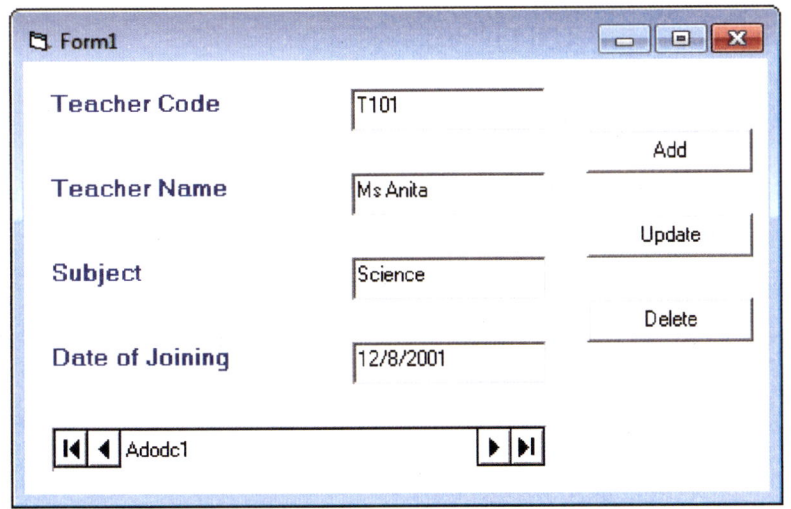

Fig. 10.18 *Changed data in the form*

The code using ADO Data Control object to allow changes in MS Access 2007 table is shown in the Code Window Figure 10.19.

TRY THIS!

Hide the adodc1 control from the form by changing the property:
Visible: False.
Add the Navigation command button to the form by using the MoveFirst, MoveNext, MovePrevious, MoveLast code after Recordset object in the coding.

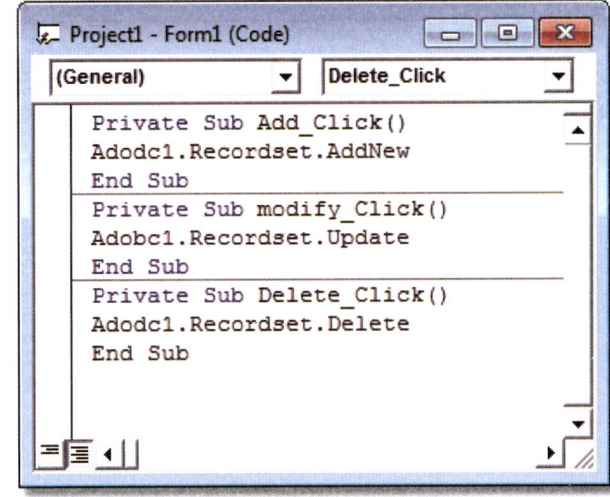

Fig. 10.19 *The Code*

ACTIVITY

Complete the following activity based on the instructions given below.
1. Try creating the updation and the navigation command buttons in the above created forms for displaying your friends' details.
2. Save the changes.
3. Execute your form.

GLOSSARY

ActiveX Data Object (ADO): It is designed as a programming interface to access a database.

NOW YOU KNOW

1. ADO is present in the form of ADO Data Control in Visual Basic and is used as a fast and easy way to connect the Visual Basic form with an MS Access 2007 Database.
2. To be able to use ADO Data Control, you need to insert it into the Toolbox by selecting it from the components option present in Project menu.
3. Follow proper steps to do the changes in the ADO Data Control properties – CommandType, ConnectionString and RecordSource.
4. After this associate each text box to the fields of MS Access 2007 table by doing changes in the DataSource and DataField properties of the text box.
5. Execute your form either by clicking on F5 function key or select Start option from Run menu or select ▶ tool present on the Standard Toolbar of Visual Basic.
6. You can do the changes in MS Access 2007 table through little coding using ADO Data Control object.

EXERCISE

A. Fill in the blanks.

1. ADO stands for ……………………… .
2. You can connect Visual Basic with MS Access 2007 using ……………………… .
3. ADO Data Control can be displayed in the Toolbox by using ……………………… menu and ……………………… option.
4. To connect VB to MS Access 2007 the property changes will be done in ADO Data Control properties ……………………… ……………………… and ……………………… .
5. To associate each text box to the fields of MS Access 2007 table the properties ……………………… and ……………………… are changed.

B. Match the following.

1.	Execute the form	a.	MoveFirst Record
2.	DataField	b.	Adds the ADO Data Control
3.	RecordSource	c.	Field of the table
4.	Project Menu	d.	F5 function key
5.	ADO Data Control	e.	Table name

C **Answer the following with proper reasons.** ◀HOTS▶

1. A telecom company wants to maintain the details of the employees in a database and when the owner wants any updation and navigation to be done then it should be displayed in a proper formatted form. How can you help the company do this?
2. The programmer was able to connect the form with Visual Basic but the records were not getting displayed in the text boxes. What steps did they miss in between? Help them to solve this problem.
3. The management does not want the ADO Data Control to be displayed on the form. Instead they want the navigation to be done by using the command buttons. Can you try the coding for these command buttons?

D **Answer the following questions.**

1. Using which control of Visual Basic can you connect a form with MS Access 2007 ? What all can you do using that control?
2. What are the three different ways of executing a Visual Basic form?
3. Give the coding for adding, modifying and deleting a record using ADO Data Object.
4. Give the steps to include ADO Data Control in VB Toolbox.
5. Give the steps for associating each text box to the fields of MS Access 2007 table.

LAB WORK

Create the table 'Teacher' in MS Access 2007.

Teacher Code	Autonumber
Name	Text
Dept	Text
Salary	Currency
Date of Birth	Date
Date of Joining	Date
Qualification	Text

Create a VB form to connect all text boxes with the fields of the table. Make a MDI form to open the above form in it. Create data navigation command buttons to move between the records.

TEACHER'S NOTES

1. Tell the students about different applications that can be connected to Visual Basic.
2. Explore the components dialog box in class. Explain the various components present there.

11 Elementary C++

SNAP RECAP

1. Operators in C++ are used to calculate and compare values and test conditions. There are three types of operators in C++: Unary, Binary and Ternary
2. Arithmetic, Relational and Logical operators are some of the commonly used operators in C++

LEARNING OBJECTIVES

You will learn about:

1. use of Unary, Binary and Ternary operators
2. Arithmetic Assignment operators
3. operators precedence
4. types of conditional statements in C++: if… else and switch… case

Introduction

In the previous lesson, you learnt about various category of operators present in C++. In this chapter, you will learn about arithmetic assignment operators and operator precedence.

Almost every correct statement in C language is correct in C++ also but the vice versa does not hold true.

Operators in C++

Symbols used to evaluate an expression, that is, to perform a calculation are called operators. Based on the number of operands, operators are classified as follows.

1. Unary operators
2. Binary operators
3. Ternary operators

Unary Operator

Unary operators work on a single operand. The three types of unary operators are given in Table 11.1.

Table 11.1 *Unary Operators in C++*

Operator	Meaning	Usage	Evaluation	Output (if int x=10)
++	It is the increment operator	X++	X=X+1	11
--	It is the decrement operator	X--	X=X-1	9
!	It is the Logical NOT operator	!(X)	!(X==5)	True

FACT FILE

The increment and decrement operator can be used in two way: as a prefix or as a postfix to a variable.

Binary Operators

Binary Operators work on two operands. They fall under the following three categories (Table 11.2).

Table 11.2 *Binary Operators in C++*

Operator	Usage
Arithmetic Operators	Used to do arithmetic calculations
Relational Operators	Used to compare two values/variables
Logical Operators	Used to combine two conditions

Ternary Operators

Ternary operators work on three operands. Ternary operators are like a conditional statement.

The syntax of ternary operator is as follows:

(condition) ? (if_true) : (if_false)

FACT FILE

The modulus operator works only with int operands.

For example,

int x=15;

int y=(x==15)? 10:20;   //here it means if x is equal to 15 then y will be assigned 10 otherwise 20

cout<<(x<=10)?"Good":"Not so good";

Arithmetic Assignment Operators

You can use assignment operator (=) to assign the value of the right operand to the left operand. An arithmetic assignment operator combines an arithmetic operator and an assignment operator. The arithmetic assignment operators present in C++ are: += , -=, *= , /= , %= . Table 11.3 shows different arithmetic assignment operators:

Table 11.3 *Different arithmetic assignment operators*

Operator	Description	Example	Explanation
+=	It adds the operands and assigns the result value to the left operand	x+= y	x= x+ y
-=	It subtracts the right operand from the left operand and stores the result in left operand	x-= y	x=x-y
*=	It multiplies the operand and stores the result in the left operand	x*= y	x=x*y
/=	It divides the left operand by the right operand and stores the result in the left operand	x/=y	x=x/y
%=	It divides the left operand by the right operand and stores the remainder in the left operand	x%=y	x= remainder of x/y

Operator Precedence

The operator precedence specifies the order in which the operator will be executed in an expression. If there are two operators with same precedence, evaluation is done from left to right. Table 11.4 specifies the precedence of different operators in C++.

Table 11.4 *Order of precedence of operators in C++*

Precendence	Operator
Brackets	[ ], ( )
Unary Operators	++,- -,!
Arithmetic Operators	*,/,%
Arithmetic Operators	+,-
Insertion/ Extraction Operator	<<, >>

Relational Operators	<, >, <=, >=
Relational Operators	==, !=
Assignment Operators	=

Conditional Constructs

Decision making can be incorporated in programs, the result of which determines the sequence of execution of the program. You can use conditional constructs to control the flow of execution of a program. Conditional constructs help us to execute a set of statements based on a condition. There are two conditional constructs present in C++.

1. if…else construct
2. switch…case construct

The if . . .else construct

In this, the if conditional construct is followed by a logical expression where the variables are compared and a decision is made.

Syntax:
```
if(condition)
{
statement 1;
}
else
{
statement 2;
}
```

For example:
```
if(a>b)
{
cout<<"a is greater than b";
}
else
{
cout<<"b is greater than a";
}
```

Nested if. . .else/ if. . .else ladder

In nested if. . .else construct, there is an if. . .else construct inside another. For every if statement there is a else statement followed by a pair of curly braces. For example,

```
if(condition1)
{
statement 1;
}
else if(condition2)
{
statement 2;
}
else
{
statement 3;
}
```

OR

```
if(condition1)
if(condition2)
.
.
if(condition3)
{
statement 1;
}
else
{
statement 2;
.
.
```

```
                    .
                    }
                else
                {
                    statement 3;
                }
                else
                {
                    statement 4;
                }
```

Note: If there is only one statement associated with a case, then the curly braces are optional.

The switch...case construct

In a switch...case construct the value of the switch variable is compared against a set of constant values. Wherever a match is found, the statements associated with that particular case are executed. If the value of the switch variable does not match any of the case constants, then the default case is executed.

Syntax:

```
    switch(switch variable)
    {
    case <constant1>: statement1;
         .
         .
         .
         statement n;
         break;
    case <constant2>: statement1;
         .
         .
         .
         statement n;
         break;
         .
         .
         .
      case <constantn>: statement1;
         .
         .
         .
         statement n;
         break;
         .
         .
         .
         default : statement1;
         .
         .
         .
         statement n;
    }
```

where,

break statement: The break keyword causes the entire switch statement to exit, and the control is passed to statement following the switch…case construct. Without break, the control passes to the statements for the next case.

 The break statement is optional in the switch…case construct.

case: This keyword gives the switch…case construct a way to take an action if the value of the switch variable does not match with any of the case constants. No break statement is necessary after default case, since the control is already at the end of switch…case construct. The default case is optional in the switch…case construct.

For example,

```
switch(choice)
{
case 1: cout<<"Sum=";
    cout<<a+b<<endl;
    break;
case 2: cout<<"Difference=";
    cout<<a-b<<endl;
    break;
case 3: cout<<"Product=";
    cout<<a*b<<endl;
    break;
case 4: cout<<"Quotient=";
    cout<<a/b<<endl;
    break;
case 5: cout<<"Remainder=";
    cout<<a%b<<endl;
    break;
default: cout<<"invalid choice";
}
```

Some solved examples

Accept a number from the user and check if it is an odd or even number

```
#include<iostream.h>
#include<conio.h>
void main()
{
clrscr();
int x;
```

```
cout<<"Enter a number";
cin>>x;
if(x%2==0)      //checks for remainder is 0
cout<<"Even Number";
else
cout<<"Odd number";
}
```

Accept an alphanumeric value from the user and check if it is in upper case or lower case

```
#include<iostream.h>
#include<conio.h>
void main()
{
clrscr();
char alpha;
cout<<"Enter an alphabet";
cin>>alpha;
if(alpha>='a' && alpha<='z')
cout<< "Alphabet in Lower case";
else if(alpha>='A' && alpha<='Z')
cout<<"Alphabet in Upper case";
}
```

Accept marks of a student in 5 subjects. Calculate the student's percentage and print a grade according to the following criteria

Percentage	Grade
90 and above	A
80 – 89	B
70 – 79	C
60 – 69	D
50 – 59	E
Less than 50	F

```
#include<iostream.h>
#include<conio.h>
void main()
{
int m1,m2,m3,m4,m5,per;
char grade;
cout<<"Enter marks in five subjects :"<<endl;
cin>>m1>>m2>>m3>>m4>>m5;
per = (m1+m2+m3+m4+m5)/500 * 100;
if(per>=90)
    grade='A';
else if(per>=80)
    grade='B';
else if(per>=70)
    grade='C';
else if(per>=60)
    grade='D';
else if(per>=50)
    grade='E';
else
    grade='F';
cout<<"Your grade is:"<<grade;
}
```

ACTIVITY

A. Accept a number from the user and check if it is positive or a negative number.
B. Accept an alphanumeric value from the user and check if it is a character or a digit.
C. Accept a number from a user and check if it is a multiple of 7 or not.
D. Accept an alphanumeric value from the user and check if it is a capital letter, then convert into small letter and if it is a small letter then convert it into capital letter.
E. Accept a character from the user and check if it is a vowel or a consonant.

GLOSSARY

Unary operators: They work on a single operand. Increment, Decrement and Not operators are examples of unary operators.

Binary operators: They work on two operands. Arithmetic, Relational and Logical operators are examples of Binary operators.

Ternary Operators: They work on three operand. They are like a conditional statement.

NOW YOU KNOW

1. Operator precedence means the order in which the operator will be executed in an expression.
2. There are two conditional contracts present in C++ if…else construct and switch…case construct.

EXERCISE

A Fill in the blanks.

1. The ……………………. operator works like a conditional statement.
2. An expression a+=5 is equivalent of …………………….
3. If there are two operators with same precedence, evaluation is done from ……………………. .
4. ……………………. and ……………………. are examples of conditional constructs.
5. ……………………. is an optional statement in switch case construct.

B Correct the errors in the following code : HOTS

```
# include <iostream>
void main()
{
clrscr;
intnum
cout<<Enter a number;
cin>>Num;
if num>100
cout<<Big number;
}
```

C Rewrite the following set of statements in terms of if…else statements: HOTS

```
switch(code)
{
case 'A':   cout<<"Accountant";
```

```
        break;
    case 'C':
    case 'G':   cout<<"Grade IV";
        break;
    default:    cout<<"Financial Advisor";
    }
```

D **Answer the following questions.**

1. What is the effect of the absence of break in a switch…case construct?
2. What is arithmetic assignment operator? Explain with the help of an example.
3. Differentiate between unary increment operator and unary decrement operator.
4. Explain the usage of ternary operator with the help of an example.
5. What is the need of operator precedence?

LAB WORK

1. Accept the class of travel as well as number of kilometres travelled to calculate the total fare. The details for calculation are:

Class	First 100 km	Next 150 km	Next 250 km	Rest
1	100	75	60	50
2	75	50	40	40
3	50	25	20	30

2. Accept the units of electricity consumed from the user and calculate the amount payable as per the following criteria:

Units	Charge per unit
First 100 units	Rs 1.20
Next 150 units	Rs 2.00
Next 150 units	Rs 2.50
Above this	Rs 3.00

TEACHER'S NOTES

1. Tell the students about similarities and differences between conditional construct/statements in Visual Basic and C++.

12 Elementary JAVA

LEARNING OBJECTIVES

You will learn about:
1. variables
2. declaration and initialization of a variable
3. data types – primitive and non-primitive
4. different types of operators
5. programming structures – sequential, selection and repetition

Variables

An area in the computer's memory reserved for storing values of specific types like numbers, text, date, Boolean, etc. is known as a variable. This value once stored in a variable can be used by the program for different purpose.

Note: All variables must first be declared before they can be used in Java.

There are two steps to be followed before a variable can be used in programming.

Step 1: Variable Declaration

Declaring a variable means reserving a memory by a specific name of a specific data type. For example,

    int a,b,c;

    float marks;

    char name;

Step 2: Variable Initialization

Initializing a variable means assigning a valid value to it. For example,

    a=3, b=5;

    marks=45.5;

    name='y';

Variables in Java can be declared and initialized at the same time.

    int a=2, b=4;

    float marks=34.5

    double do=20.22d;

Rules for assigning name to a variable

- Variable can either begin with an alphabet, dollar sign ($) or an underscore (_).
- It cannot contain spaces in between.
- No special characters like @, #, %, ^, etc. are allowed in a variable name.

Data Types

Data type is defined as the type of data a variable can hold. Java supports two types of data types:

1. Primitive data type
2. Non-Primitive data type

Primitive data type

A primitive type is predefined by the language and is named by a reserved keyword. The eight primitive data types supported by the Java programming language are:

- *byte:* The byte data type is an 8-bit signed two's complement integer. It has a minimum value of – 128 and a maximum value of 127 (inclusive).
- *short:* The short data type is a 16-bit signed two's complement integer. It has a minimum value of – 32,768 and a maximum value of 32,767 (inclusive).
- *int:* The int data type is a 32-bit signed two's complement integer. It has a minimum value of –2,147,483,648 and a maximum value of 2,147,483,647 (inclusive).
- *long:* The long data type is a 64-bit signed two's complement integer. It has a minimum value of –9,223,372,036,854,775,808 and a maximum value of 9,223,372,036,854,775,807 (inclusive).
- *float:* The float data type is a single-precision 32-bit IEEE 754 floating point. Float is mainly used to save memory in large arrays of floating point numbers. It is never used where precision is required to be more accurate.
- *double:* The double data type is a double-precision 64-bit IEEE 754 floating point. It is generally used as the default data type for decimal values. It is also never used where precision is required to be more accurate.
- *boolean:* The boolean data type has only two possible values: True or False.

- *char:* The char data type is a single 16-bit Unicode character. It has a minimum value of '\u0000' (or 0) and a maximum value of '\uffff' (or 65,535 inclusive). It is used to store single character.

Non-primitive Data type

Non-primitives are **reference-types**. These include objects and arrays which are defined in the program. The value assigned to variables of reference-type will either be a reference to an object (instance of a class) or null. A null value, meaning it does not currently refer to any instance in memory. For example, java.lang.String is a non-primitive data type and can be used to store string by creating an object of it. String objects once created cannot change their values.

Operators in Java

There are number of operators in Java. Following is the list of operators available in Java.

Arithmetic operators

These operators are used to perform arithmetic operations. Table 12.1 lists the arithmetic operators present in Java.

Let us assume int a=20, b=10;

Operator	Usage	Example	Output (if a = 20 & b = 10)
+	It adds the two operands	a+b	30
–	It subtracts the two operands	a–b	10
*	It multiplies the two operands	a*b	200
/	It divides the two operands	a/b	2
%	It gives the remainder of the division(modulus operator)	a%b	0

Assignment Operator

It is used to assign a value to a variable lying to the left side of the assignment operator. But, if the value already exists in that variable then it will be overwritten by the assignment operator (=). This operator can also be used to assign the references to the objects. For example,

    int x=5;
    String name="abc";
    booleanans=true

You can also assign a value to the more than one variable simultaneously. For example:

    a=b=c=10;
    a=b+c;

Compound Assignment operator

These operators perform shortcuts in common programming operations. For example,

Operator	Usage	Example	Output (if a = 20 & b = 10)
+=	It adds right operand to the left operand and assign the result to left operand	a += b means a=a+b	a=30
–=	It subtracts right operand from the left operand and assign the result to left operand	a –= b means a=a–b	a=10
*=	It multiplies right operand with the left operand and assign the result to left operand	a *= b means a=a*b	a=200
/=	It divides left operand with the right operand and assign the result to left operand	a /= b means a=a/b	a=10
%=	It takes the remainder using two operands and assign the result to left operand	a %= b means a=a%b	a=0

Unary Operators

These operators operate on only one operand. Like increment (++) operator and decrement (––) operator. They can either be used before a variable(prefix) or after a variable(postfix).

For example,

   int a=10;

   b=++a

Here, b=11, a=11; the value of 'a' is increased before it is assigned to 'b'. It works as prefix unary operator.

   b=a++

Here, b=10, a=11; the value of 'a' is first assigned to 'b' and then incremented. It works as postfix unary operator.

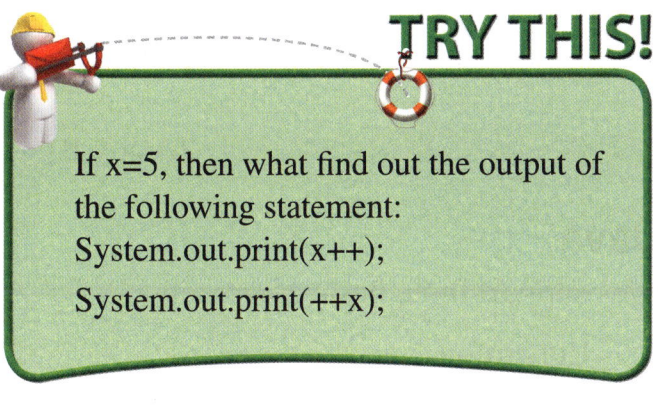

TRY THIS!

If x=5, then what find out the output of the following statement:
System.out.print(x++);
System.out.print(++x);

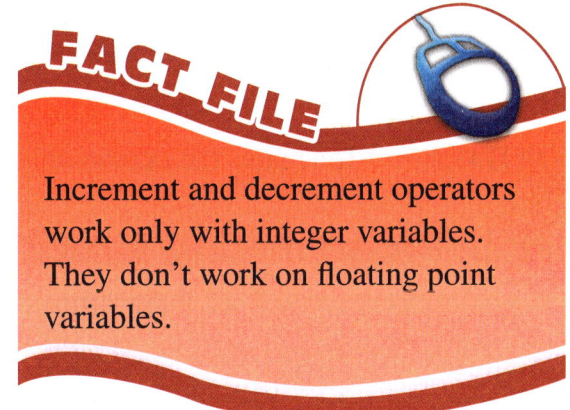

FACT FILE

Increment and decrement operators work only with integer variables. They don't work on floating point variables.

Relational Operators

They compare two values and return the logical value as True or False

Operator	Usage	Example	Output (if a = 20 & b = 10)
==	Checks if the value of two operands are equal or not, if yes then condition becomes True	(A == B)	False
!=	Checks if the value of two operands are equal or not, if values are not equal then condition becomes True	(A != B)	True
>	Checks if the value of left operand is greater than the value of right operand, if yes then condition becomes True	(A > B)	True
<	Checks if the value of left operand is less than the value of right operand, if yes then condition becomes True	(A < B)	False
>=	Checks if the value of left operand is greater than or equal to the value of right operand, if yes then condition becomes True	(A >= B)	True
<=	Checks if the value of left operand is less than or equal to the value of right operand, if yes then condition becomes True	(A <= B)	False

Logical operators

They are used when a decision is required to be taken based on multiple conditions.

Operator	Usage	Example
&& (AND)	If both the operands/expression are True, then it returns True	(A && B)
|| (OR)	If any of the two operands/expression is True, then it returns True	(A || B)
! (NOT)	It negates the condition	!(A && B)

Simple Programming structure in Java

As we have done earlier, all programming languages support three basic constructs :
- Sequential
- Selection
- Repetition

Sequential Programming

Any program that executes the instructions one by one in a specific order then it follows the sequential programming construct. For example, accept two numbers (Fig. 12.1) and print the sum (Fig. 12.2).

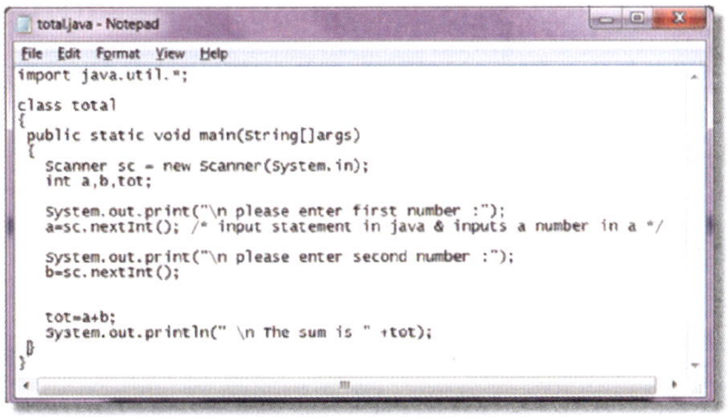

```
total.java - Notepad
File Edit Format View Help
import java.util.*;

class total
{
 public static void main(String[]args)
 {
   Scanner sc = new Scanner(System.in);
   int a,b,tot;

   System.out.print("\n please enter first number :");
   a=sc.nextInt(); /* input statement in java & inputs a number in a */

   System.out.print("\n please enter second number :");
   b=sc.nextInt();


   tot=a+b;
   System.out.println(" \n The sum is " +tot);
 }
}
```

Fig. 12.1 *Input*

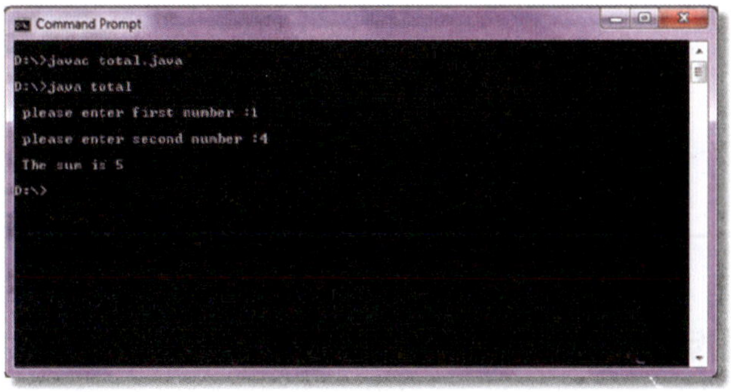

```
Command Prompt
D:\>javac total.java
D:\>java total
 please enter first number :1
 please enter second number :4
 The sum is 5
D:\>
```

Fig. 12.2 *Output*

ACTIVITY

A. **Accept a name from the user and print a welcome message.**
B. **Accept marks of two subject and print the percentage.**
C. **Accept first name and last name and print the full name.**

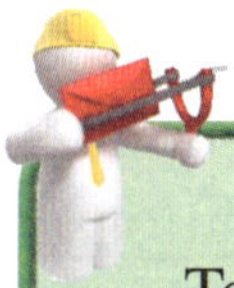

TRY THIS!

To accept string value use sc.nextLine();

To accept float value use sc.nextFloat();

Selection Programming

It means the flow of execution in a program depends upon a condition. Based on the condition, the decision is taken. For example, the if. . .else construct:

```
if (condition)
{
True statements
}
else
{
False statement
}
```

For example, to accept two numbers and print the largest of two numbers, the input (Fig. 12.3) and the output (Fig. 12.4) are given.

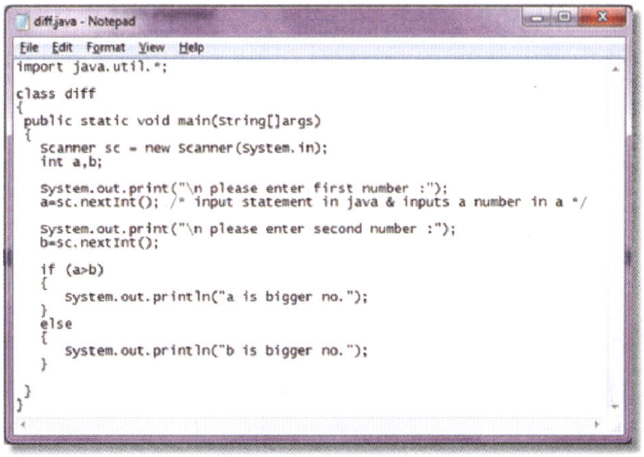

```
diff.java - Notepad
File Edit Format View Help
import java.util.*;

class diff
{
 public static void main(String[]args)
 {
   Scanner sc = new Scanner(System.in);
   int a,b;

   System.out.print("\n please enter first number :");
   a=sc.nextInt(); /* input statement in java & inputs a number in a */

   System.out.print("\n please enter second number :");
   b=sc.nextInt();

   if (a>b)
   {
      System.out.println("a is bigger no.");
   }
   else
   {
      System.out.println("b is bigger no.");
   }

 }
}
```

Fig. 12.3 *Input*

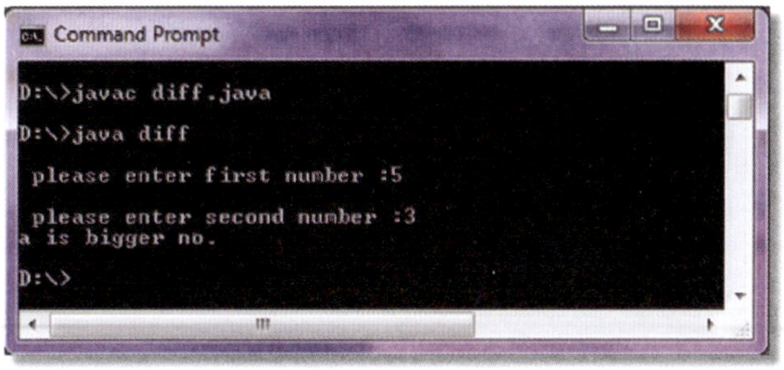

```
Command Prompt
D:\>javac diff.java
D:\>java diff
 please enter first number :5
 please enter second number :3
a is bigger no.
D:\>
```

Fig. 12.4 *Output*

ACTIVITY

A. Accept a number and find out whether it is divisible by 5 or not.
B. Accept a number and print whether it is even or odd.
C. Accept three numbers and print the smallest of all.

TRY THIS!

We can also use **switch… case** for conditional programming.

Repetition Programming

Any block of statement that repeats itself based on a condition is known as repetition. This repetition works in a loop so it is also known as looping construct. Java supports various types of looping.

Using while loop: The while loop allows the programs to repeat a block of statements, till the test condition is True. The test condition is checked first. If the condition is True, then it executes the block of statement. After executing the statement, the condition is checked again. As long as the condition is True, it will keep executing the block of statement. When the condition becomes False, it exits the loop.

It is also known as **entry controlled loop** as the condition is pre-tested and then the block of statement is executed. The syntax is :

while(test condition)
{
block of statements;
}

For example, to print natural numbers from 1 to 5 the input (Fig. 12.5) and the output (Fig. 12.6) are given below.

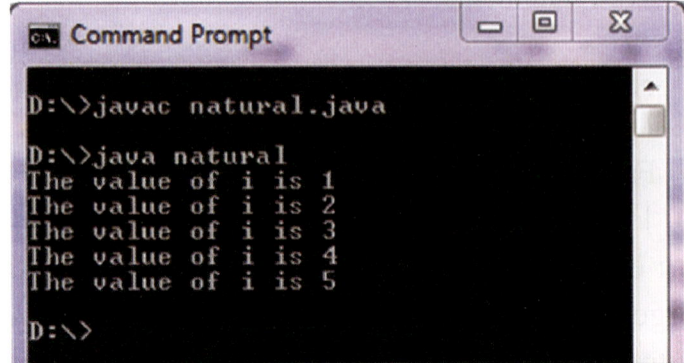

Fig. 12.5 *Input*   Fig. 12.6 *Output*

Using do...while loop: It work just like while loop except that the condition is evaluated at the end. That is why it is also known as **exit controlled loop** where the condition is post-tested. The syntax is:

    do
    {
    block of statements;
    }
    while(test condition)

For example, to print even numbers from 2 to 10, the input (Fig. 12.7) and the output (Fig. 12.8) is given.

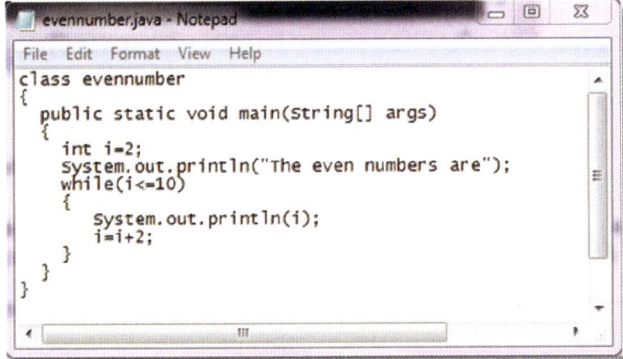

Fig. 12.7 *Input*

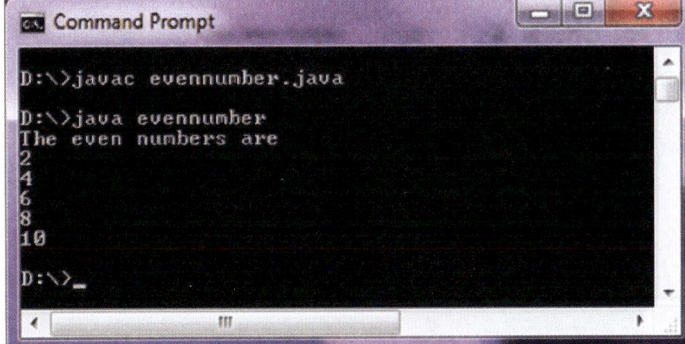

Fig. 12.8 *Output*

Using for loop: The for statement is used to repeat a block of statement a fixed number of times. The syntax is

    for (start ; condition ; step value)

where,

start specifies starting point for the counter variable. It is executed once, as the loop begins
condition specifies the number of times the loop will execute. When the condition evaluates to False, the loop stops.
step value increment/decrement the counter variable to keep the loop running for specific number of times. It is invoked after every iteration.

For example, to print numbers 1 to 10 in reverse order, the input (Fig. 12.9) and output (Fig. 12.10) are given.

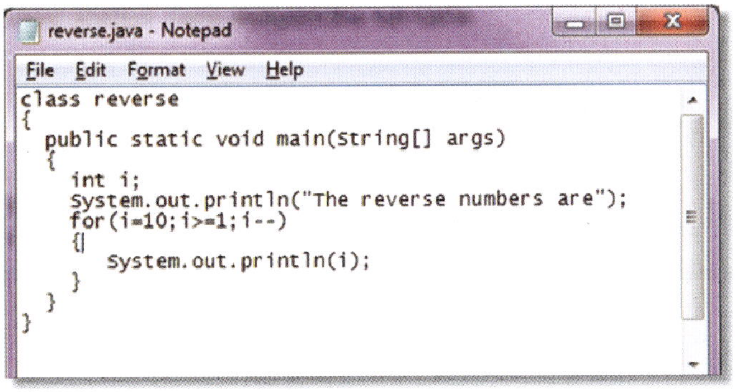

Fig. 12.9 *Input* 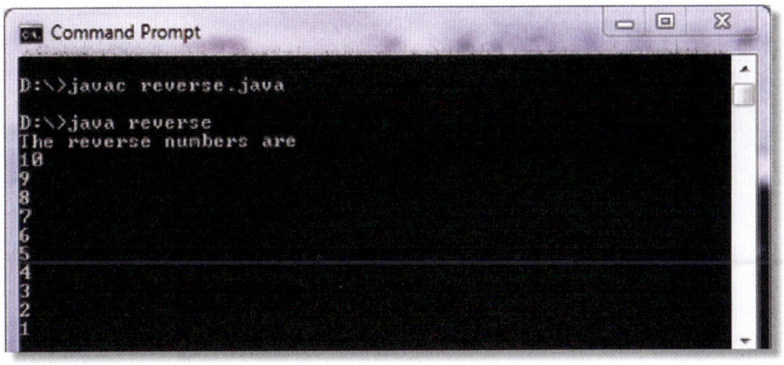   **Fig. 12.10** *Output*

ACTIVITY

A. Print odd numbers from 1 to 10.

B. Print the square of multiples of 3.

GLOSSARY

Non-primitive data types: They are reference-type data types and include objects and arrays which are defined in the program.

Primitive data types: They are predefined by the language and are named by a reserved keyword.

Repetition Programming: It means the flow of execution works in a loop, that is, any block of statement is repeated till the condition is true.

Selection Programming: It means the flow of execution in a program depends upon a condition.

Sequential Programming: It means the flow of execution is in a specific order and statements are executed one-by-one.

NOW YOU KNOW

1. Variables are named memory locations used for storing a value that needs to be declared and initialized.
2. There are two types of data type: Primitive and Non-Primitive.
3. Addition, subtraction, multiplication, division and remainder are arithmetic operators in Java.
4. Relational operators are used to compare two values or variables.
5. Logical operators are used when a decision is required to be taken.
6. Java supports three basic constructs: Sequential, Selection and Repetition.

EXERCISE

A. Fill in the blanks.

1. ……………… is the area reserved in a computer's memory.
2. Initializing a variable means ……………… .
3. A variable name can begin with an ……………… or a ……………… .

4. The two types of data types are .... and ....
5. Int is a .... data type.

B **Find out which of the following variable names are valid and which are invalid. Also give reasons.**

1. address
2. 6phone
3. Formal school
4. Mynumber
5. &User id

C **Answer the following questions.**

1. Explain in short the 8 primitive data types in Java.
2. What are the rules for creating variables in Java?
3. What are two different steps before we use a variable in Java?
4. Explain if construct with example.
5. Differentiate between while and do while with example.

LAB WORK

A. Accept the marks from the user and find out whether he is fail or pass.
B. Accept a number and generate the table of a number.
C. Print the sum of 1 to 5 natural numbers.
D. Print the count of even and odd numbers entered by the user. Let the total number entered are 10.
E. Accept a number from 1 to 7 and display the name of the week in words.

TEACHER'S NOTES

1. Give the students as many examples of looping as possible.
2. Tell the students the usage of break and continue statements in looping.

13 Virus and Anti-Virus

LEARNING OBJECTIVES

You will learn about:
1. computer virus
2. what a virus cannot do
3. how do computer virus spread
4. symptoms of computer virus
5. types of computer virus
6. other harmful programs
7. how to protect your computer from virus
8. anti-virus software

Computer Virus

A computer virus is a destructive software program. All computer viruses are man-made. These can spread from one computer to another through disks, networks, email links, etc. A computer virus may corrupt or delete data on a computer. It may even delete everything on the hard disk, and can interfere with computer operations.

The term VIRUS stands for Vital Information Resources Under Seize.

Some viruses remain active even when you shut down the computer while some become active only when the infected program or application is executed, or you have started your computer from a disk that has infected system files. Once a virus is active, it loads onto the computer's memory and is saved there. It then replicates (makes copies of itself) in your hard drive or applications or system files on the disks you use.

Some viruses are programmed specifically to damage the data on your computer. Many viruses are not very harmful as they only display a message, or produce sound when active. Other viruses make your computer system behave erratically, corrupt programs, delete files or crash the computer system frequently.

It is interesting to know how the computer virus got this name. Let us draw an analogy between computer and biological virus:

- A biological virus destroys the cells of the body, likewise a computer virus is a program that is secretly put onto a computer in order to destroy the information that is stored in it.
- Like a biological virus, it can form multiple copies of itself inside another computer. It needs some other program or document in order to launch. Once it is running, it can infect other programs and documents.
- Like a biological virus, you do not realise the presence of a computer virus until your computer has already been affected.

 If your computer is not operating properly, it is a good practice to check for virus with a latest and updated virus checking program.

What a Virus Cannot Do

Look at the following to see when the computer system is not affected by a virus:

- Computer virus cannot infect write-protected discs (CD–ROMs) or infect written documents.
- Virus do not infect compressed files, unless the file was infected prior to compression.
- No virus can do a physical damage to computer hardware, such as chips, boards and monitors.
- In addition, Macintosh virus do not infect DOS/Window computer software and vice versa. For example, the Melissa virus of 1998 worked only on Windows based machines and could not operate on Macintosh computers.

FACT FILE

The Creeper was the first virus that was detected. It was detected on ARPANET, in the early 1970s.

How Does a Computer Virus Spread

Computer virus can spread in several ways. Few ways are explained here:

- A computer virus begins to work and spread whenever you start up the infected program or application. For example, any word processing application that contains the virus will place the virus in memory every time the program is run.
- Once the virus is copied onto the computer memory it may get programmed to attach to other applications, disks or folders. It may also infect a network.

- These viruses behave in different ways. Some stay active only till the infected application is running. They become inactive when the computer shuts down. Other viruses operate every time you start your computer after they have infected a system file or network.

FACT FILE

Before the easy accessibility of the Internet, virus were typically spread by infected floppy disks.

Symptoms of a Computer Virus

You can detect the presence of a virus in your computer. The following are some primary indicators that a computer may be infected:

- The computer runs slower than usual.
- The computer stops responding, or it locks up frequently.
- The computer crashes, and then it restarts every few minutes.
- Applications on the computer do not work correctly.
- Disks or disk drives are inaccessible.
- You see unusual error messages.
- You see distorted menus and dialog boxes.
- You cannot print items correctly.
- There is a double extension on an attachment that you recently opened, such as a .jpg, .gif or .exe extension.
- New icons appear on the desktop that you did not place there, or the icons are not associated with any recently installed programs.
- Strange sounds or music plays from the speakers unexpectedly.
- A program disappears from the computer even though you did not intentionally remove the program.

Types of Computer Viruses

Computer viruses are classified depending upon the infection methods. A few of them are discussed here.

Boot sector virus

Boot sector is that area of the computer that is accessed when the computer starts. A boot sector virus infects this part. This allows the virus to spread fast and cause damages. Once the boot sector is infected, the virus is loaded onto the memory when the computer starts. This virus then infects boot sectors on floppies or other removable media. Boot sector viruses have become less common as floppy disks have become rarer.

The best way of avoiding boot sector virus is to ensure that floppy disks are write-protected, and you never start your computer with an unknown floppy disk in the disk drive. A few examples of boot sector virus are Polyboot.B, Form, Disk Killer, Michelangelo and Stoned.

FACT FILE

The first PC virus was a boot sector virus named Brain, created in 1986 by the Farooq Alvi brothers.

Program Virus

The file infector virus infects files that contain executable codes like .exe, .com, .dll, .bin, .sys and many more files. Some file infectors are **memory resident**. This means that the virus will stay in memory, and continue to infect other programs. Other file infector viruses only infect the files when they are executed.

The file infector virus can cause irreversible damage to the files. By overwriting the files, it permanently destroys the content of these files. Some file viruses operate as email Worm virus and Trojan horse as well. You will learn about these later.

The only way to disinfect files from the file virus is to ensure that the files affected with the virus are deleted and restored if they have been taken from the back up.

Examples of known file infector virus include Jerusalem and Cascade.

Macro computer virus

Macro is a set of commands written by the user to be executed later. Macros can be created in several application software like Word, Excel, Visual Basic, Access, etc. This virus infects the macro files and whenever any macro is executed they show their effect by altering the macro code.

The existence of the **autoexec macro** makes it possible to create many macro viruses. The **autoexec** macro is executed in response to some event, and does not depend on the user command. Other existing macro viruses are those which replace command names like Save, Open, etc. with their code. Unlike the auto macros which can be disabled, commands cannot be disabled. Once the macro virus uses these commands, it can copy itself to other files and even delete those files.

The auto macros are disabled if you use the **DisableAutoMacros** command in any macro that is written. It can also be disabled by holding down the Shift key while opening a document.

A word document cannot contain macros, only word templates can. You can mask a template as a document file to prevent it from infection.

Examples of macro virus include W97M.Melissa, WM.NiceDay and W97M.Groov.

Multipartite virus

Some computer viruses appear to behave like many other viruses and sometimes more than one type. These are **hybrids** and are called as multipartite computer virus.

Multipartite virus infects both boot records and program files. These are particularly difficult to repair. If the boot area has been sanitised but not the files, the infection would recur in the boot area. The same holds true for sanitising the program files. If the virus has not been removed from the boot area, any file that you have sanitised will be infected again.

Examples of multipartite virus include One_Half, Emperor, Anthrax and Tequilla.

Polymorphic virus

Polymorphic viruses are written in such a way that they change their code whenever they pass to another machine. Polymorphic viruses infect the computer with encrypted copies of it. Thus, making it difficult for an anti-virus scanner to locate them. Flaws in the program code make it easy to track down this virus.

FACT FILE

Any destructive program written for causing damage to the computer and the network is also known as malware. Virus, worms, Trojan horse, etc. are all examples of malware.

Other harmful programs

Malware stands for **Malicious Software**. It is used or programmed to infiltrate a computer, gather secret information and disrupts its functioning. Malware includes Virus, Worms, Trojan Horses, etc.

Worms

Computer worms are destructive software programs designed to spread through computer networks. Anyone can install the worm inadvertently by opening an email attachment or message that contains executable scripts.

A virus is dependent upon the host file or boot sector, and transfer of files between computers to spread. On the other hand, a computer worm can execute independently and spread on its own through network connections. They replicate themselves from system to system without the use of a host file, and can lead to negative effects on your system. Unlike computer virus, worms do not corrupt files and folders.

Being embedded inside everyday network software, computer worms easily penetrate most firewalls and other network security measures. Due to their high replication rate, worms consume a large part of the system memory and network bandwidth. This in turn leads to a significant slowdown in the speed of web servers, network servers and individual computer.

You might have heard of specific computer worms, like Sasser worm, the Blaster worm and the Conficker worm.

Trojan Horses

Trojan horses are harmful programs that unlike virus do not reproduce by infecting other files, nor do they self-replicate like worms. They claim to be something desirable. Trojan horses contain malicious code. The code when triggered causes loss or even theft of data. Trojan horse spreads when you open an email attachment or download and run a file from the Internet.

The name of the virus comes from Greek mythology. It is based on Trojan War where the Greeks fooled the Trojan by presenting a horse (wooden) as gesture of goodwill. But this horse actually brought the downfall of Troy. Similarly, the code pretends to be friendly but actually the harmful code is presents inside apparently harmless programming. It acts in such a way that it can get control and do its chosen form of damage, such as ruining the file allocation table on your hard disk.

Trojan.Vundo is a very common example of Trojan horse.

Logic Bombs

A logic bomb is a destructive program which lies dormant until a specific piece of program logic is activated. They are different from viruses as they do not replicate. They are not even programs in their own right but rather camouflaged segments of other programs.
In some ways, a logic bomb is the most civilised programmed threat, because a logic bomb must be targeted against a specific victim. Their objective is to destroy data on the computer once certain conditions have been met.

Spyware

Spyware is a software that secretly gathers information about a person or an organization without their knowledge. It passes on this information to advertisers or third parties.

Spyware can be installed when a user downloads something from the Internet or clicks on something leading to a pop-up window opening up. It uses a lot of the computer memory and in turn makes it slow. It also steals the personal information of the user and sends it to its source.

Adware and tracking cookies are examples of spyware.

ACTIVITY

Who Am I?

1. I can infect files that contain executable codes.
2. I know how to be like many other viruses and I am a hybrid virus.
   I can infect both boot records and program files.
3. I am a destructive software program designed to spread through computer networks.
4. My name resembles an animal.
   I contain malicious codes.
   I aim at causing loss, or even theft of data.

Protection Against Computer Viruses
Using an anti-virus software

Anti-virus software is used to prevent, detect, and remove destructive programs, including computer viruses, worms, and Trojan horses. To help prevent the most current virus, you must update your anti-virus software regularly. You can set up most types of anti-virus software to update automatically. These software's can also be set to automatically scan diskettes when inserted into the disk drive, scan files when downloaded from the Internet, or scan emails when received.

The advent of anti-virus programs spelled a death blow to many common types of computer virus those were written by the various tools to generate types of computer virus. Some anti-virus software can be availed for free and some have to be bought. Some anti-virus vendors maintain websites with free online scanning capability of the entire computer or for critical areas like, local disks, folders or files only.

Independent testing on all the major virus scanners consistently shows that none provide 100 percent virus detection.

Some of the famous anti-virus software are Norton, McAfee Virus Scan, Panda, PC Tools, Quick Heal, etc.

General steps to run and update an anti-virus

You can get your system installed with a good anti-virus software. To run the scan, you generally follow the steps given below:

1. Open the Anti-virus program's main window. Initiate virus scan by clicking on the scan options.
2. Once the scanning is complete, you get a detailed list of viruses in your system and the infected files. You will be asked to repair, delete or quarantine the infected file.
   a. *To repair:* It eliminates the virus and repairs the infected file.
   b. *Delete option:* It removes or erases the virus and the infected file completely from the system.
   c. *Quarantine option:* It can be used when you are not sure of the virus present on the file. In this way, you can separate the infected file from the non-infected files.

The more the number of viruses are known to the anti-virus database, the easier it becomes to detect them on your system. For this, it is important to keep the anti-virus you use updated. To update the anti-virus, you may follow the steps given here:

1. Connect to the Internet.
2. Click on the available update options. Wait till it progresses.
3. Restart your computer.

You can also protect your computer from a virus by keeping the following points in mind:

1. Load a software from original disks or CDs. Pirated or copied software always comes with a risk of a virus.
2. Do not open email attachments if you do not recognise the sender (though you may also receive virus from people you know). Scan the attachments with anti-virus software before opening or saving them.
3. Computer uploads and changes in the System Configuration should always be performed by the person who is responsible for the computer. Password protection should be employed.
4. Download files only from reputed Internet sites, and be a little judicious while exchanging diskettes or other media with friends.
5. Purchase an anti-virus program that runs as you boot or work on its own on your computer. Update it frequently.
6. Install a **firewall** on your system. It is a security system that can protect software or hardware or both. It monitors the movement of information both in and out when turned on.

GLOSSARY

Anti-virus software: It is a software used to prevent, detect and remove destructive programs.
Boot sector: It is the area of the computer that is accessed when the computer starts.
Boot sector virus: It is the virus that infects the boot sector.
Firewall: It is a security system that protects hardware or software or both.
Logic bomb: It is a destructive program that lies dormant until the target program logic is activated.
Macro computer virus: It infects the macro files.
Multipartite virus: It infects both boot records and program files.
Trojan horses: It is a harmful program containing malicious codes.
Worms: It is a destructive software programs designed to spread through computer networks.

NOW YOU KNOW

1. A computer virus may corrupt or delete data on a computer.
2. A virus is inactive until you have executed an infected program or application.
3. A computer virus acts in a destructive manner like a biological virus.
4. Computer virus cannot infect write-protected discs.
5. Virus cannot do a physical damage to computer hardware.
6. Computer virus can spread in several ways.
7. Some common types of computer virus: Boot sector virus, Macro computer Virus, Multipartite virus, Polymorphic virus.
8. Do not open email attachments if you do not recognise the sender.

EXERCISE

A Fill in the blanks.

1. ………………………. is a destructive software program.
2. The virus does not infect …………………. and damage …………………. .
3. …………………. is that area of the computer that is accessed when the computer starts.
4. ……………… virus infects files that contain executable code like .exe, .com, .dll, etc.
5. ……………………. destructive software program designed to spread through computer networks.

B **Fill in the blank with the correct option.**

1. Computer virus are similar to biological virus because...............................
   a. medicines are effective against them
   b. they spread when you come in contact with an infected computer
   c. they are very dangerous for us
   d. they pass from computer to computer

2. Melissa virus can infect only... .
   a. Windows based machine
   b. DOS based machine
   c. Windows as well as DOS based machine
   d. Macintosh machine

3. Disk Killer is an example of ....
   a. Boot sector virus
   b. Macro virus
   c. Multipartite virus
   d. Polymorphic virus

4. Software that prevents, detects, and removes destructive program is ....
   a. Worm
   b. Trojan horse
   c. Virus
   d. Anti-virus

5. One_Half and Emperor are the examples of ....
   a. Boot sector virus
   b. Macro virus
   c. Multipartite virus
   d. Polymorphic virus

C. Give the difference between:

1. Virus and Anti-virus
2. Multipartite virus and Polymorphic virus
3. Computer virus and Biological virus
4. Worms and Trojan horse
5. Virus and Logic bombs

D. Answer the following questions.

1. What is a computer virus? Why are they named as virus?
2. List the damages that cannot be caused by viruses.
3. How does a virus spread? Explain in brief.
4. What are the symptoms of a computer virus?
5. How can you protect your computer from a virus?

LAB WORK

A. Make a list of the anti-virus software installed in your school lab.
B. Ask your teacher if there is a separate type of an anti-virus software installed for the server.
C. Check out the latest list of virus and the anti-virus software available on the Internet.
D. Note down the list of steps to scan the files on your system that your anti-virus software follows.

TEACHER'S NOTES

1. Tell the students about Stuxnet Viruses that attacked the software that controls industrial programs, thus causing real life damage.
2. Talk to the students about online virus protection.

14 Troubleshooting

LEARNING OBJECTIVES

You will learn about:
1. computer troubleshooting
2. importance of computer maintenance
3. areas to troubleshoot
4. steps of troubleshooting
5. some common problems and their troubleshooting

Introduction

As wonderful as computers can be, at times they can also be incredibly troublesome. Sometimes it is worth having a look to see if you can solve simple PC problems yourself before calling a technician. In this chapter, you will learn about a few simple tips on how you can avoid some of the most common problems that you face while working on computers.

Troubleshooting

Troubleshooting is the identification of trouble in a system caused by a failure of some kind. The problem is initially described as symptoms of malfunction, and troubleshooting is the process of determining the causes of these symptoms. You can also say that troubleshooting is a process of identifying a computer problem so that it can be fixed.

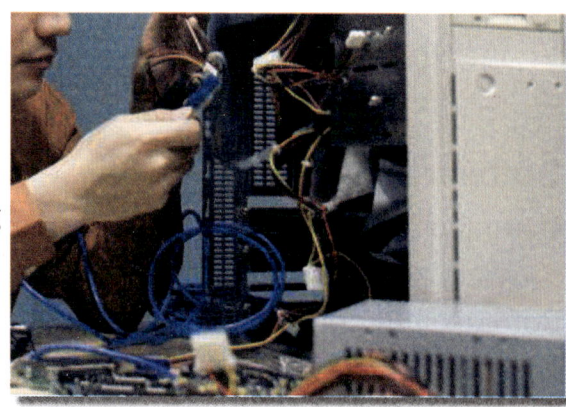

Some people use their instincts while others use advice from experts to get an idea about different types of troubleshooting. A few common steps are then followed to find out the problem in the computer. You can try these steps whenever you come across any problem in your computer. If these steps do not help you, then you can call an expert, that is, a computer engineer, to troubleshoot.

FACT FILE

The term **debug** is used when the problem is within the software program. The process of finding and reducing the number of bugs, or defects in a computer program is known as **debugging**.

Importance of Computer Maintenance

It is important to take proper care of your computer for the following reasons.

- It will increase the speed and the life of your PC.
- It prevents errors.
- It secures your data and information from any unwanted damages.
- Lastly, it saves you precious time.

Areas to Troubleshoot

There are three areas to troubleshoot. These are discussed here.

Hardware

Computer hardware is the physical part of a computer and it is not frequently changed or updated. Most computer hardware is in-built and cannot be seen by normal users. There are a large number of the computer hardware devices including hard disk, CD-ROM, RAM, motherboard, monitor, printer, and other peripheral devices. In order to identify the problem with your system hardware, you need to identify the type of the hardware first.

Some of the basic hardware problems that you may face are:

- Power failure in the computer.
- Device problem like keyboard, mouse, and printer not recognised.

Software

Computer software can be any program file or an application running on the computer. The software problems could be of any form such as unexplained crashes or strange error messages. Before calling up a software expert, you need to identify the problem.

Some of the basic software problems that you may face are:

- You are unable to install a program.
- Program or utility does not load. It has an error when you attempt to load it.
- The system crashes when you are working with a specific software.

FACT FILE

You can speed up your computer by increasing the system RAM, deleting the temporary files, running the **Disk Cleanup** utility and emptying the Recycle Bin.

Operating System

Probably the most frustrating problem computer users run into are startup problems where your computer fails to boot up properly.

Some of the commonly faced problems involving the operating system of a computer are:
- Windows restarts without warning.
- Windows starts in a safe mode.
- Windows stops responding.
- Windows slows down.
- Windows file do not boot.

Steps of Troubleshooting

Let us find out how you should handle any problem that crops up in your computer.

Step 1: Find out the problem

This is a very important step as it gives you an idea of just how frequently you face this problem. On the basis of your findings you can also decide if it needs attention. Once you are able to answer these two questions, you can think of troubleshooting your computer system.

Some of the common problems that you may face are:
- The system is not getting proper power supply.
- The system restarts on its own after a few minutes.
- Sometimes the system stops responding.
- System is running slow.
- Some flashy error message is displayed.
- Windows does not get loaded.

Step 2: Categorize your problem

Once you have figured out whether the problem is related to the hardware or the software, then half of the work is done.

For hardware related problems
- Check the power supply points.
- Check whether devices like keyboard, mouse, printer and system unit are connected properly.
- Ensure that during the startup process all the peripherals attached are recognised properly.

For software related problems
- Check the operating system files.
- Check the software files that are frequently used.
- The device drivers should be properly installed.

Step 3: Check the service manual

You have learnt to figure out the type of problem that your computer system may be facing. The service manuals contain instructions for troubleshooting and service information. Almost every computer and peripheral made today has a set of service documentation in the form of books, service CD-ROMs and websites. Websites are growing in popularity as more service centers get connections to the Internet. For example, if the computer is not able to recognise any device attached, like a printer, then take out the CD for the device driver installations. Insert it in your CD-ROM and install it.

Step 4: Back to its original state

When you troubleshoot, make one change at a time in the problem sector. If the change does not solve the problem, restore back to the original state. You must not make many alterations at a time as this may lead to more complications. Whenever changes are made with no results, then it is always advisable to undo the changes.

Step 5: Call an expert

If you feel that you will not be able to solve the problem in your computer then it is always advisable to call a technician. It ensures that you do not end up creating more complications rather than solving the problem.

Some Common Problems and Their Troubleshooting

The computer locks up

If the computer is frozen and does not respond to any commands then follow the steps given below:

1. Press **Ctrl + Alt + Del** (all three keys at the same time).
2. Click on the **Start Task Manager** option in the list (Fig. 14.1)

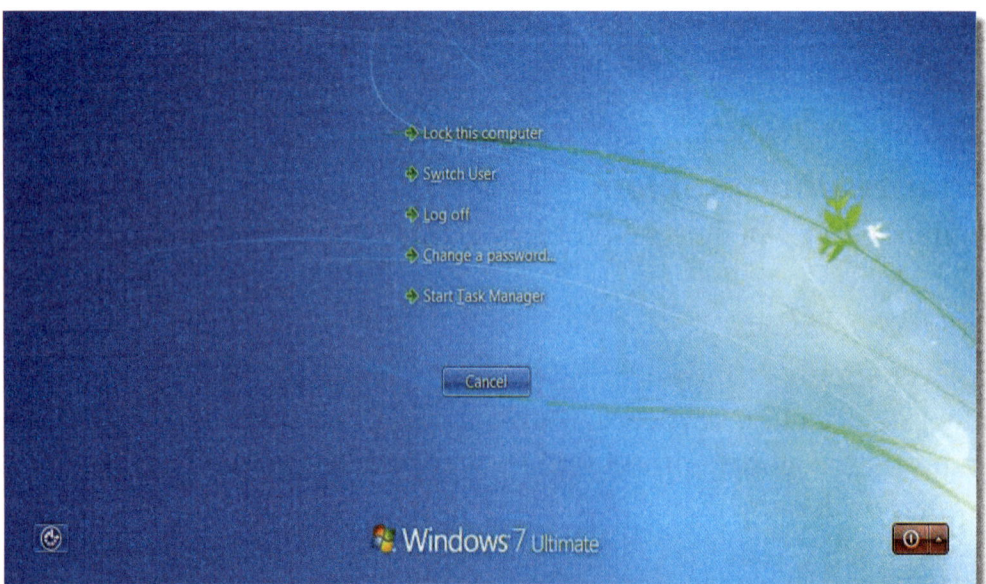

Fig. 14.1 *Start Task Manager*

3. The **Windows Task Manager** window displaying the **Task** list appears (Fig. 14.2).
4. Select any program that says 'Not responding' in the **Status** section.
5. Click on the **End Task** button. Repeat until all such tasks come to an end.

If this does not work, shut down the computer, wait for several seconds, turn the computer on and scan the disks, files and folders to check for any virus.

Error messages displayed on the monitor

If any error message is displayed on your monitor screen, you must **reboot** it, that is, restart your computer. A majority of problems that occur while you are using your computer can be fixed by rebooting.

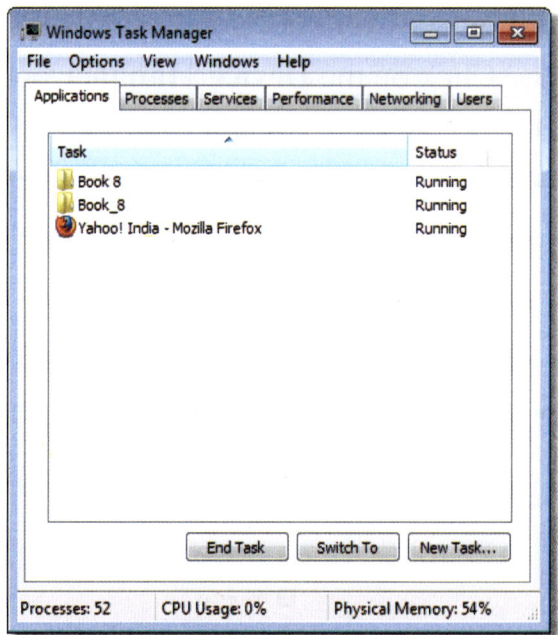

Fig. 14.2 *Windows Task Manager*

Applications sometimes do not release memory like they should when they are closed. This at times results in the computer acting in an unexpected manner. When you reboot, memory space is cleared of any application that is not in use and most of the things are reset.

The computer is completely dead with no power supply

Under adult supervision, check all the connections, the cables between the CPU, the monitor and all the electrical cables. Check the wall socket. After doing so, keep the following options in mind:

- If you have a green light on your monitor but not on your CPU, then there is a problem with your CPU.
- If there is a green light on your CPU but not on your monitor, then you have a problem with your monitor and your CPU may be fine.
- If you have another monitor in working condition, the quickest way to test is to put another monitor on the machine and see if you get an image on the screen.
- If you have a light on both the monitors and the CPU, ask an adult to check the pins of the data cable between the monitor and the CPU. A single bent pin can also cause an image problem.

The mouse and keyboard does not work

Check the connection of the computer mouse and the computer keyboard wire with the computer. If the wire is plugged in yet the device is not detected, you may have to reboot your computer.

You can also check the following:

1. Click on the **Start** button.

2. Select **Control Panel** from the list.
3. Click on the **Device Manager** option from the list of tasks given.
4. The **Device Manager** window appears (Fig. 14.3).

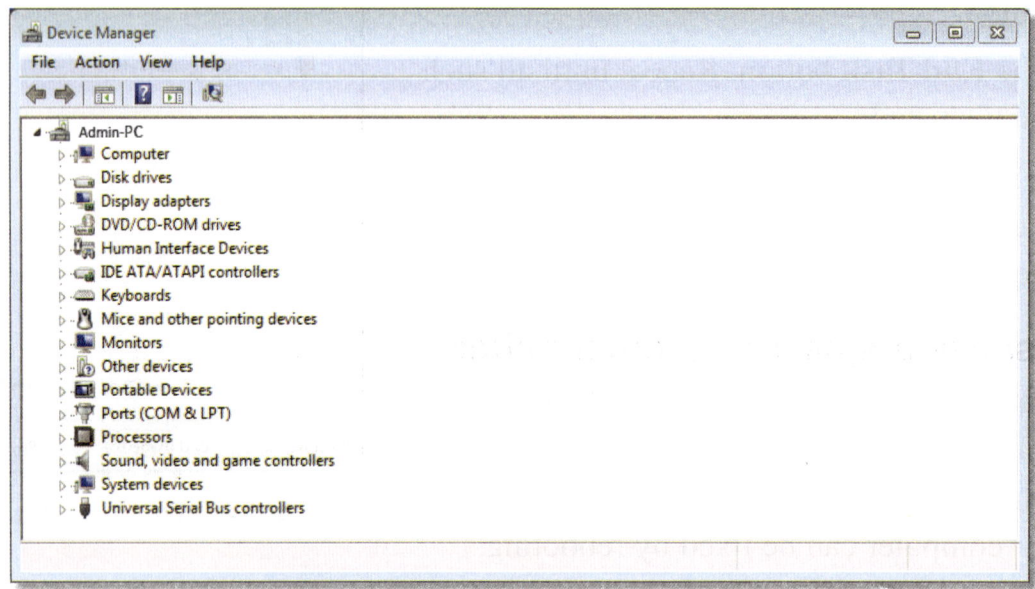

Fig. 14.3 *Device Manager window*

 There can be other possibilities for the devices not working. At times dust particles may hamper the functioning of your devices. To prevent this you must always keep your computer covered and clean it regularly.

The computer displays a disk error or non-system disk message

You must check your disk drives for any floppy disk or CD left inserted. If any, remove it and reboot the computer.

If you do not have any disk in the drive, and the message is accompanied by some sound, shut down your computer and call a technician.

The computer starts up in Safe Mode

If any problem occurs with the operating system, the system files get loaded in the safe mode to avoid system crash. Only the minimum necessary programs will load thus avoiding working of any unnecessary program. You may then try solving the problem by running a scan of the disks.

When scan is over, reboot your computer to see if the problem has been fixed. Along with scanning your system, you may also try defragmenting the files by following the steps given below:

1. Click on the **Start** button.
2. Type **Disk Defragmenter** in the **Search programs and files** box.
3. Click on **Disk Defragmenter** in the **Search Results** list.
4. Once the defragmentation is over restart your computer and check.

 Defragmenting frees up the files that were overlapping.

5. You must call a technician if the problem still persists.

The printer does not work

If there is some error in the printing of files, first find out whether it is due to any damage in the printer or an incorrect command from the computer.

Many printer models have a built-in self test option which allows you to print a test page by holding down the feed button for a few seconds. The power button will begin to flash and a test page will print. If the printer self test fails, then the problem is with the printer itself rather than the printer cable or the computer. If this occurs, you need to contact a technician.

If the printer self test prints, the next step is to have Windows print a test page. You must follow the steps given below:

1. Click on **Start** ⟹ **Control Panel** ⟹ **Devices and Printers**, and right-click on the **Printer** icon.
2. Select **Printer properties** and press the **Print Test Page** button. If the test page fails to print, make sure the printer cable is firmly fixed in both the computer and the printer.
3. You should also check the ends of the printer cable to make sure that none of the prongs are bent.
4. If the test print fails, or if the print consists of unwanted characters or a few characters printed over many pages, you need to uninstall and then reinstall the drivers for your printer.

A lot of computer problems can be solved at your end with the above explained ways. However, you must always remember that juggling with the system files and computer hardware may sometimes lead to more errors. Therefore, when you feel that the problem is too complicated then you should always attempt to solve it only under the supervision of an adult or a computer technician.

ACTIVITY

A. Annie has opened several files and applications on her computer. She noticed that her MS Word 2007 window has suddenly stopped responding. What can she do to prevent data loss?

B. Maya's hardware devices are attached to her computer. But some of them are still not working. Can you suggest where all she should check to see that devices are connected properly?

GLOSSARY

Troubleshooting: It is identification of trouble in a system caused by a failure of some kind.
Reboot: It is restarting a computer.

NOW YOU KNOW

1. It is important to take proper care of our computer.
2. The three areas to troubleshoot are – Hardware, Software and Operating system.
3. The steps of troubleshooting help you to deal with the problem in a more systematic way.
4. If the computer is frozen or any program is not responding, press Ctrl + Alt + Del keys at the same time and start the Task Manager.
5. When the problem is too complicated, you should attempt to solve it only under the supervision of an adult or a computer technician.

EXERCISE

A Fill in the blanks.

1. The .... is the identification of trouble in a system caused by a failure of some kind.

2. ...., ... and .... are the areas to troubleshoot.

3. In case of a problem with the operating system, the files are loaded in a ....

4. When Windows restart without warning then it is .... type of troubleshoot.

5. To deal with the computer lock problem, press the keys .... and .... at the same time.

B. Choose the correct answer.

1. Categorising your problem as related to hardware and software is
   a. Step 1. ☐   b. Step 2. ☐   c. Step 3. ☐   d. Step 4. ☐

2. The printer does not work.
   a. Hardware problem ☐   b. Software problem ☐
   c. Both ☐   d. None ☐

3. Windows start in a safe mode.
   a. Hardware problem ☐   b. Software Problem ☐
   c. Operating system Problem ☐   d. None ☐

4. It is important to ensure that your computer is free of troubles because
   a. nobody likes a technician. ☐
   b. it will not cause a break in your work. ☐
   c. data loss cannot be easily recovered. ☐
   d. it increases the speed and life of the computer. ☐

5. Disk defragmenter is available in
   a. Control Panel ⟹ Settings. ☐
   b. Accessories ⟹ System. ☐
   c. Start button ⟹ System. ☐
   d. Start button ⟹ Search programs and files box. ☐

C. Give the solution to deal with the given problem:

1. Some error messages are displayed on the monitor.
2. The computer locks up.
3. The keyboard does not work.
4. The mouse does not work.
5. The computer displays a disk error or non-system disk message.
6. The computer starts up in safe mode.
7. The printer does not work.

D **Answer the following questions**

1. What is troubleshooting? Name different types of troubleshooting.
2. Why is good maintenance important for a computer?
3. Write about two types of hardware problems you often come across.
4. Write briefly the steps to troubleshoot your computer before calling a technician.
5. Write about two commonly faced problems related to the operating system that you might have also faced.

LAB WORK

A. Find out if any of the system or printer is not working in your lab class. Talk to your school technician to find out the problem with the non-working device.

B. Make a list of the common problems you may come across with computers at home or in your school.

C. Make a list of the problems that you think you can easily be resolved without taking the help of a technician.

D. Make a presentation on the topic Steps of Troubleshooting. Use the Internet for collecting more information and images.

E. Make a list of day-to-day troubles that you encounter during your lab classes.

TEACHER'S NOTES

1. Tell the students about Problem Steps Recorder which records your problem step-by-step and compile it in one file. Demonstrate in class how they can start the recorder by simply typing 'psr' in Run dialog box.
2. Tell the students about Microsoft Fix It Solution Centre, which is an online tool that quickly find and fix system problems.